Loyal Dissent

Brief Lives from Westminster School

Loyal Dissent

Brief Lives from Westminster School

Edited by

Patrick Derham

The University of Buckingham Press

First published in Great Britain in 2016 by

The University of Buckingham Press
Yeomanry House
Hunter Street
Buckingham MK18 1EG

A CIP catalogue record for this book is available at the British Library

The images are all provided by and reproduced with the kind permission
of Westminster School.

ISBN 978-1-908684-74-5

Editor's Acknowledgement

I owe a huge debt to two colleagues, Tom Edlin and Elizabeth Wells, whose wisdom, passion for Westminster and forensic eye were invaluable in putting together this book.

All royalties from sales of *Loyal Dissent* will go towards the Westminster School Bursary Fund.

CONTENTS

James Campbell

Dr James W P Campbell is the Seear Fellow in Architecture and History of Art at Queens' College, Cambridge. He studied architecture at Trinity College, Cambridge and practised as an architect before returning to do a PhD on Sir Christopher Wren, the Royal Society and the development of structural carpentry. This led later to his book *Building St Paul's*. He has published widely on seventeenth-century building construction and presented a Radio 3 programme on Hooke's architecture that was featured on *Pick of the Week*. His other books include a history of library buildings (*Library: a World History*) and an exploration of the use and development of brick in architecture (*Brick: a World History*) both in collaboration with the architectural photographer Will Pryce. These been very well received and have been translated into many languages. He is a Fellow of the Society of Antiquaries and Chairman of the Construction History Society.

Nick Clegg

Nick Clegg MP is a Liberal Democrat politician who served as Deputy Prime Minister in Britain's first post war Coalition Government from 2010 to 2015 and as Leader of the Liberal Democrats from 2007 to 2015.

He is a Member of Parliament for Sheffield Hallam, where he was first elected in 2005. Prior to his entry into British politics, he served as a Member of the European Parliament and as an international trade negotiator in the European Commission dealing with the accession of China and Russia into the World Trade Organisation. He has also held part time positions at Sheffield University and won a writing prize at the Financial Times in the early 1990s.

Nick Clegg is fluent in five European languages and studied at Cambridge and Minnesota Universities and the College of Europe in Bruges. He is married to Miriam González Durántez, an international trade lawyer, and they have three sons.

He attended Westminster School 1979-1985.

Peter Cox

Peter Cox is now a writer and oral historian, something he began only after working for the John Lewis Partnership for thirty-five years. He joined them initially as a computer programmer in 1968 after university. At John Lewis in the 1970s he was in the teams that developed the first electronic point-of-sale system in UK department stores, and for Waitrose the first entirely computerised food ordering system in Britain, before moving into computer system management. He retired in 2003 as the Waitrose Systems Director. In the last ten years he has written five books of non-fiction on different subjects, of which *Spedan's Partnership* was the third. The first was about cricket, a childhood obsession and a sport he still plays: *Sixty Summers – English Cricket Since World War II*, and the most recent *Growing Up In London 1930-1960*, based on interviews with Londoners born between the two world wars. He was born and brought up in Croydon, where he went to Whitgift School, about which he has written an anecdotal history *Memories of Whitgift – The Boys' Own Tales 1880-1980*, derived from personal memoirs and a century of school magazines. He says that anyone who wants to understand the preoccupations of any period can't do much better than examine school debates: Westminster's are recorded, as were Whitgift's, in ample detail in the school archive, and are ripe for research.

Patrick Derham

Patrick Derham has been Head Master of Westminster School since September 2014. After studying History at Cambridge he taught at Cheam and Radley before becoming Head Master of Solihull School in September 1996 and Rugby in September 2001.

Passionate about widening access Patrick set up the Arnold Foundation for Rugby School in 2003 which provides a boarding education at Rugby to under-privileged children and was instrumental in the setting up of the SpringBoard Bursary Foundation, a new national charity closely modelled on the Arnold Foundation, in November 2012. He is also Deputy Chairman of Trustees of **Into**University and a Trustee of the Gladstone Library. At Westminster Patrick is closely involved with Harris Westminster Sixth Form, an academically selective free school which has as its key objective to transform the education of the most able London students.

Patrick co-edited *Liberating Learning Widening Participation* with Michael Worton (2010) and *Cultural Olympians* with John Taylor (2013), both published by UBP.

Ian Donaldson

Ian Donaldson is the author of *Ben Jonson: A Life,* published by Oxford University Press in 2011, and is a General Editor, with David Bevington and Martin Butler, of *The Cambridge Edition of the Works of Ben Jonson*, published in 7 volumes in 2012 by Cambridge University Press, and in greatly expanded online format in 2014-15. He has taught at Oxford, Cambridge, Edinburgh, and Melbourne Universities, and at the Australian National University, Canberra. He is a former Fellow of Wadham College, Oxford and of King's College, Cambridge and is at present an Honorary Professorial Fellow of the University of Melbourne, and Fellow of Trinity College, Melbourne. He was the founding Director of the ANU's Humanities Research Centre and of the Centre for Research in the Arts, Social Sciences, and Humanities (CRASSH) at Cambridge. He is a Fellow of the British Academy and the Royal Society of Edinburgh, and a Fellow and Past President of the Australian Academy of the Humanities.

A. C. Grayling

A. C. Grayling is the Master of the News College of the Humanities, London, and its Professor of Philosophy, and the author of over thirty books of philosophy, biography, history of ideas, and essays. He is a columnist for Prospect magazine, and was for a number of years a columnist on the Guardian and Times. He has contributed to many leading newspapers in the UK, US and Australia, and to BBC radios 4, 3, 2 and the World Service, for which he did the annual 'Exchanges at the Frontier' series; and he has often appeared on television. He has twice been a judge on the Booker Prize, in 2015 serving as the Chair of the judging panel. He is a Vice President of the British Humanist Association, a Fellow of the Royal Society of Arts, and a Fellow of the Royal Society of Literature.

Dominic Grieve

Dominic Grieve was first elected as MP for Beaconsfield in 1997, entering Parliament from a career as a barrister and having served as a councillor in Hammersmith and in the Territorial Army. He was appointed to the opposition front bench in 1999 as spokesman on Constitutional affairs and moved to the Home affairs team covering criminal justice in 2001 before being made shadow Attorney General by Michael Howard in 2003. In 2008 he was made shadow Home Secretary and shadow Justice Secretary in 2009. After the General Election of 2010 he was appointed a Privy Councillor and Attorney General holding that office until July 2014. Mr Grieve is currently a member of the Standards and Privileges Committee of the House of Commons and Chairman of the Intelligence and Security Committee of Parliament.

His work in Parliament on civil liberties and the Rule of Law was recognised by two awards - Parliamentarian of the Year in 2005 and in 2014 by a Lifetime Achievement award from Liberty. He has specialised on issues relating to Law and Order, civil liberties and international affairs as well as having an interest in environmental issues.

He is married to Caroline, also a barrister and they have two sons at university. He has been a deputy church warden. He enjoys mountain walking, scuba diving, skiing and architecture in his spare time.

He attended Westminster School 1969 – 1974.

Leslie Griffiths

Leslie Griffiths is a Methodist minister with a wide and varied background. He has degrees from three of our leading universities and half a dozen honorary fellowships. He preaches from John Wesley's pulpit in London as the minister of Wesley's Chapel, has a stall in St Paul's Cathedral as an Honorary Canon, and a seat in the House of Lords as a Life Peer. He has written seven books and innumerable articles on religion, history, ideas, his beloved Haiti and life in general. He has been broadcasting with the BBC for over a quarter of a century. And he's been writing his column for the "Methodist Recorder" for even longer. He is President of the Boys' Brigade and Chair of Trustees of the Central Foundation Schools of London. He is married with three children who have all become his best friends. He identifies his interests as "fun and friendship spiced with occasional moments of solitude."

Conrad Keating

Conrad Keating is the Writer-in-Residence at the Wellcome Unit for the History of Medicine at the University of Oxford. As a writer and historian, Keating seeks to place the science and art of medicine in a social context, freeing it from accusations of impenetrability and making it understandable to the general reader. Following more than a decade working a researcher, writer and producer at the BBC, and across other media, Keating produced the widely-acclaimed authorised biography of Richard Doll, *Smoking Kills: The Revolutionary Life of Richard Doll* (Signal Books, 2009), and has since gone on to explore the field of medical history more broadly, creating a number of podcast series, writing journal articles and delivering lectures in the UK, US and Australia.

In 2013, he published *Great Medical Discoveries: An Oxford Story*, which accompanied the exhibition 'Great Medical Discoveries: 800 Years of Oxford Innovation' which he curated for the Bodleian Library. He has recently completed work on an ambitious book project entitled *Kenneth Warren and the Great Neglected Diseases of Mankind Programme: The Transformation of Geographical Medicine in the US and beyond*, to be published by Springer New York in 2016.

Keating is currently working on a long-term collaboration with *The Lancet*, looking at the history of randomised controlled trials and their contribution to improving health and reducing the burden of illness. His next book will be a social history of neglected tropical diseases which will tell the remarkable story of the sacrifices and achievements of doctors and scientists who have made a real difference in identifying and treating disease. He lives in Oxford.

Zareer Masani

Zareer Masani is the author of *Macaulay: Britain's Liberal Imperialist* (Bodley Head, 2014). He has an Oxford history doctorate and is the author of three other historical books: *Indira Gandhi: A Biography* (Hamish Hamilton, 1975), *Indian Tales of the Raj* (BBC, 1987) and *India from Raj to Rajiv* (BBC, 1988). He has also written a widely acclaimed family memoir, *And All Is Said: Memoir of a Home Divided* (Penguin, 2013).

Zareer spent two decades as a current affairs radio producer for the BBC and is now a freelance historian, journalist and broadcaster. His particular area of interest is imperial history, including the legacies of the Raj in India today.

Sarah Mortimer

Sarah Mortimer is Student and Tutor in Modern History, Christ Church, and University Lecturer in Modern History. Her research focuses on the relationship between political and religious ideas in the early modern period; she is currently writing a book on global political thought from 1517-1625 for Oxford University Press. Her monograph, *Reason and Religion in the English Revolution* (2010), won the Forkosch prize for the best first book in intellectual history and she has also edited, with John Robertson, *The Intellectual Consequences of Religious Heterodoxy 1600-1750 (2012)*.

Gareth Stedman Jones

Gareth Stedman Jones is Director of the Centre for History and Economics, Cambridge, and a Fellow of King's College, Cambridge since 1974. He was Professor of Political Science, History Faculty; Cambridge from 1997 and in 2010 became Professor of the History of Ideas at Queen Mary, University of London. He is a Fellow of the Royal Historical Society and a Fellow of the British Academy.

His publications include the books *Outcast London*, (Oxford, 1971, new edition Verso 2013) *An End to Poverty? (2004);* Karl Marx and Friedrich Engels, *The Communist Manifesto* (2002); *Religion and the Political Imagination*, co-edited with Ira Katznelson (2010) and the *Cambridge History of Nineteenth-Century Political Thought*, co-edited with Gregory Claeys (2011). His next major work *Karl Marx: Greatness and Illusion, A Life* will be published by Penguin in August 2016.

His major research interest is the history of British and European political thought from the aftermath of the French Revolution to the First World War.

Philip Waller

Philip Waller was Fellow and Tutor in History at Merton College, Oxford, from 1971 to 2008, and is now an Emeritus Fellow. His books include *Democracy and Sectarianism: A Political and Social History of Liverpool 1868-1939* (1981), *Town, City, and Nation: England 1850-1914* (1983; 1999), and *Writers, Readers, and Reputations: Literary Life in Britain 1870-1918* (2006; 2008). He is a former editor of the *English Historical Review.*

Helen Wilcox

Helen Wilcox is Professor of English Literature at Bangor University, Wales. She grew up in Nottingham, attended the Universities of Birmingham (B.A.) and Oxford (D Phil), and lectured at the University of Liverpool before being appointed a professor at the University of Groningen, The Netherlands. She returned to the UK to take up her chair at Bangor in 2006, and has also been a visiting professor in Spain, Singapore and the USA. Her teaching and research focus on English Renaissance literature, with particular interests in Shakespeare, devotional poetry, literature and music, women's writing, and early autobiography. Among her publications are the acclaimed annotated edition of *The English Poems of George Herbert* (Cambridge, 2007) and the recent monograph *1611: Authority, Gender and the Word in Early Modern England* (Blackwell, 2014). She is the co-editor (with Andrew Hiscock) of the forthcoming *Oxford Handbook of Early Modern English Literature and Religion*, and (with Suzanne Gossett) of the forthcoming Arden (3) edition of Shakespeare's *All's Well That Ends Well*. She is a Fellow of the Royal Society of Literature and of the Learned Society of Wales.

Ruth Winstone

Ruth Winstone edited all ten volumes of the political diaries of Tony Benn, published by Hutchinson between 1987 and 2010. She was also editor to Chris Mullin, Labour MP for Sunderland South, whose diaries were published by Profile Books in three volumes: *A Walk-On Part 1994-99,* A *View from the Foothills 1999-2005* and *Decline and Fall 2005-2010*; she has worked on other political biographies. From 1997 to 2007 she was also a senior researcher in the House of Commons Library. She most admires the works of Anthony Trollope and Ian McEwan.

Brian Young

Brian Young is Charles Stuart Student and Tutor at Christ Church, Oxford. He is the author of *Religion and Enlightenment in Eighteenth-Century England* (Oxford, 1998) and *The Victorian Eighteenth Century* (Oxford, 2007), and co-editor of a number of books about intellectual history. He is currently Junior Censor at Christ Church and is completing a study of relations between believers and unbelievers in eighteenth-century England.

Patrick Derham

Its history, location and ethos reinforce the fact that Westminster is no ordinary place. It is interesting that when one joins an institution such as this school, whether as pupils or staff, we become part of a thread of history running back at least 456 years to the year 1560 when Queen Elizabeth re-founded the school, continuing the long tradition of scholarship established by the monks of the Abbey. When we look around at the school today, we see the results of the endeavours of all those who, before us, have been part of that thread. Represented in this volume are former pupils who have been a part of that; shaped and influenced by the distinctive nature of a Westminster education.

Is it possible though to uncover what is distinctive about the thread of education that has been provided here for centuries? Perhaps the answer lies in one of the many stories about Dr Busby, Westminster's finest Head Master, and arguably this country's first great Head Master. The story goes that walking in St James's Park the staunchly Anglican Dr Busby bumped into a former pupil, Philip Henry, who had become a nonconformist preacher. Dr Busby asked him why, only to be told that he was himself to blame, for, Henry said, "You taught me those things which hindered me from conforming."

That is the Westminster way. Throughout its history Westminster pupils have been encouraged to express what we would see as loyal dissent, by seeking every opportunity to enter debate, to challenge the orthodoxy, to question, to have an understanding of the uncertainties in life, and above all to respect genuine scholarship. Westminster pupils have always known that learning is a complex, demanding and often painful process because it is challenging to open one's mind, to change one's views, to try the unfamiliar.

This has come about because the Westminster way has been to provide an unrivalled liberal education that recognises the fundamental importance of critical, reflective, informed debate. Although there have been moments in the school's history where this has not always been clear, these sentiments find notable resonance in the words of the Elizabethan Charter of 1560:

> "The youth, which is growing to manhood, as tender shoots in the wood of our state, shall be liberally instructed in good books to the honour of the state." (Elizabeth I)

So Westminster pupils have in the main demonstrated humility rather than arrogance. They have been respectful, accepting, interested in being of service to others. Westminster measures success by the adults they become and by the service they give beyond the school. This is amply illustrated by the lives of those Westminsters featured in this book.

Interestingly, Westminster has stood apart from the other so-called leading schools. By bypassing the Arnoldian revolution of the nineteenth century, by not leaving London, by not becoming a day school, by not remaining single sex, by not having a typically Victorian school chapel, by its connection with the Abbey, by wearing its traditions lightly, by being part of a vibrant community, by not being an ivory tower, by tolerating and encouraging individuality among both pupils and staff, it has trodden its own path. This has undoubtedly helped shape the distinctive ethos.

Few schools can match Westminster's academic, cultural, political and spiritual heritage and sense of place. Some of the country's most distinguished thinkers, writers, theologians, scientists, politicians, artists and musicians are included among its former pupils. What follows is just a sample of these, but the "loyal dissenters" featured, share a connection to their place of education (although not all enjoyed or appreciated their time here), but they were shaped by an education that stresses the importance of liberalism and the Westminster way of doing things. They have benefitted from an education that challenges convention, encourages individuality, respects originality of mind and action, and perhaps above all inculcates an inclination towards dissent and nonconformity.

John Owen, Oliver Cromwell's nominee as Dean of Christ Church, was perhaps articulating a shrewd awareness of the distinctive nature of a Westminster education when, fearing for his narrow vision of a future "Godly England", he thundered that "it will never be well with the nation, until Westminster School is suppressed." We were, at that time, leading dissenters against prescriptive dissent, refusing to conform to an official nonconformity. Loyal dissent indeed, and a thread that is cherished and nurtured to this day.

Introduction

Nick Clegg

From the whimsical inventor of Winnie-the-Pooh, A. A. Milne, to the father of British liberalism, John Locke; from the medic with communist sympathies who discovered the carcinogenic effects of tobacco, Sir Richard Doll, to Shakespeare's troubled contemporary, Ben Jonson; from the greatest writer of Hymns in the English language, Charles Wesley, to the restless constitutional and penal reformer, Jeremy Bentham; all of them in different ways possessed the unusual contradictions which have long characterised Westminster School, and all of them are described in glorious detail in this excellent collection of essays.

Westminster School has never conformed to expectations: located in the physical heart of the political establishment, opposite the Houses of Parliament, it has produced legions of anti-establishment figures; providing a private education to children born into affluence, it has a long tradition of radicalism and reform; soaring high against national and international competition, it refuses to be defined by league tables; open to the big, wide world, it nonetheless remains quintessentially British.

It is also a quintessentially liberal institution – liberal with a small "l" (I wouldn't dare to foist a party political affiliation on a school whose independent turn of mind escapes political conformities). "Loyal dissent" is at the very heart of British liberalism: a belief in reform rather than revolution; reason and evidence rather than violence and upheaval; and the give and take of debate rather than shrill polemic. All of those enduring, liberal values are embodied in Westminster School.

I first arrived as a pupil at Westminster School in 1979 from a highly conventional prep school in the Home Counties countryside. Rugby was the lifeblood of that prep school and the ferocity of a crunching tackle on a muddy rugby pitch was admired and rewarded more generously than your performance in the classroom. So when I arrived at Westminster School, I felt I'd landed on another planet: no rugby; a somewhat haughty disregard for the fresh air and innocence of the countryside; clever, wordy pupils wearing trendy "winkle picker" shoes and fake cockney accents; girls – girls! – in the sixth form; and an effortless swagger on the grimy streets of London.

I had been used to a school culture where authority was unquestioned, rules meticulously obeyed, hierarchy strictly enforced. Suddenly, I found myself in a school culture where authority was constantly questioned, independence of thought celebrated and individualism always trumped conformity.

And I loved it.

Looking back, I think Westminster School taught me, above all, to be sceptical: of unchallenged assertions, bogus prejudices, untrammelled authority, evidence free theories, pompous traditions, outdated institutions and all forms of stale convention.

There is, of course, a fine line between healthy scepticism and unhealthy cynicism. Scepticism can be a spur to action, a catalyst for change. Cynicism merely devalues initiative and erodes the belief that things can be improved at all. Scepticism is a precursor to change; cynicism destroys the potential for change. The sceptical turn of mind at Westminster School could occasionally topple into grumpy, teenage cynicism. But that is probably a universal tendency of adolescence rather than a specific failing of the School.

I certainly wouldn't have taken the course I did in politics if Westminster School had not inculcated in me a scepticism about the status quo. My generation grew up under the stifling grip of a two-party system in which everyone was either in the red or blue team. There was little choice, few alternatives. Power was – and still is – administered in woefully outdated Westminster institutions, by way of a lopsided electoral system and an opaque means of funding political parties. When I became Deputy Prime Minister, I tried – and failed – to reform all of them whilst continuing to co-pilot the Government of the day. A form of "loyal dissent" in action, I suppose.

Indeed, Coalition Government is the political epitome of "loyal dissent": it sustains the mandate of Government while undermining the convention of one-party authority; it creates political stability while dissenting from the convention of winner-takes-all politics; it enables difficult decisions to be made, but believes that two heads can be better than one. In short, plural, multi-party coalition politics is a challenge to, and a continuity of, the status quo all at once.

It is fascinating to read in this collection of essays how many alumni of Westminster School have sought to strike the balance between loyalty and dissent, continuity and challenge, authority and reform down the ages: Charles Wesley committed himself to the Church of England on his death bed even though his evangelism challenged it in so many ways throughout his life; A. A. Milne produced one of the most homely, comforting cast of characters of all time yet he was an anguished radical and pacifist; John Locke's emphasis on the primacy of the individual remained, in the end, subservient to his religious beliefs; Ben Jonson condemned and celebrated the theatre in equal measure, dissented from and flattered the writ of the King's authority at different times.

The values that these great men embodied - given that girls first entered Westminster in 1973, I assume a later edition of *Loyal Dissent* will celebrate the achievements of the remarkable women who were pupils at the School – are timeless. Independence of mind, a fearless desire to challenge orthodoxy, ingenuity, compassion – all of these qualities are on ample display in these essays. The individuals described here helped not only to sustain the unique ethos of Westminster School, but to shape our country too. Philosophy, medicine, literature, theology – not to mention some of Walt Disney's greatest cartoons – would all be the poorer without the unique contribution of each of them.

At a time when extremism, globalization and political populism are coming together to create a profound sense of unease and volatility it is also good to be reminded of the humanity and common sense of this unusual cast of individuals. It is difficult to know what John Locke, Sir Richard Doll or Winnie the Pooh for that matter would make of Donald Trump and Marine Le Pen. But I think one can safely assume that the finger-jabbing politics of blame which is now on the rise across North America and Europe would not find favour with any of the alumni described in these essays.

Because, in the end, whilst they all hail from different centuries and vocations they are all united by a belief in open inquiry, intelligent discourse and respect for other faiths and ideas. There is a balance to "loyal dissent" – challenging and moderate at the same time - which stands in stark contrast to the imbalance of the politics of identity which is now rearing its ugly head across the democratic world.

If this collection of essays helps remind people of that moderate, reformist, liberal tradition which has always infused Westminster School as well as so much of our national life, it will provide a wider lesson beyond the confines of Little Dean's Yard.

Ian Donaldson

Loyal dissent: the oxymoronic title of this volume nicely captures the essential spirit of Ben Jonson, distinguished alumnus of Westminster School, a man whose life was deeply marked by paradox and contradiction. The greatest dramatist of his age, next to his friend William Shakespeare, Jonson viewed the theatre of his day with open contempt, as a place where "nothing but ribaldry, profanation, blasphemy, all license of offence to God and man is practised": uttering this verdict in a year now regarded as a supreme moment in the history of the English stage.[1] The son of an Anglican minister who had lost his estate from Marian persecution, Jonson converted unexpectedly to the religion under which his father had suffered, and – in a further acrobatic move – chose then to serve at a Protestant court at a perilous time for Catholics in England. A scornful critic of the court's extravagances, he was obliged, through a painful irony, to devise many of its most lavish entertainments. Charged with treason and sedition for plays he had written for the public stage, he won in the end a laureate role as the king's own poet. The anointed spokesman for royal policies that, as time went by, seemed increasingly at odds with the mood of the country, he shared many of the gravest concerns of close friends in parliament and the judiciary as troubles mounted throughout the land, but maintained his loyalty to the reigning monarch. "Indeed, when had Great Britain greater cause/ Than now, to love the sovereign and the laws?", he wrote in 1629, as Charles prepared to dissolve parliament and embark on an eleven-year period of personal rule which would lead inevitably to civil war.[2]

Jonson was a dissenter, then, but a loyalist too: a combination which – as the present gathering of essays implies – may be not untypical of former pupils of Westminster School. Loyalty and dissent (as we shall see) were two qualities that Jonson would certainly have learnt to value at Westminster, along with other skills and attitudes destined to stay with him throughout his long career as a writer. Yet the influence of Jonson's early schooling, powerful as it was, does not wholly explain his curiously divided temperament: the many opposed impulses and allegiances which informed his private as well as his professional life. He was a man "passionately kind and angry", according to his friend, the Scottish poet William Drummond of Hawthornden, yet an advocate too of stoical

---

[1] Lines 28-9 of the Epistle prefixed to the 1607 quarto edition of *Volpone*, in *The Cambridge Edition of the Works of Ben Jonson*, ed. David Bevington, Martin Butler, and Ian Donaldson, print edition, 7 vols. (Cambridge University Press, 2012); online edition (Cambridge University Press, 2014/ 2015); hereafter *CWBJ*. All quotations from this edition. The theatrical moment on which Jonson is reflecting is examined by James Shapiro: *1606: William Shakespeare and the Year of Lear* (2015).
[2] "An Epigram To Our Great and Good King Charles On His Anniversary Day, 1629", *The Underwood*, 64.7-8 (*CWBJ*, 7.212).

restraint. A boisterous talker, especially in his cups, he wrote eloquently in praise of taciturnity. A believer in reason as the ultimate guide to all human action, he was haunted by fanciful dreams and wild delusions. "He hath consumed a whole night lying looking to his great toe", William Drummond reported, "about which he hath seen Tartars and Turks, Romans and Carthaginians, fight in his imagination". He was (in short) a notably conflicted figure, as Drummond's records of his visit to Hawthornden Castle over the Christmas season in 1618-19 vividly testify.[3]

Jonson's family origins lay in Scotland, and his visit to Drummond that winter – the culmination of a famous walk from London to Edinburgh in the late summer – was his first venture into the land of his forebears. His grandfather, so he informed Drummond at this time, "came from Carlisle, and he thought from Annandale to it" (*Informations*, 177, *CWBJ*, 5. 371). The Johnstones or Johnstouns of Annandale – the name was spelt in at least thirteen different ways in Scotland at this time, but always with a "t"[4] – were a powerful border clan, notorious for their constant feuding with their chief rivals, the Maxwells, and their marauding raids throughout the "debateable lands" between Scotland and England. Jonson's grandfather may have been one of a group of Scottish leaders captured by the English after the battle of Solway Moss in 1542, taken to a garrison in Carlisle, and cajoled into the service of Henry VIII.

His son – Jonson's father – was the Anglican minister who had been imprisoned during Mary's reign and obliged to forfeit his entire estate. Having married and made his way south, he died a month before Ben's own birth on June 11th 1572. Jonson's own early years were therefore difficult. He was "brought up poorly" by his widowed mother, who, while he was still a "little child" in "his long coats", married again, this time to a bricklayer named Robert Brett: a man of sufficient means who would rise

---

[3] *Informations to William Drummond of Hawthornden*, 559, 247-9 (*CWBJ*, 5.391, 375). On reason and the passions: "Epode", *The Forest*, 11; *Discoveries,* 22-3. On taciturnity, *Discoveries*, 235-79 (*CWBJ*, 5.230; 7.500, 7.511).

[4] C. L. Johnstone, *History of the Johnstones 1191-1909* (Edinburgh, 1909). When he came to adult life Ben was to favour the spelling 'Jonson', the version of his name that appears in his published work from 1604 and all surviving examples of his holograph.

in time to become Master of the Tylers' and Bricklayers' Company.[5] The family moved to live in Hartshorn Lane, near Charing Cross, a narrow alleyway prone to flooding which ran from the Strand down to the Thames, often bearing sewage in its passage: an unwholesome area inhabited by many families connected with the building trade, who laboured on grander nearby sites in the soon-to-be-fashionable area of the Strand.

As a child Ben attended the small elementary school maintained by the church of St Martin-in-the-Fields, where children were taught to read and write and master basic grammatical skills. At the age of about seven his real education began, when he was "put to school by a friend (his master, Camden)" (*Informations*, 181-2). The great antiquarian scholar William Camden was Under Master at Westminster at this time. Drummond's characteristically ambiguous note probably means that Camden was Jonson's teacher at the School, rather than being the "friend" who sponsored his education; though the syntax leaves this matter unclear. In one fictional re-imagining of this episode Camden is pictured strolling one afternoon through Charing Cross when he comes upon a group of small boys teasing one of their little companions, who is clad grotesquely in an adult greatcoat. He pauses to watch the scene.

> Unconscious that he was observed, the tormented child stopped in the middle of the square, and taking a deep breath, screamed in a terrifying voice.
> *"Scelerati! Detestabiles! Catilinae!"*

Unable to "resist this combination of Latin and misery", Camden goes to console the boy, discovers his name, his talents, and his circumstances, and impulsively recruits him as a student at Westminster.[6] Perhaps it was indeed through a chance meeting of such a kind that Jonson gained entry

---

[5] *Informations*, 178-81 (*CWBJ*, 5.371); Thomas Fuller, *The History of the Worthies of England* (1662), *CWBJ* online Life Records, LR95b (Early Lives). For the identification of Jonson's stepfather as Robert Brett, see J. B. Bamborough, *Times Literary Supplement*, April 8th 1960.

[6] Byron Steel (= Francis Steegmuller), *O Rare Ben Jonson* (New York and London, 1928), 10-13. "Scoundrels! Abominations! Conspirators!" (The real Ben Jonson would have more to say about Catiline and his conspiracy against Rome in his tragedy of 1611.)

to the School; more probably, however, the "friend" was a teacher or churchwarden at St Martin's who had spotted the young boy's gifts, and shrewdly placed him in a school that would fully extend his native abilities.

By whatever means Jonson entered the School, he retained a lifelong sense of indebtedness to William Camden: "most reverend head", as he later hailed him, "to whom I owe/ All that I am in arts, all that I know/ (How nothing's that?)".[7] It was Camden who introduced Jonson and his fellow-pupils not just to the great poets of Greece and Rome but to those of England too, whom he saw as their equals: styling Chaucer (for example) as "our English Homer". He told them about contemporary writers as well as those from the distant past, extolling Sir Philip Sidney, with whom he had been personally acquainted at Oxford, as "the miracle of our age".[8] Under Camden's guidance, Jonson and his classmates were encouraged to translate Greek and Latin poetry into English verse: a regular (and educationally innovative) practice at the School at this time, whose continuing impact can be seen in Jonson's later work and in that of other Westminster poets: George Herbert, Henry King, Richard Corbett, Abraham Cowley, John Dryden, and others.[9] Camden encouraged the boys' own attempts at verse composition, urging them to set out their thoughts first in prose, before rendering them in verse (*Informations*, 293

---

[7] *Epigrams*, 14.1-3, *CWBJ*, 5.119. For a more detailed account of Jonson's time at Westminster School (and other matters mentioned in the present chapter) see my *Ben Jonson: A Life* (Oxford, 2011). On the early history of the School see in particular R. Ackermann, *The History of the Colleges of Winchester, Eton, and Westminster* (London, 1816); John D. Carleton, *Westminster School: A History* (rev. edn. 1965; first published 1938); John Field, *The King's Nurseries: The Story of Westminster School* (London, 1987); John Sargeaunt, *Annals of Westminster School* (London, 1898); Lawrence E. Tanner, *Westminster School: A History* (London, 1934).

[8] Camden, *Remains Concerning Britain* (1614).

[9] C. Hoole, *A New Dictionary of the Old Art of Teaching Schools* (1660), speaks of this as a new educational practice, requiring justification: T. W. Baldwin, *William Shakspere's Small Latin and Lesse Greeke* (University of Illinois Press, 1944), vol. 2, p. 395. Jonson was later to read or recite to William Drummond his translations of Horace, Martial, and other classical poets: *Informations*, 54-7, 74, etc. (*CWBJ*, 5. 363-4.) On the strength of the Westminster poetic tradition throughout the seventeenth century see Margaret Crum's introduction to her edition of *The Poems of Henry King, Bishop of Chichester* (Oxford, 1965), 5.

(*CWBJ*, 5. 378). He instructed them too in another art destined to be of crucial significance in Jonson's professional life. For Camden was also responsible for Westminster's Latin Play, which since the time of Alexander Nowell (Head Master 1543-55) had been a regular event at the School.[10] Nowell believed that the comedies of Terence helped in "the better learning the pure Roman style", and these comedies, together with those of Plautus, became particular favourites at the School – and of Jonson himself.[11] It was therefore a significant compliment when, later in life, Jonson – comparing ancient and modern writers in the manner Camden himself had practised – declared in his memorial poem prefixed to Shakespeare's first folio that the author of these works, "My Beloved, the Author, Master William Shakespeare", had now surpassed the achievement of these great classical masters:

> Neat Terence, witty Plautus, now not please,
> But antiquated and deserted lie,
> As they were not of nature's family.[12]

Camden's example had encouraged Jonson to compare not only ancient and modern authors but ancient and modern nations as well. During Jonson's time at Westminster Camden was putting the finishing touches to his monumental work *Britannia* (first published in Latin in 1586): a study of the history, languages, and customs of the entire British archipelago, through much of which he had journeyed, county by county, on his antiquarian researches; and which he regarded as an empire comparable in reach and power to that of ancient Rome, as celebrated by Virgil under the emperor Augustus. Successive enlarged editions of Camden's *Britannia* were dedicated in 1600 to Elizabeth – the *Annals* of whose reign Camden would shortly begin to write – and in 1607 to James, who was to draw gratefully on Camden's work in promoting his own vision of a newly United Kingdom flourishing under the name Britannia, or Great Britain.

Westminster School (otherwise known as the Royal College of St Peter in Westminster) had long been associated with royal interests, and,

---

[10] Wyman H. Herendeen, *William Camden: A Life in Context* (Woodbridge, UK, Rochester, NY, 2007), pp. 56-8.
[11] Carleton, *Westminster School*, p. 3.
[12] "To the Memory of My Beloved, the Author, Master William Shakespeare, and What He Hath Left Us", 52-4 (*CWBJ*, 5.641).

since its re-founding by Elizabeth in 1560, with the broad ambitions of the Elizabethan Settlement. Camden's teaching and scholarship both strengthened and exemplified that association. The School itself stood at its present site at the very heart of the nation, alongside the Abbey and close to the Palace of Westminster, the seat of law and government. Elizabeth took a close personal interest in the School's affairs. In new statutes drawn up at its re-founding she made provision for forty Queen's Scholars and their stipend (£3 0s. 10d.) was paid from the College's income. On at least two recorded occasions she attended performances of the Latin play. From time to time she visited the School to see for herself how the boys were progressing with their studies. The boys in return composed verses in celebration of her birthday and other notable occasions in her life. Their loyalty to the monarch was instinctive and assured, a deeply embedded part of the School's educational fabric.

And as for *dissent*, that too was an essential part of Westminster routines in Ben Jonson's day, involving the teaching of dialectical skills through regular exercises in wrangling and formal disputation, which drew often on strategies laid down by the Roman rhetorician, Quintilian. These led to contests with other church schools and to the annual three-day ritual of oral examination known as the Election, by which younger boys were selected for entry into College and senior boys picked out for advancement to Christ Church, Oxford, or Trinity College, Cambridge, the two academic institutions most closely linked at this time with Westminster. Visiting Paris with the young son of Sir Walter Raleigh in September 1612, Jonson had occasion to draw on experience gained at the School when invited to act as a formal witness to a seven-hour debate concerning the nature of the real presence: in which two protagonists summoned their opposed arguments as to whether Christ was literally, or merely symbolically, present in the wine and wafer of the mass. Jonson was required to testify, along with another witness, that the two debaters had followed the somewhat elaborate rules of procedure set down on this occasion.[13] These disputational skills, often requiring a capacity to argue on either side of a given proposition, were regularly practised at leading schools in England at this time and at the two universities. John Milton a few years later would write his twin poems *L'Allegro* and *Il Penseroso* in praise respectively of the sociable and the retired lives, having learnt this form of rhetorically opposed argumentation at St Paul's School, whose

---

[13] Donaldson, *Life*, p. 299.

curriculum closely resembled that followed at Westminster. In writing his seventh Prolusion – "That Learning Makes Men Happier Than Ignorance" – Milton is known to have been ready, in similar spirit, to argue for the contrary proposition: that learning (alas) does nothing of the sort.[14]

Such skills could also, however, be abused, as Jonson was sharply aware, and turned to more sinister or trivial ends. In Jonson's great comedy *Volpone*, Mosca, the insinuating parasite, flatters the advocate, Voltore, by saying how his master, Volpone, has praised his rhetorical dexterity, and that of his silver-tongued colleagues.

> I oft have heard him say how he admired
> Men of your large profession, that could speak
> To every cause, and things mere contraries,
> Till they were hoarse again, yet all be law;
> That with most quick agility could turn
> And re-turn; make knots, and undo them;
> Give forkèd counsel; taking provoking gold
> On either hand, and put it up: these men
> He knew, would thrive, with their humility.
> *Volpone*, 1.3.52-60 (*CWBJ*, 3. 59)

In *Bartholomew Fair* these arts of oppositional argument are further debased into a mindless game of "vapours", *"which is nonsense"* (as Jonson explains in a marginal note, 4.4.24-8, *CWBJ*, 4. 372), *"every man to oppose the last man that spoke, whether it concerned him or no"*. Later in the same play the Puritan preacher, Zeal-of-the-Land Busy, finds himself drawn into a similarly ludicrous rhetorical contest with a wooden puppet whose rights to perform in the fairground Busy has challenged. As the debate proceeds, the puppet-master, Lantern Leatherhead, contributes a few observations of his own.

BUSY	Yet I say, his calling, his profession, is profane: it is profane, idol.
PUPPET DIONYSIUS	*It is not profane.*
LANTERN	It is not profane, he says.
BUSY	It is profane.

---

[14] D. L. Clark, *Milton at St Paul's School* (New York, 1948); E. M. W. Tillyard, *The Miltonic Setting* (Cambridge, 1938), p. 15.

PUPPET DIONYSIUS	*It is not profane.*
BUSY	It is profane.
PUPPET DIONYSIUS	*It is not profane.*
LANTERN	Well said, confute him with 'not' still. – You cannot bear him down with your base noise, sir.

Bartholomew Fair, 5.5.51-60 (*CWBJ*, 4. 412-13)

Religious dissent and disputation in England too often proceeded in just this fashion, as Jonson's friend the jurist John Selden – "the law-book of the judges of England, the bravest man in all languages", Jonson had called him: *Informations*, 483-4 (*CWBJ*, 5.388) – later remarked.

> One says one thing, and another another; and there is, I say, no measure to end the controversy. 'Tis just as if two men were at bowls, and both judged by the eye: one says 'tis his cast, and the other says 'tis my cast; and having no measure, the difference is eternal. Ben Jonson satirically expressed the vain disputes of divines by Inigo Lanthorn disputing with a puppet in *Bartholomew Fair*. It is so; it is not so; it is so; it is not so; crying thus one to another a quarter of an hour together.[15]

Dissent needed to proceed through reasoned argument, not by a series of flat denials; through patient searching of a kind Jonson saw exemplified in the scholarly enquiries of Selden himself:

> What fables have you vexed! What truth redeemed!
> Antiquities searched! Opinions disesteemed!
> Impostures branded, and authorities urged!
> "An Epistle to Master John Selden",
>   *The Underwood*,14.39-41 (*CWBJ*, 7. 116)

John Selden's form of dissent was always in one sense *loyal*, being always conducted within a legal framework whose constitutional origins it was simultaneously attempting to verify and strengthen. But it would at times prove discomfiting for the king, whose claims upon ancient rights and

---

[15] *Table-Talk: Being the Discourses of John Selden Esq.* (London, 1689), ed. Edward Arbor (1868), pp. 103-4.

privileges Selden was obliged on occasions to question. Having queried in his *History of Tithes* in 1618 the king's power to levy ecclesiastical tithes by virtue of divine right, Selden found himself summoned abruptly by James to the royal palace at Theobalds to debate this matter with him. Selden arrived at Theobalds accompanied by his chamber-mate Edward Heyward and his friend Ben Jonson, *poetarum ille facile princeps*, as Selden called him ("easily the foremost of poets"). Faced by this formidable trio, James – who had not previously heard of John Selden or known of his forensic talents – decided to avoid debate. He set Selden instead some playful penitential tasks: to write verses about the significance of the number 666 in the Book of Revelation, and the proposition that Christ had been born on 25 December.

Jonson's decision to accompany Selden on this occasion nicely exemplifies his position on the matter of loyal dissent. A faithful servant of the King, Jonson was prepared to stand firmly in the royal presence in support of a friend, equally loyal in his intentions, who had questioned the reach of kingly power, and, by implication, the doctrine of divine right, so central to James's beliefs. For all his loyalty, Jonson, like Selden, was ready to defend these opinions in a face-to-face meeting with the monarch himself.[16]

After leaving Westminster School around 1587, Jonson appears to have studied briefly at St John's College, Cambridge, before a family crisis called him back to London to join his stepfather in the bricklaying trade: an occupation which, as he later frankly reported to William Drummond, "he could not endure".[17] Jonson laboured for a time with Robert Brett on buildings around Holborn and Lincoln's Inn Fields, but then recruited impulsively with an English expeditionary force bound (probably early in 1591) for the Low Countries to support the Protestant troops of the United Provinces in their struggle against the armies of Catholic Spain. Jonson's greatest feat in the campaigns that followed, of which he boasted many years later to William Drummond (*Informations*, 184-6, *CWBJ*, 5.372), was to defeat in single combat "in the face of both the camps" a chosen champion from the Spanish forces, and to have "taken *opima spolia* from him" – *opima spolia* being the arms or spoils

---

[16] G. J. Toomer, *John Selden: A Life in Scholarship*, 2 vols. (Oxford, 2009), vol. 1, ch 8; Donaldson, *Life*, pp. 362-3.

[17] Fuller, *CWBJ* online Life Records, LR95b (Early Lives); Drummond, *Informations*, 182-3, *CWBJ*, 5. 372.

that in ancient Roman custom were traditionally stripped by the victor from his conquered adversary. To have been picked as the Protestant champion, to have won such a striking victory in the sight of both armies, is testimony to Jonson's unusual courage and physical strength: qualities which would soon, however, be tested in less fortunate ways.

Returning to England probably in the autumn of 1592, Jonson looked about for other means of livelihood. New playhouses were being constructed in and around London in the final decades of the century, and new theatrical companies were forming to meet the rapidly growing demand for dramatic entertainment in London. Having some knowledge of the theatre through his experiences at Westminster, Jonson began to work as a "hired man" (or jobbing actor) at various metropolitan playhouses and with a company travelling in the provinces, playing the famous part of the bereaved father, Hieronimo, in Thomas Kyd's hugely popular play, *The Spanish Tragedy*. Before long he was asked to contribute to new scripts being put together, usually at high speed, by small groups of collaborating writers. Most of the plays Jonson co-wrote at this time are now lost, and known only through their titles. One of these now-missing plays, *The Isle of Dogs*, written in 1597 in collaboration with Thomas Nashe – evidently a satirical comedy, possibly aimed at Elizabeth's treasurer, William, Lord Burghley, and his son Robert Cecil, but conceivably glancing at the Queen herself – caused a particular sensation. Jonson was arrested at the behest of the Privy Council, and imprisoned along with two fellow-actors, then questioned by Elizabeth's chief interrogator, Richard Topcliffe. Nashe, forewarned of the troubles, fled to the safety of Norfolk. The Council issued instructions for the closure of all playhouses throughout the city, and, more startlingly, their immediate demolition. But no firm evidence against the players or their company could be found, for all texts of the play had (unsurprisingly) vanished. In due course the three men were released, and the companies across London began playing once more. Though theatrical business in the capital had suffered, no playhouse, happily, had been "plucked down".

Not long afterwards, however, Jonson was back in gaol on a different charge. In September 1598, while his new comedy, *Every Man In His Humour*, was enjoying some success at the Curtain theatre, one of the actors with whom Jonson had recently been imprisoned at Marshalsea, a notoriously quarrelsome man named Gabriel Spenser, challenged him to a duel in Hoxton Fields: in the course of which fight Jonson – equipped, as

he later protested, with a weapon ten inches shorter than Spenser's –
fatally wounded his challenger. Duelling was an illegal pursuit in England
at this time, and Jonson found himself charged with manslaughter. While
awaiting sentence he was visited in gaol by a Catholic priest, and
persuaded to convert to the Roman faith. His decision is not at first easy to
understand. Jonson was not only at the threshold of a promising theatrical
career, but ambitious to enter the service of Queen Elizabeth, who, after
numerous plots and continuing fears and rumours of a new post-Armada
invasion by Spain, had introduced ever more severe penalties and
disabilities for Catholics in England, and for those who attempted to
convert her Protestant subjects to Rome.

Two factors may have affected Jonson's decision to convert at this
time. Believing that he faced a certain and imminent death, he might
(firstly) have recalled that the Catholic church, through its Sacrament of
Penance, offered a more assured form of Absolution than was available in
the Church of England; and, for that reason alone, been tempted to
undergo a last-minute conversion.[18] But Jonson finally escaped the
gallows through an archaic legal device known as benefit of clergy, by
which first-time offenders were spared after conviction if they showed
they could read a single verse from the Bible (usually Psalm 51, verse 1:
Miserere mei, Deus. . . : "Have mercy upon me, O God. . ."). After
passing this simple test – originally introduced in England to protect
ordained clergy from criminal sentencing, and later extended to other
classes – Jonson was released immediately from gaol: branded on the
thumb with a hot iron to denote his status as a convicted felon, but in other
respects a free man. By that time, however, his decision to convert had
already been made. He would persevere in his new faith for another dozen
years

Awaiting sentence in his cell at Newgate, Jonson must also however
have pondered the paradox presented by the title of this book: that of *loyal
dissent.* Was it possible to be simultaneously a true subject of the Queen
of England and a faithful member of the Church of Rome? This dilemma
was often presented to Catholics in England at this time in the form of
what was known as "the bloody question". Were they prepared (it was
asked) to take up arms against the Pope – who had excommunicated

---

[18] Absolution was also available at this time to members of the Anglican Church,
but in a less assured form, being vested not in a sacrament but in the possibly
fallible judgement of an individual minister.

Elizabeth and supported Spanish designs against her country – if he sent an army to invade England?[19] The Jesuits answered roundly that in such an eventuality they would stand by the Pope and not fight against him. Other sections of the Catholic community in England wavered and differed in their loyalties. On this all-important issue Jonson is likely to have been guided by the priest who visited him in gaol and persuaded him to convert. This man has been plausibly identified in recent years as Father Thomas Wright, a notably independent Yorkshireman who had studied at various Catholic seminaries throughout Europe, been admitted to the Jesuit Order in Rome and ordained as priest in 1586. In 1594, however, the Jesuits had moved to expel Wright from their Order for expressing "extravagant opinions" in a tract exploring the hot question of the day: "Whether Catholics in England may use arms and other means in defence of the Queen and the kingdom against the Spanish". Wright's answer to this question was emphatically affirmative. He is fiercely mistrustful of Spanish intentions, which he sees as driven not by religious motives by "lust of ruling", and openly disdainful of the Pope's intervention in what he sees as purely secular matters of political allegiance. When the Jesuits' attempt to expel Wright from their Order failed, he resigned of his own volition, and returned to England. His staunchly loyalist position is one that Jonson is likely to have found especially congenial. It offered the encouraging hope that he himself might become a good Catholic while remaining at heart a patriotic Englishman.[20]

Throughout the decade or so following his conversion, however, Jonson's own loyalties were often acutely divided. He had many friends within the English Catholic community, and was alert to their needs and causes, as several of his early poems testify. But he had also now entered

---

[19] In Elizabeth's day an answer to the question could not legally be enforced, and there was no stipulated penalty for a refusal to answer. The Oath of Allegiance introduced under James in 1606, posed this question in more emphatic form, and carried stiffer penalties and conditions.

[20] Theodor Stroud, "Ben Jonson and Father Thomas Wright", *English Literary History*, 14 (1947), 274-82 identifies Wright as the priest who visited Jonson in gaol. An English text of Wright's tract, *An licitum sit catholicis in Anglia arma sumere, et aliis modiis, reginam et regnum defendere contra Hispanos,* is given in John Strype, *Annals of the Reformation*, 7 vols. (Oxford, 1874), vol. 3, pp. 2, 583-97 (but misattributed there to another Father Wright).

the service of the new King, James VI and I, with whom many members of that community, initially hopeful of royal support, were feeling increasingly disenchanted. In a series of court masques and entertainments of brilliant ingenuity and splendour, Jonson and his scenic collaborator Inigo Jones extolled the policies and achievements of the Stuart dynasty. Yet his plays, by witty indirection, sometimes told a different story. For his Roman tragedy, *Sejanus*, he was summoned by the Privy Council to answer charges of "popery and treason" (*Informations*, 251-2, *CWBJ*, 5. 375). For jokes about King James and his Scottish followers in their jointly-written comedy, *Eastward Ho!* Jonson, George Chapman, and John Marston were imprisoned and treated with severity: "The report was that they should then had their ears cut and noses", Drummond noted in his account of the episode (*Informations*, 207-15; *CWBJ*, 5. 373-4). This was a dangerous moment in Jonson's career, which might (once again) have led directly to the gallows. When the three men were finally released – thanks in all likelihood to the intervention of Jonson's patron, Esmé Stewart, a cousin of the King – Jonson celebrated their escape in the company of his closest friends, including his former Master from Westminster School and the prodigiously talented young jurist who was soon to become the country's leading authority on questions of free speech and constitutional authority.

"After their delivery he banqueted all his friends", wrote Drummond; "there was Camden, Selden, and others." Present at this gathering too was Jonson's formidable mother.

> At the midst of the feast his old mother drank to him, and show him a paper which she had, if the sentence had taken execution, to have mixed in the prison among his drink, which was full of lusty strong poison. And that she was no churl, she told she minded first to have drunk of it herself.

Light-hearted jokes about Scottish knights, their Scottish king, and "a few industrious Scots. . . dispersed over the face of the whole earth" (*Eastward Ho!, 3.3.30-5*) may seem scarcely deserving of the response that was threatened on this occasion. But anti-Scottish feeling ran strong in England at this time, and was often associated in particular with the discontent of English Catholics, who were closely associated in the official mind with the plots that had been uncovered, soon after James's accession, to dislodge or destroy the newly installed king. Shaken by these threats, James issued a proclamation early in 1604 ordering all Jesuits and seminary priests to leave the country, a measure that further angered the Catholic community. In November of the following year an even more spectacular plot was detected on the very eve of its execution: to blow up the House of Lords on the occasion of the State Opening of Parliament, thus destroying King James, his son Prince Henry, and his leading ministers; a scheme intended, in the words of one of its leaders, Guy Fawkes, "to have blown them back into Scotland".

Jonson was well acquainted with the leading conspirators in the Gunpowder Plot, and must have had prior knowledge of the Plot's existence. For on or about October 9th 1605, less than a month before the intended coup on November 5th, he attended a supper party at William Patrick's hostelry in the Strand, the Irish Boy, in the company of many of its ringleaders, including Robert Catesby, Francis Tresham, Thomas Wintour, John Ashfield, Sir Josceline Percy, and Lord Mordaunt. What can Jonson have been doing in this company? That he was himself party to a conspiracy to murder the king and leading figures at court upon whom his very life and livelihood depended is hardly conceivable; that he had infiltrated the group as a government spy operating on behalf of Robert Cecil seems an equally fanciful conjecture. Jonson had a particular loathing of spies and spying, and held Cecil himself in contempt.[21] He was to persevere in the Catholic faith for another five years after the Gunpowder Plot, remaining on close and friendly terms with those in the Catholic community, none of whom ever accused him of duplicity. His role on this occasion may rather have been to restrain and perhaps negotiate on behalf of his more extreme co-religionists.

In the immediate wake of the Plot Jonson was instructed by Cecil to search out an unnamed Catholic priest – possibly Father Wright himself – to assist the Commission in its enquiries. The priest, it was hoped, would persuade Guy Fawkes, then in strict custody in the Tower of London, that it was now his duty to reveal the names of his co-conspirators. In due course Jonson reported that he had been unable to locate the priest. Father Wright was eventually brought before the commission, but by that time the services of a priest were no longer required. The hitherto silent and

---

[21] *Informations*, 194-7, 274, *Epigrams*, 59, 101.36, etc. (*CWBJ*, 5. 373, 377, 141, 168). The improbable scenario of Jonson as spy is set out by B. N. De Luna, *Jonson's Romish Plot* (Oxford, 1967), ch. 4.

stoical Guy Fawkes had at last broken down under torture, and confessed the names of his fellow conspirators. While many details of this episode remain obscure, the acute embarrassment of Jonson's position at this moment, caught between sharply opposed demands for loyalty and dissent, is all too evident.[22]

Jonson finally returned to the Anglican Church after the assassination in Paris in May 1610 of the French King Henri IV by a Catholic fanatic named François Ravaillac: an event which prompted James to introduce new anti-Catholic legislation in England of even greater severity than hitherto. The new laws, which forbade Catholics all access to his court, would otherwise have swiftly ended Jonson's court career. Jonson's old mentor, William Camden, was recruited at this moment to serve as historical advisor at Chelsea College at Thameshot, a Protestant "spiritual garrison" newly established by James to combat Catholic propaganda. Camden's successor as Head Master of Westminster School, Richard Ireland, a convert to Catholicism, made a contrary choice, abandoning his post and fleeing to France to avoid further exposure.[23] It was an acutely difficult time to remain a good Catholic in England: to be loyal to one's faith, loyal to the king, and judged worthy of maintaining the highest office. Jonson celebrated his return to the Anglican Church by drinking the entire chalice of wine at his first communion.

Jonson's Catholic years, for all their difficulty, coincided with the rapid flourishing of his career. His sometimes tempestuous collaborations at court with the designer Inigo Jones began spectacularly with *The Masque of Blackness* in 1605, which, at Anne's own request, presented the Queen and eleven other ladies of the court 'all painted like blackamoors, face and neck bare', dazzlingly bejewelled, seated on a scallop shell drawn into the Banqueting Hall on the crest of a moving wave, escorted by sea monsters. Further triumphs were soon to follow, and Jones and Jonson continued to work together in a productive if at times uneasy partnership over three decades. Jonson's Catholic years also saw the performance of some of his most successful comedies, by which he is best remembered today: *Volpone, Epicene, The Alchemist,* and in all probability, the revised version of *Every Man In His Humour,* its location

---

[22] For details, see Donaldson, *Life*, chs. 10, 11, 13.
[23] Thomas Fuller, *The Church History of Britain*, ed. J. S. Brewer, 6 vols. (Oxford, 1645), vol. 5, p. 387; Herendeen, *William Camden*, pp. 425, 516; Field, *The King's Nurseries*, p. 31.

now shifted from Florence to London. Amazingly and amusingly intricate in their plotting, such comedies, like those that soon followed – *Bartholomew Fair*, *The Devil is an Ass,* and (a decade later) *The Staple of News* – focus on the frauds, projects, and pretensions of contemporary city life, reflecting the follies of Londoners back to the very audiences that flocked to enjoy them.

For all his successes in the playhouse, however, Jonson did not work primarily, as Shakespeare did, for a single company, or even primarily within the theatre. At intervals he forsook altogether the "loathèd stage" (as he called it in a moment of vexation, after the failure of his comedy *The New Inn* in 1629) for other creative and scholarly pursuits. In the course of a notably varied career Jonson wrote (perhaps) two dozen plays for the public stage, but much else besides. He completed more than thirty masques and entertainments for royal and aristocratic patrons, for the City of London, for leading guild companies, and for wealthy individuals. He compiled three substantial collections of poetry, and completed two translations of Horace's *Ars Poetica* along with other classical translations and occasional verses. He wrote two English Grammars, along with numerous historical essays and miscellaneous reflections on "men and matters" – on questions of statecraft, theology, philology, rhetoric, poetics, personal conduct – in his commonplace book, *Discoveries*. He began, but did not complete, an epic poem "of the worthies of his country roused by fame" (*Informations*, 1-2, *CWBJ*, 5. 359). Through the sheer versatility of his work, and his quick realisation of the value of its publication, he became in his lifetime a writer who was more widely and variously known, in Britain and abroad, than was Shakespeare, only half of whose plays were in print by the time of his death in April 1616. Early that same year, Jonson had been granted a royal pension to serve as James I's laureate poet; in November 1616 he published an imposing folio edition of his collected *Works*. Many regarded Ben Jonson as the greatest writer that England had ever produced: as the figure who defined and dominated the present age. In his poem to Shakespeare's memory prefixed to the First Folio in 1623 Jonson offered a contrary opinion, hailing his now-dead friend as "Soul of the age!" and a writer of transcendent genius. "He was not of an age, but for all time", Jonson wrote (*CWBJ*, 5. 639). No one until that moment had offered such a powerful tribute to Shakespeare, or so confidently predicted his enduring fame.

Severely disabled by a stroke in 1628, Jonson returned in his final years to live close to the School where he had studied in his youth, lodging in "the house under which you pass as you go out of the churchyard into the old Palace".[24] Visiting him at this time George Morley, future Bishop of Winchester – a fellow Old Westminster – describes Jonson as sharing his pension with "a woman that governed him with whom he lived and died near the Abbey in Westminster; and that neither he nor she took much care for next week, and would be sure not to want wine, which he usually took too much before he went to bed, if not oftener and sooner".[25] The great antiquarian scholar, Sir Robert Cotton, an old friend of Jonson's since their days at Westminster under Camden's tutelage, lived nearby until his death in 1631; Jonson often borrowed books from his magnificent library before it was forcibly closed by Charles I in 1629. Robert Cotton and his friend John Selden had incurred the King's displeasure through their outspoken criticism of the growing power wielded by the royal favourite, George Villiers, Duke of Buckingham. Those in authority evidently associated Jonson with his friends' critique: for when the highly unpopular Buckingham was assassinated in 1628 he was sharply questioned by the Attorney General for his suspected authorship of verses written in praise of Buckingham's assassin, John Felton: a charge that Jonson flatly denied. By this stage of his life he had learned discretion. During his final years he repeatedly affirmed his unswerving loyalty to Charles and his consort, Henrietta Maria. He must have shared many of the doubts and fears of his closest friends about Charles's leadership, but had no wish, at this fragile moment in his own life and that of the nation, to play the heroic role of a vocal dissenter.

Jonson died on August 6th 1637, at the height of summer, when many of his friends and acquaintances were out of town. But the crowd that assembled at his house in Westminster to accompany his body on its short journey across to the Abbey included none the less "all or the greatest part of the nobility and gentry then in town".[26] In the months and years that followed, Jonson's death was widely mourned, by none more strongly than those who counted themselves "the sons of Ben": members of his so-

---

[24] John Aubrey, *Brief Lives*, ed. Kate Bennett, 2 vols. (Oxford, 2015), vol. 1, pp. 357-8.

[25] Aubrey, *Brief Lives*, ed. Bennett, vol. 1, p. 363.

[26] Sir Edward Walker, Life Records 103, LR 92, online *CWBJ*.

called "tribe", who pledged to his memory a firmer loyalty they might at this moment have been ready to pay the reigning King. "When time has made/Slaughter of kings that in the world have swayed', wrote one such follower, glimpsing (one might almost think) the cataclysmic events soon to come in England, "A greener bays shall crown Ben Jonson's name'.[27] Jonson himself, who liked to believe that poets were at least as important as kings and their influence far more enduring, would no doubt have been comforted by this pleasing thought.

---

[27] Owen Felltham, "To the memory of Immortal Ben", 67-9, in *Jonsonus Virbius*, Literary Record, online *CWBJ*.

Among the many distinguished churchmen and important writers produced by Westminster School, there is only one about whom it can be said that he was both a revered model of priesthood and probably the greatest devotional poet in our language: George Herbert. His influence in the fields of both religion and literature has been extensive and profound: his life, work and writings established an enduring template of pastoral ministry at its most saintly, while his lyrical verse set a standard for poetic conversation with God which has since been emulated by writers from Henry Vaughan to Rowan Williams. As Sir Francis Bacon wrote in 1625, Herbert was one in whom "Divinitie, and Poesie met", a view confirmed by the dedication of a day in the Anglican liturgical calendar, 27 February, to "George Herbert, priest, poet".[1] In the following brief account of Herbert's significance in uniting spirituality and poetry, I first outline his life and education, particularly his experience of Westminster School, then look closely at what makes his poetry special and, finally, suggest several ways in which the Westminster heritage of loyalty and dissent may be seen in his approach to God and the world.

George Herbert, though claimed as an English poet, was in fact Welsh by origin and ancestry. His parents both came from distinguished Welsh families: his mother was a descendant of the princes of upper Powys, and his father's Welsh ancestors were described as a "*Generous*, Noble, *and Ancient Family*" by Herbert's first biographer.[2] Among his Herbert cousins were the Earls of Pembroke, who were connected by marriage to the great literary family of Mary Sidney and her brother Philip, and by patronage to the leading writer of the period, William Shakespeare. Herbert, a generation younger than Shakespeare, was born in 1593 at Montgomery, in the county for which his father and grandfather had both previously served as Sheriff and Member of Parliament. Within four years of his birth, Herbert and his siblings had moved across the border into England with their mother, Magdalene Herbert, to live at her family home in Shropshire after the premature death of her husband. By 1601, Magdalene Herbert established herself and her children in a house at Charing Cross, and a more settled period of George's young life ensued.

---

[1] Sir Francis Bacon, *The translation of certain Psalmes into English Verse* (London: Hanna Barret and Richard Whittaker, 1625), A3v; www.churchofengland.org, Holy Days. See also Clarke 1992.

[2] Barnabus Oley, "A Prefatory View of the Life of Mr. Geo. Herbert", *Herbert's Remains* (London: Timothy Garthwait, 1652), b6ʳ. For further early biographical information on Herbert, see Walton 1670, and among modern biographies, Charles 1977, Drury 2013, Malcolmson 2004, Powers-Beck 1998 and Wilcox 2004.

London itself, however, was far from settled. The dramatic Essex rebellion against Queen Elizabeth I had taken place in London in the spring of 1601, and although the revolt was suppressed and the Earl of Essex executed, the court at Whitehall continued in a state of uncertainty as the ageing Elizabeth had no direct heir. The threat of plague also was never far away: there was a major outbreak in the city early in 1603 which killed almost a quarter of the population. In that same year, the old Queen died, and was succeeded by her Stuart cousin, James VI of Scotland. When James VI/I and his Queen made their royal entry into London (delayed by the plague) in March 1604, the Jacobean era began in earnest. One of the most significant events of 1604 was the Hampton Court Conference, called by James as an attempt to resolve tensions within the Church of England, primarily between the bishops and the Calvinist puritans. The most notable outcome of these discussions was the commissioning of a new translation of the English Bible, leading eventually to the 1611 publication of the King James Version. Meanwhile, in 1604, the auspicious year of the new King's formal welcome to London and the conference on the future of the church, the eleven-year-old Herbert was enrolled as a day pupil at Westminster School.

When Herbert began his connection with Westminster, the School was benefiting from the inspiring presence of the great scholar, linguist and preacher, Lancelot Andrewes. He had become Dean of Westminster in 1601, the year in which Herbert and his family began living in nearby Charing Cross. As a result of the Hampton Court conference, Andrewes would go on to become the leading translator among the many working on the new Bible. In the meantime, although he was officially only the titular head of the School by virtue of his position as Dean, Andrewes exercised a major influence on the pupils there. Herbert's contemporary, John Hacket, gave a detailed account of Andrewes, whom he honoured as "the first that planted me in my tender Studies, and water'd them continually with his Bounty".[3] Hacket makes clear how Andrewes directed the masters and shaped the curriculum:

---

[3] John Hacket, *Scrinia Reserata* (London: Samuel Lowndes, 1693), p. 45. Hacket's account of the education he shared with Herbert appears in this memoir of John Williams, the Welsh-born bishop to whom Hacket was chaplain before becoming Bishop of Lichfield and Coventry.

> I told ... how strict that excellent Man [Andrewes] was, to charge our Masters, that they should give us Lessons out of none but the most Classical Authors; that he did often supply the Place both of Head School-master and Usher for the space of an whole week together, and gave us not an hour of Loitering-time from morning to night. How he caused our Exercises in Prose and Verse to be brought to him, to examine our Style and Proficiency. (Hacket 1693: 45)

Lancelot Andrewes – that "strict" but "excellent" pedagogue – clearly had the School firmly under his benevolent control. In addition to the fundamental spiritual and musical training integral to the experience of Westminster, the distinctive qualities of the education insisted upon by Andrewes were twofold. First, the boys must show scholarly discipline: Hacket points out that they were permitted no

> "Loitering-time", and refers elsewhere to the boys' ordered life of "rising betimes, and constant study".[4] The second element of Andrewes' educational vision was to teach his pupils a range of classical and biblical languages. Hacket notes that Andrewes would give additional tutoring to the scholars in his own lodgings in the evenings, "sometimes thrice in a week": [he] kept them with him from eight till eleven, unfolding to them the best Rudiments of the *Greek* Tongue, and the Elements of the *Hebrew* Grammar, and all this he did to Boys without any compulsion of Correction; nay, I never heard him utter so much as a word of Austerity among us. (Hacket 1693: 45)

While other schools at the time were particularly focused on Latin, Andrewes was giving Westminster a distinctive curriculum with its emphasis on a plurality of ancient languages. It was into this atmosphere of scholarship, intellectual discipline and awareness of the spirituality of learning that Herbert was drawn as a day pupil from 1604, and to which he became a King's Scholar in 1605.

That same year, one of the most regularly commemorated events of British history took place – or rather, did not. On November 5th 1605, Guy

---

[4] From the biography of Hacket by Thomas Plume, appended to Hacket's *Century of Sermons* (London: Robert Scott, 1675), p. iv.

Fawkes and his fellow plotters made a foiled attempt to blow up the King and Parliament in what became known as the Gunpowder Plot. A devastating actual explosion may have been avoided, but the plot still blew a great hole metaphorically in the King's hopes for religious harmony. The effects of the conspiracy, not to mention the executions of its leaders, must have overshadowed Herbert's early years at the school. At the time, his brother Edward – the philosopher, poet and future Lord Herbert of Cherbury – was following the family tradition as Member of Parliament for Montgomery, and would normally have been attending the ceremonial Opening of Parliament. Writing later about the Gunpowder Plot, he claimed to have had a premonition of the danger facing the king and his parliament on November 5th: "The night before this horrible Conspiracy was to bee acted I was two severall tymes warned in my sleepe not to goe to the Parliament that day."[5] This first-hand experience of the near miss and ensuing crisis of the "Gunpowder Treason" would have been conveyed directly to his younger brother George, highlighting the topographical and emotional proximity of the young Westminster scholar to the urgent political and religious issues of his day.

Meanwhile, King and Parliament continued unscathed, and Herbert pressed ahead with his studies along with his friend John Hacket, whose account of Lancelot Andrewes' role at Westminster School extends even to their rare moments of leisure. Hacket reports that, while Andrewes was Dean, he liked to walk to Chiswick "for his Recreation" but never did so "without a brace of this young Fry". Even though Andrewes and his youthful companions were indulging in 'way-faring Leisure', the Dean still taught those who accompanied him on his walk, always showing a "singular dexterity to fill those narrow Vessels with a Funnel" (Hacket 1693: 45). Herbert and his fellow scholars may have been "narrow vessels", but they were filled to the brim with learning by Andrewes and by their experience of School life. Andrewes' beneficial influence undoubtedly lingered long after he left Westminster at the end of 1605 to become Bishop of Chichester and, subsequently, Winchester. The School's masters (including Richard Ireland) and the new Dean (Richard Neile) evidently continued the rich classical curriculum that Andrewes had fostered, the legacy of which training may be discerned in the formal inventiveness and linguistic precision of Herbert's English verse. It should

---

[5] From an early draft of Edward Herbert's autobiography, cited in Charles 1977: 50.

not be forgotten, however, that Herbert wrote accomplished Latin and Greek verse in addition to his better-known English poetry. He was entrusted with translating part of Bacon's *Advancement of Learning* into Latin, and his earliest publications were Latin poems.[6] It is fitting that among Herbert's Latin compositions is an epistle written to Lancelot Andrewes soon after his consecration as Bishop of Winchester in 1619. As Herbert's brother, Edward later remarked of George's accomplishments, the English poetry for which he was most famed fell "far short", in Edward's view, "of expressing those perfections he had in the Greek and Latin Tongue".[7] While George Herbert's great literary predecessor at Westminster, Ben Jonson, wrote that he "owed" to the first Head Master of Westminster School, William Camden, "All that I am in arts, all that I know", George Herbert could well have said the same of Lancelot Andrewes.[8]

Herbert's formative period at Westminster (1604-9) thus coincided with the aura of Andrewes, the impact of the Hampton Court Conference and the drama of the Gunpowder Plot just outside the walls of the School. However, it was also concurrent with a remarkable cultural moment in London. The Globe playhouse on the opposite bank of the river witnessed the first performances of *King Lear, Macbeth* and *Pericles* during these years, as well as Jonson's *Volpone* and Thomas Middleton's *The Revenger's Tragedy*. Elsewhere in the vicinity, comedies such as Middleton's *A Mad World, My Masters* and Marston's *The Dutch Courtesan* were keeping Herbert's fellow-Londoners entertained, while the new works for sale at the booksellers around St Paul's Cathedral in these years included *Hamlet*, Drayton's *Poems* and Joseph Hall's *Arte of Divine Meditation*. It is difficult to discern the extent to which Herbert and his fellow Westminsters were aware of the flourishing cultural life of the world beyond the walls of their intensely scholarly and almost monastic existence at the school – but the knowing wit, rhetorical appeal and

---

[6] The translation was published as *De augmentis scientiae* in 1623; Herbert's first published poems were Latin elegies contributed to volumes on the deaths of Prince Henry (1612) and Queen Anna (1619).

[7] Edward Herbert, *Life ... written by himself*, ed J. W. Shuttleworth (London: Oxford University Press, 1976), p. 8.

[8] Ben Jonson, "To William Camden", *Poems*, ed Ian Donaldson (Oxford: Oxford University Press, 1975), p. 13.

worldly irony of Herbert's later writings certainly mark him as a product of that thrilling literary moment.

Herbert left Westminster School in 1609 at the age of sixteen, he and John Hacket having been elected to scholarships at Trinity College, Cambridge.[9] Hacket's biographer later recounted the parting words of the Head Master to the two young men:

That he expected to have credit by *them two* [sic] at the *University*, or would never hope for it afterwards by any while he lived: and added withal, that he need give them no counsel to follow their Books, but rather to study moderately, and use exercise; their parts being so good, that if they were careful not to impair their health with too much study, they would not fail to arrive at the top of learning in any *Art* or *Science*.[10]

Both these excellent pupils did indeed achieve academic success at Cambridge, but "*Master Ireland*" knew Herbert well: he suffered from ill health throughout his time as a student, possibly through excessive study. Certainly, Herbert's letters home – particularly to his new step-father, Sir John Danvers, whom his mother had married in 1608 – often refer to health matters, and even more frequently request money for reading matter. The books were clearly worth the expenditure of time as well as money (if not, perhaps, health), for Herbert gained the second highest marks in the university when he graduated in 1613, aged twenty. He was almost immediately made a Minor Fellow of Trinity College and, two years later, a Major Fellow. It is evident that he was the outstanding classicist of his generation: by 1618 he was "praelector" in rhetoric, and in 1619 he was deputising for the University Orator, the position he described in a letter to Danvers as "the finest place in the University".[11] He became Orator himself in 1620, and his duties included Latin orations to King James I, the Prince of Wales and many other visiting dignitaries. He had become, as his Westminster Head Master had anticipated and hoped, a "credit" to his School and University.

Biographers of George Herbert disagree about the underlying motivations and trajectory of his life in the 1620s. He was moving in courtly circles and in 1624 became, like other Herberts before him, the

[9] The third university scholar in that year, who went to Christ Church, Oxford, was Henry King, future poet (author of "The Exequy" in memory of his wife) and Bishop of Chichester.

[10] Plume in Hacket 1675: v.

[11] Herbert, *Works*, ed F. E. Hutchinson (Oxford: Clarendon Press, 1941), p. 369.

Member of Parliament for Montgomery. However, he did not pursue the political and diplomatic career of which this might have been the beginning; neither did he remain in Cambridge and put his prodigious linguistic talents to further academic use. While some critics interpret these choices as signs of failure or disappointment, it seems clear to me that Herbert had divinity and poetry in view from the earliest days of his adult life. In a letter to his mother in 1610, he announces a "resolution" that "my poor Abilities in *Poetry*, shall be all, and ever consecrated to Gods glory"; in another, to his stepfather in 1617, he explains that he is "setting foot into Divinity" in order to "lay the platform" of his own "future life" (Herbert 1941: 363, 364). It is therefore not surprising to find that, after a brief period in the rush of political debate, Herbert fulfilled his longer-lasting spiritual intentions and was ordained Deacon. What *is*, perhaps, surprising is that Herbert did not seek a more prominent position in the church – such as the bishopric that his early mentor Lancelot Andrewes achieved, or the post of Dean of St Paul's filled by Herbert's friend and fellow poet, John Donne. When Herbert did finally settle into a priestly function in 1630, it was as rector of the small church of St Andrew's, Bemerton, between the cathedral city of Salisbury and Wilton House, the home of his cousins, the Earls of Pembroke. To be a rural parish priest was Herbert's ultimate vocation, his own "top of learning" – though not quite the kind of achievement that Ireland had predicted. As Herbert asserted, the library to which every country parson should aspire is not a collection of learned books but a "holy Life".[12] As some of his contemporaries apparently observed, Herbert "did not manage his brave parts to his best advantage and preferment"[13] – a comment that may be interpreted either as criticism or high praise.

Herbert had been the rector of Bemerton for less than three years when his chronic ill health finally took its toll: he died of consumption in 1633, one month before his fortieth birthday. He had married his stepfather's cousin, Jane Danvers, in 1629, but they had no children; the legacy that has kept his name alive is textual. Very soon after his death, Herbert's collection of English poems, *The Temple*, was published by the press of his own university, Cambridge. Nearly twenty years later, in 1652, his prose handbook *The Countrey Parson: His Character and Rule of Holy Life* was published under the supplementary title *The Priest to the*

---

[12] Herbert, *The Countrey Parson, Works*, p. 278.
[13] Oley 1652: a11$^\text{v}$-a12$^\text{r}$.

Temple, thereby linking it with Herbert's volume of poems which by then was already into its sixth edition. In fact, the poems were so popular among a wide spectrum of early readers – including King Charles I, the nonconformist minister Richard Baxter, the diarist Lady Anne Clifford, and Oliver Cromwell's chaplain, Peter Sterry – that *The Temple* had gone through at least thirteen editions by the beginning of the eighteenth century.[14] The poems appealed to such contrasting readers because they seemed to cut across the disagreements that were dividing the nation in the mid and later seventeenth century. Herbert's lyrics do not court controversy or write *about* God in doctrinal or polemical tones; they are addressed *to* God in a personal and conversational manner. As Richard Baxter wrote succinctly in 1681, "*Herbert* speaks to *God* like one that *really believeth a God ... Heart-work* and *Heaven-work* make up his Books".[15]

One of George Herbert's later seventeenth-century admirers, the nonconformist preacher Oliver Heywood, paid him one of the highest compliments possible for a devotional poet: that Herbert was "the incomparable sweet singer of our *Israel*".[16] This magnificently expressive phrase sums up much that is still valued in Herbert's work, and forms the basis for the following account of his qualities as a poet.[17]

Heywood begins with a claim that Herbert is "incomparable", suggesting something of the depth of admiration that his poetry has evoked for nearly four centuries. In many ways, the adjective is strictly accurate, since Herbert was indeed doing something bold and untried with his verse, which cannot be directly compared with the work of any other poet at the time. His starting-point was a rejection of contemporary secular poetry – a daring move, considering the fact that he was growing up when sonnet sequences and love lyrics were all the rage. In his early years at Cambridge, Herbert lamented that poetry seemed to be wearing only "*Venus* Livery", and asked God, almost plaintively, "Why are not

---

[14] For further discussion of the phenomenon of Herbert's broad readership, see Ray 1986 and Wilcox 2009.

[15] Richard Baxter, *Poetical Fragments* (London: B Simmons,1681), A7ᵛ.

[16] Oliver Heywood, *The sure mercies of David* (London: Tho Parkhurst, 1672), p. 119.

[17] For two comprehensive studies of Herbert's verse, see Summers 1981 and Hodgkins 1993.

Sonnets made of thee?"[18] By the time he was writing the more mature verse of *The Temple*, Herbert had put this right and was "making" poems, including sonnets, about God, written in a style that deliberately avoided the "enchanted groves" and "purling streams" of contemporary verse, as he described them in his poem "Jordan" (I). His preference was for the "beautie" exemplified by "truth" itself, or discovered in the plain biblical phrase with which the poem concludes: '*My God, My King*' (200). It is fascinating to think of the former Orator taking such a radical step towards a transparently expressive poetic mode, and saying farewell (in his poem "The Forerunners") to the "lovely enchanting language" (612) with which he worked so adeptly. Of course, it takes greater rhetorical skill to write with exquisite simplicity than with fancy embellishment, and Herbert's writing, though often using everyday vocabulary, is highly crafted and richly expressive. What he was eager to avoid was the *excess* of artistry that can obscure the very subject that it seeks to honour, especially when that subject is divine. At the end of "Jordan" (II), Herbert's speaker receives a piece of tantalisingly good advice on how to write poetry about the love of God: "*There is in love a sweetnesse readie penn'd: / Copie out onely that, and save expense*" (367). This is no easy task, but Herbert's English poems explore with unprecedented openness the complex process of "copying" God's love in word and deed. Herbert writes to, and about, his "deare angrie Lord" as naturally as worldly poets contend with their lovers ("Bitter-sweet", 587). "Dulnesse", for example, opens with a sense of desperation – "Why do I languish thus, drooping and dull, / As if I were all earth?" – but moves swiftly to a joyful declaration of love: "Thou art my lovelinesse, my life, my light" (410-11). This is sacred love poetry with a difference: delightfully fluent, accessibly honest, and addressed to God as if he were the speaker's best friend. The mid-seventeenth century poet Henry Vaughan, who was inspired to write devotional poems through reading *The Temple*, asserted that Herbert was "the first" to take this new direction, giving "check" with his "holy *life* and *verse*" to what had been the "most flourishing and admired *wit* of his time".[19] Herbert was thus

---

[18] George Herbert, *English Poems*, ed Helen Wilcox (Cambridge: Cambridge University Press, 2007), p. 4. All further quotations from Herbert's poems are taken from this edition with page numbers supplied in the text.

[19] Henry Vaughan, "The Author's Preface", *Silex Scintillans* (1655), *The Complete Poems*, ed Alan Rudrum (Harmondsworth: Penguin, 1976), p. 142.

"incomparable": a pioneer, developing a new kind of poetic dialogue with God.

Heywood's second adjective for Herbert's writing was "sweet", a word suggesting the fine lyrical beauty of the poems. There is indeed a purity of phrase about his lyrics – a sense that, as he puts it in "The Forerunners", the language they employ has been "washed" (612) of its sour or worldly associations. The word "sweet" was itself a favourite of Herbert's, making it all the more apt that Heywood should use it of *The Temple*.[20] In Herbert's usage, 'sweet' does not have any sugary or sentimental meanings; as we have seen, he finds in God's own love, which is stronger than death, "*a sweetnesse readie penn'd*". Herbert's verse is "sweet" because it is rhetorically beautiful to read and hear, but also because it celebrates the resilient "sweetnesse" of redemptive love in action. The Holy Spirit is said to make up for human errors with its own "sweet art" ("Easter", 140), and when Herbert's God reappears after an apparent absence, that "return" is greeted as "sweet and clean" ("The Flower", 567). Herbert's most intense exploration of sweetness is "Vertue":

> Sweet day, so cool, so calm, so bright,
> > The bridall of the earth and skie:
> The dew shall weep thy fall to night;
> > > For thou must die.
>
> Sweet rose, whose hue angrie and brave
> > Bids the rash gazer wipe his eye:
> Thy root is ever in its grave,
> > > And thou must die.
>
> Sweet spring, full of sweet dayes and roses,
> A box where sweets compacted lie;
> > My musick shows ye have your closes,
> > > And all must die.
>
> Onely a sweet and vertuous soul,
> > Like season'd timber, never gives;

---

[20] On the significance of the word "sweet" to Herbert, see Herbert 2007: xliv-xlv and Sherwood 1989: 57-76.

> But though the whole world turn to coal,
>> Then chiefly lives. (316)

The poem is sweet in itself: sensual yet lucid, and elegantly constructed with its subtle repetitions and partial half-line refrain. It presents a variety of kinds of sweetness: innocent freshness (the new day), visual beauty (the rose), the promise of renewal (spring) and sensual experience (the sweet-smelling herbs "compacted" in a box). The greatest example, however, is saved for the final stanza. The reader expects the concluding moral to be *carpe diem* – seize this sweet day (and the rose and the spring) before it fades – but the climax turns out to be something altogether different. The familiar, temporary sweetnesses are trumped by the spiritual, eternal sweetness, that of the "vertuous soul" which does not die along with the rest of the transitory world, but "chiefly lives". In its modest and understated way, "Vertue" turns the worlds of poetry and logic upside down.

When Herbert writes in "Vertue" that his "musick shows ye have your closes", he is ostensibly reminding us that all things "must die" and that music, in particular, makes this clear with its cadences, the closing chords bringing a musical phrase so firmly to an end. In addition, his reference to "my musick" reveals that he thought of his poems as words which themselves made music with their own forms and sounds, a perception evidently shared by Heywood since he describes our poet as an "incomparable sweet *singer*". This idea of Herbert as a "singer" was a widely held view among Herbert's early readers, and highlights the especially lyrical quality of his verse.[21] His poems have titles such as "A true Hymne", "A Dialogue-Antheme" and "Antiphon", drawing attention to their musical conception, and Herbert makes particularly expressive use of features common to music and poetry: sophisticated rhythms and melodic sounds. In "Deniall", the miserable speaker's soul is said to lie like an abandoned musical instrument, "out of sight, / Untun'd, unstrung", and the final line of each stanza hangs "Discontented" (288), breaking the expected pattern of both metre and rhyme. The poem gives vent to grief and frustration: "O that thou shouldst give dust a tongue / To crie to thee, / And then not heare it crying!" (289). When, finally, there is a tentative

---

[21] Barnabus Oley, for example, refers to Herbert as the "sweet singer of the Temple" (Oley 1652: a11ᵛ), and in 1697 Daniel Baker praised Herbert's poems as the "Songs" and "Anthems" of "our sweet Psalmist" (Baker 1697: 87-8, 86).

turn from deep sorrow to prayerful optimism, the lines are no longer "untun'd":

> O cheer and tune my heartlesse breast,
> Deferre no time;
> That so thy favours granting my request,
> They and my minde may chime,
> And mend my ryme. (289)

In this last stanza, for the first time in the poem, the second, fourth and fifth lines rhyme with one another. The fact that this symbolic threefold rhyme carries meaning is highlighted by the presence of the word "chime" among the rhyming sounds, for this is what rhymes naturally do. Here it represents the aligning of the speaker's "minde" (the assonance of "my" and "minde" anticipating the ensuing rhyme) with God's purpose: both the poem and the speaker's heart have been "mended" even before the prayerful request could be fully made. The speaker and God are once more in tune with one another. The underlying purpose of *The Temple* is to move from discord to poetic and spiritual harmony, and so to sing: as Herbert wrote in the opening lines of "Easter", "Rise heart; thy Lord is risen. Sing his praise / Without delayes" (139).

Herbert's lyrics, whether lamenting or praising, are profoundly musical; their structures use rhythmic and harmonic sounds; their language resounds with musical metaphors; many of their stanza forms resemble those of song lyrics, and indeed the written texts anticipate being sung. There is evidence that Herbert himself set some of his poems to music (though the actual scores do not survive), and many of his lyrics have subsequently taken their place in the musical repertoire as the words of hymns and anthems.[22] In all these ways, Herbert's lyric poems resemble the Psalms, and when Heywood described Herbert as the "incomparable sweet singer of our *Israel*", this is undoubtedly what he had in mind. As David gave voice to the experiences of the original

---

[22] In his *Life* of Herbert, Izaak Walton described the poet singing his own lyrics to the accompaniment of "one of his Instruments" before he died (Walton 1670: 77), and by the end of the century, *Select hymns, taken from Mr Herbert's Temple* had been published (London: Thomas Parkhurst, 1697). For further discussions of Herbert's poems in relation to music, see Charles 1967, Jackson 2013/14, McColley 1997, Schleiner 1984 and Wilcox 1987.

chosen people, so Herbert speaks for seventeenth-century believers. There are numerous important parallels between *The Temple* and the Book of Psalms – not least the title of Herbert's collection, and the quotation from Psalm 29 on the title-page of the first edition, "In his Temple doth every man speak of his honour". Herbert's poetic *Temple* echoes with the sounds of God's "honour", especially in the extensive sequence of shorter poems (just over 150, the number of biblical Psalms) forming its central section, "The Church".[23] Most importantly, these poems resemble the Psalms by expressing the range of moods, from intense joy to painful suffering, that characterise the spiritual life. Like the Psalms, Herbert's lyrics speak in such a way that readers can find their own varied experiences reflected in them. His observation on the power of the Bible may be applied to the effect of Herbert's own poems on those who read them: "Thy words do finde me out, & parallels bring, / And in another make me understood" ("The H. Scriptures II", 210).

It is a great tribute to devotional poets to suggest that their work is Psalm-like, since the existence of the Psalms has long been seen as evidence for the divine approval of poetry.[24] Herbert's poems provided a new Psalter for his era – he was the David of "our *Israel*" – but they have a further scriptural quality about them, simply by being so full of biblical echoes.[25] This is not only to be discerned in the more obvious places, such as his versification of "The 23 Psalme", or the poem entitled "Coloss. 3.3" within which a biblical verse is ingeniously "hidden" (305). The majority of his poems discreetly echo, mix and meditate upon biblical passages, not announcing these connections but simply building brilliantly on a firmly scriptural foundation. Take, for example, "Redemption":

> Having been tenant long to a rich Lord,
>   Not thriving, I resolved to be bold,
>   And make a suit unto him, to afford
> A new small-rented lease, and cancell th' old.

---

[23] *The Temple* consists of three sections: "The Church-porch", "The Church" (containing all the lyric poems) and "The Church Militant".

[24] See, for example, Philip Sidney, *An Apology for Poetry* (1595), ed Geoffrey Shepherd (Manchester: Manchester University Press, 1973), p. 99.

[25] For an excellent book-length discussion of Herbert and the Bible, see Bloch 1985.

In heaven at his manour I him sought:
    They told me there, that he was lately gone
    About some land, which he had dearly bought
Long since on earth, to take possession.

I straight return'd, and knowing his great birth,
    Sought him accordingly in great resorts;
    In cities, theatres, gardens, parks, and courts:
At length I heard a ragged noise and mirth

Of theeves and murderers: there I him espied,
    Who straight, *Your suit is granted*, said, & died. (132)

The poem begins as a parable, using the familiar narrative style from the Gospels, and ends, startlingly, at the foot of the cross. The story of the old arrangement with the landlord, and the "new small-rented lease" with which the speaker hopes to replace the old, is an allegory of the old and new covenants; in fact, Herbert condenses into fourteen lines virtually the entire Old and New Testaments of the Bible. This is no dry sermon, however, but a startling depiction of the complacency of human beings: the speaker is a bustling know-all who actually knows nothing and, in the astonishing last line, is confronted by the shocking generosity of God.

When Heywood identified Herbert as the poet who spoke for "our *Israel*", he drew attention to one final way in which *The Temple* has had an impact on the lives of its readers. By referring to "*Israel*", Heywood was indicating that he and his fellow nonconformists in the 1670s were suffering a kind of internal exile in England (being legally prevented from preaching or gathering for worship) just as the Israelites were in exile when the Psalms were first sung. "By the waters of Babylon we sat down and wept", begins Psalm 137, and the parallel drawn by Heywood between the early Israel and "ours" reminds us that Herbert's lyric poetry, similarly, can give powerful expression to feelings of spiritual abandonment in any period or context. It is very revealing that, while *The Temple* includes several poems sharing the same title (as we have seen with "Jordan" (I) and (II), for example), the most frequently repeated title is "Affliction", used five times. These poems unflinchingly face up to the darker aspects of spiritual experience: the sense that "Sorrow was all my soul" (162), for example, or the need to cry out in desperation to God,

"Kill me not ev'ry day" (224).[26] Herbert does not turn away from the difficulties of his relationship with God, and described his poems as a "picture" of "spiritual Conflicts" between God and the soul (Walton 1670: 74).

The opening stanza of "Affliction" (IV) brings together many facets of the misery that can be faced in the spiritual wilderness, including isolation, fear, self-pity, and Hamlet-like perplexity at the human condition:

> Broken in pieces all asunder,
>   Lord, hunt me not,
>   A thing forgot,
> Once a poore creature, now a wonder,
>   A wonder tortur'd in the space
>   Betwixt this world and that of grace. (328)

Yet despite this sense of torture and brokenness, Herbert's poems rarely end in despair. As God brought Israel out of the wilderness, so blessings are shown to abound for the speakers in his verse. The difficulty they encounter is in accepting that God's love is all-encompassing. This realisation is given particularly vivid expression in "The Flower", celebrating the "return" of God into the speaker's consciousness, causing him to emerge from a winter of the spirit like a flower reappearing in the spring:

>   Who would have thought my shrivel'd heart
> Could have recover'd greennesse? It was gone
>   Quite under ground; as flowers depart
> To see their mother-root, when they have blown;
>   Where they together
>   All the hard weather,
> Dead to the world, keep house unknown.
>
>   ...
>
>   And now in age I bud again,
> After so many deaths I live and write;

---

[26] Herbert gave all his lyrics titles, many of which play an important part in the poem's meaning. He was the first poet in English to do this (Bauer 1995) – another aspect of his "incomparable" art.

I once more smell the dew and rain,
And relish versing: O my onely light,
It cannot be
That I am he
On whom thy tempests fell all night.
(568, ll. 8-14 and 36-42)

In this poem, the "incomparable sweet singer of our *Israel*" once again finds the unique tone, form, vocabulary and faith to convey poetically the incredible joy of a restored – or resurrected – relationship with God.

The foundations for Herbert's achievements as a devotional poet were undoubtedly laid during his time at Westminster School. His capacity for the hard work of scholarship, and his commitment to mental and devotional improvement in spite of physical weakness, both seem to stem from those early years.[27] His skill in languages, poetic forms and rhetorical techniques, and the knowledge that it was possible to combine devout priesthood with discreet learning, derive from his school days.[28] Herbert also gained his experience and love of music, particularly liturgical singing, from the School and Abbey; furthermore, as a result of the events of 1604-5 in the vicinity, he became aware of the destructive potential of political and religious divisions. Bearing in mind this profound heritage, it is fitting to conclude with a brief enquiry into the ways in which Herbert's life and work upheld the Westminster tradition of loyalty combined with dissent. To what people, principles or things was he loyal, and in what ways did he creatively or constructively dissent from them?

Fundamentally, Herbert was loyal to two main maternal presences in his life – his mother, and the church. The immensely capable Magdalene Herbert made possible his education and that of her other nine children, all of whom she brought up single-handedly and saw safely into adulthood. Herbert remained close to her and, after her death, wrote a set of poems in Latin and Greek devoted to her memory.[29] Herbert's second

---

[27] One indication of this is Herbert's painstaking revisions of his poems; see Lull 1990.

[28] See Drury 2013: 62-7 for a detailed analysis of a sermon by Andrewes in relation to Herbert's own writing.

[29] *Memoriae Matris Sacrum* was published with Donne's *Sermon of Commemoration of the Lady Danvers* (London: Philemon Stephens, 1627). For a

mother, the Church of England, is addressed in his poem "The British Church" as the "dearest Mother" whose beauty is an ideal of moderation between the sombre Calvinists and the "painted" Roman Catholic church (390-1). Herbert was said by his friend Nicholas Ferrar of Little Gidding to have shown unbroken "obedience and conformitie" to the church.[30] Yet, loyal though Herbert was to both these mothers, his was not the normal route through life that might have been expected by them. He did not follow the courtly career of political prominence for which his position as Orator appeared to be preparing him, and when he entered the service of the church he chose the role of a country parson in an obscure parish. The unexpected humility demonstrated in the life of this most promising gentleman and scholar is echoed in his poetry, which praises a modest calling and asserts, in the well-known words of "The Elixer", "Who sweeps a room, as for thy laws, / Makes that and th'action fine" (174). Herbert's brother Edward commented that George was so devoted to his priestly vocation that he was "litle [sic] less than Sainted", but George's first biographer noted that some thought he had "*lost himself* in an humble way".[31] Herbert certainly hid himself away as a writer, too, even though the excellence of his poems would have been to the credit of both his mothers. He did not publish any of his English devotional poems, but left them behind at his death with the instruction that the poems should be burnt, unless they could be "turned to the advantage of any dejected poor Soul" (Walton 1670: 74). This was a devoted son who nevertheless knew his own mind.

Herbert was equally independent in terms of the religious politics of his lifetime. It was an age of ecclesiastical tensions, encapsulated while he was at Westminster by the Gunpowder Plot and the Hampton Court Conference, but intensifying through the early seventeenth century at such a rate that the country spiralled into civil war less than ten years after his death. Remarkably, Herbert did not openly take sides but wrote poetry exploring the spiritual experiences that unite rather than divide believers – thus giving rise to the enormously wide-ranging readership for *The*

---

recent verse translation of Herbert's Latin poems, see Freis, Freis and Miller 2015.

[30] "The Printers to the Reader", prefaced to *The Temple* (Herbert 2007:42). In his sonnet "Prayer" (I), Herbert defines prayer not as private dialogue with God but as "the Churches banquet" (178).

[31] Edward Herbert, *Life*, p. 9; Oley 1652: a11ʳ.

Temple which continues to this day. It took great strength to dissent from the polemical tones of his time. While debates were raging around him concerning the true nature of the Holy Communion, Herbert simply celebrated in firm yet homely language the generous action of God who "by way of nourishment and strength / ... creep'st into my breast" ("The H. Communion", 182). As the role of the sermon became increasingly controversial, Herbert quietly favoured a pulpit that was no higher than the lectern, to ensure that preachers of all varieties knew that they were never more important than the scriptural word of God.[32]

In literary terms, too, Herbert was loyal to the power of poetry and the traditions of lyric verse, but still went his own "incomparable" way. Writing in an era of complex literary artistry, he demonstrated the capacity to construct ingenious poetic forms and designs, including poetry whose shape on the page underscores its meaning, yet some of his greatest lines are of the utmost simplicity.[33] In his sonnet "Prayer" (I), Herbert spends almost all the poem attempting to find metaphors for prayer itself – a challenging task, but one to which he rises magnificently with phrases such as "heaven in ordinarie, man well drest" to encapsulate the reciprocal nature of prayer. However, in the last line he abandons the attempt to find descriptive vocabulary for this profound experience, and ends with a suggestion of prayer simply as "something understood" (178). It is clear that Herbert could use all the tools available to him as a poet and rhetorician, but he rejected artistry for its own sake. What mattered more than any poetic sleight of hand was the ultimate engagement of the writer and reader, whose hearts, minds and – above all – souls must "bear a part" (140) in the literary and devotional process. This was his radical re-definition of genuine poetry: as he wrote in "A true Hymne", "The fineness which a hymne or psalme affords, / Is, when the soul unto the lines accords" (576).

Finally, Herbert's paradoxical dissenting loyalty applies even to his relationship with God. Despite the poet's deeply loyal faith, the speakers

---

[32] The material evidence for this is the church at Leighton Bromswold, Huntingdonshire, renovated during Herbert's time as prebendary there.

[33] See, for example, the expressively shaped poems "The Altar" and "Easter wings", and the witty devices such as pruned or broken words ("Paradise", "Jesu"). These exist side by side with simplicity, as in the opening of "The Temper" (II), the rhetorical questions in "Mattens", or the monosyllabic last line of "Love" (III), the final lyric in "The Church": "So I did sit and eat" (661).

in his poems struggle with dismay at their own shifting spiritual moods and perplexity as to how to respond to God's loving "welcome" (661). The last line of "Affliction" (I) wittily condenses this uncertainty and puzzlement: "Let me not love thee, if I love thee not" (163). Herbert's most outspoken moment of dissent is expressed in "The Collar":

> I struck the board, and cry'd, No more.
>   I will abroad.
>   What? shall I ever sigh and pine?
>   My lines and life are free; free as the rode,
>   Loose as the winde, as large as store.
>   Shall I be still in suit? (526)

The speaker's anger and frustration boil over in these dynamic lines of complaint and self-justification. Yet, as the poem lurches forward in a tirade of defiance, the words becoming "more fierce and wilde" as it proceeds, suddenly God is heard through all the noise, calling *"Childe"* – "And I reply'd, *My Lord*" (526). As we have seen, the endings of Herbert's poems often deliver a startling rhetorical punch. Here, the speaker's dramatic submission and the renewal of relationship demonstrate that the bond between the human speaker and God may be strained in *The Temple*, but is never broken. The pull of protest and the force of fidelity constantly interact in the poems, and both are vital to their effect. Often dissenting but never less than loyal – in faith, poetry and life – Herbert was a Westminster through and through.

In closing a brief letter to Richard Busby from Worcester in October 1689, Thomas Severne, a clerical tutor at Christ Church, Oxford, observed to his old Head Master, 'Lord! how I tremble to send this to you! I see you have me in awe still and ever will.'[1] In this particular, Severne spoke for the great majority of Busby's former pupils, whether they were scholars or otherwise. Often it was his scholarship that produced such awe; sometimes it was the memory of the beatings he enthusiastically administered, and here it is customary in all writing about Busby to adduce a tribute from a fictional figure, Joseph Addison's Sir Roger de Coverley, as evinced in the *Spectator* in 1712: 'As we stood before Busby's tomb, the knight uttered himself again after the same manner: "Dr Busby! a great man: he whipp'd my grandfather; a very great man! I should have gone to him myself, if I had not been a blockhead: a very great man!"'[2] Sir Roger's tribute also bears witness to Busby's legendary longevity in office, covering fully two generations, from his appointment aged thirty-two n 1638 to his death in harness in his eighty-ninth year, fully fifty seven years later, in 1695. Busby sustained Westminster School's standing as the leading academic school in the country, educating personally many of the leading figures of the seventeenth and early eighteenth centuries.

Before Keate of Eton, and the great Victorian headmasters – Arnold of Rugby, Thring of Uppingham, Vaughan and Butler of Harrow – had begun to dominate histories of public school education, Busby long held sway as the greatest of English schoolmasters. But before returning to Westminster, where he had himself been a King's Scholar, Busby had enjoyed fourteen years of study and teaching at Christ Church, with which institution, along with Trinity College, Cambridge, the school had long enjoyed an intimate association. And Busby continues to preside at Christ Church with richly-deserved authority; for not only did he supply the college with some of its most distinguished members - from John Locke and his contemporary the controversial divine Robert South, to two future Deans of Christ Church, Henry Aldrich, literally the architect of the college's eighteenth-century fortunes and Francis Atterbury, ultimately and stylishly attainted for Jacobite plotting - but he also founded lectures in Oriental studies and funded its first Common Room. But classical scholarship, even when imbibed through on Busby's principles and his own direct instruction, could go wrong: it was his pupils Aldrich and

---

[1] Severne to Busby, Oct. 21, 1689 in John Nichols ed., *Illustrations of the Literary History of the Eighteenth Century* (8 Vols, London, 1817-58), iv. 406.
[2] *The Spectator* 329, March 18, 1712 in *The Spectator* (8 vols., London, 1797), v. 56.

Atterbury who were instrumental in causing the battle between the ancients and the moderns, in which they were completely routed by the altogether more modestly-educated, if rather more scholarly, Richard Bentley, the Master of Trinity College, Cambridge.[3]

It is, therefore, entirely right and fitting that the Old Common Room at Christ Church should be dominated by a bust of Busby, where he stands sentinel over the fireplace, acting as a testimony to the fact that, as a Student of Christ Church between 1624 and 1638, he had become all too aware of the barely tolerated manner in which the Students, that is the tutors of Christ Church, were frequently treated by the Chapter of Christ Church, that is the Dean and his clerical allies, the Professors of divinity and variously assorted canons of the cathedral. Secure in their redoubts in college, respectively, in the Deanery and the Canonries - themselves considerable properties with extensive gardens - the Chapter was well looked after domestically, but the Students were not. Being considered as merely the hired hands routinely and necessarily brought in to teach the undergraduates, the Students did not even possess a common room, let alone the common rights accorded to tutors everywhere else in Oxford and Cambridge. It was Busby who supplied the necessary money for his immediate successors at Christ Church to hire the space that became known in time as Old Common Room. He understood from the inside their lack of standing and institutional dignity; a sensible man who understood the lie of the land, he took holy orders, becoming a Prebendary of Westminster Abbey when Head Master, later holding *in commendam* both the position of Canon-Treasurer at Wells Cathedral and the Archdeaconry of Westminster.

Elsewhere in Oxford (and likewise in Cambridge), the Fellows of colleges had a right to an annual share in the profits made by college lands; not so the Students of Christ Church, who did not even eat at High Table, but were roughly set aside on their own table, lower down in Christ Church Hall. When Dr Johnson, an old member of Pembroke College, stated characteristically, 'Sir, it is a great thing to be invited to dine with the Canons of Christ-Church', even he, aware of every slight he had ever

---

[3] See Joseph E. Levine, *The Battle of the Books: history and literature in the Augustan age* (Ithaca, New York, 1991), pp. 47-84; and more generally, Kristine Louise Haugen, *Richard Bentley: poetry and Enlightenment* (Cambridge, Mass., 2011).

suffered, made no reference to the poor Students of Christ Church.[4] But then, denied most conceivable rights by the Chapter it is highly doubtful that any of their number would have considered an invitation to dine with the Canons a great thing. The commanding, if posthumous, portrait of Busby and a favourite pupil (variously identified as Philip or Matthew Henry or Robert South), that has long hung in Christ Church Hall is thus an elegant commentary on his ascent in status from a poor lay Student to a rich clerical grandee.[5]

This distinctive disparity was to remain the state of affairs at Christ Church until, in the year of reform in 1867, the 'Revolt of the Students' secured them membership of Governing Body and all rights thereby accruing. The crucial meetings in that revolt were held in Old Common Room in February 1867, 'almost exactly' two hundred years after Busby's endowment of that space.[6] Busby was to prove as generous to Christ Church as it had been to him. A poor Lincolnshire boy by origin, his education at Westminster School had been paid for by patrons and the rewards of a King's Scholarship some years after his family had moved to the parish of Westminster when Busby was a very young child. Busby was a signally strong scholar, and he worked equally hard at Oxford, both in languages, in which he had been rigorously trained, but also in mathematics, a subject he had not been taught at school; it was in these fields that he subsequently endowed two lectureships at Christ Church. Mathematics fared little better at Oxford than it did at Westminster School, whereas his support for a lectureship in oriental languages strengthened a subject already very successfully promoted at Christ Church by Edward Pococke, the Regius Professor of Hebrew; as a condition of his largesse Busby required all undergraduates to be present at the oriental lecture.[7] A typically able product of Busby's Westminster,

---

[4] James Boswell, *Life of Johnson*, ed. R.W. Chapman (Oxford, 1980), p. 693.

[5] On the complex nature of the portrait, see G.F. Russell Barker, *Memoir of Richard Busby D.D. (1696-1695) with some account of Westminster School in the seventeenth century* (London, 1895), p. 46 and note, and a pamphlet *Commemoration of the Bicentenary of the Death of Richard Busby, Westminster School, Nov. 18 MDCCLXXXXV* (London, 1895), p. 9.

[6] E.G.W. Bill and J.F.A. Mason, *Christ Church and Reform 1850-1867* (Oxford, 1970), p. 172.

[7] E.G.W. Bill, *Education at Christ Church, Oxford, 1660-1800* (Oxford, 1988), pp. 198, 302-3.

Humphrey Prideaux, elected to a Westminster Scholarship at Christ Church in 1666, subsequently turned down the succession to Pococke, in 1691, but his Hebrew researches, begun at school and continued at Oxford, were maintained during a busy period as Dean of Norwich, and he paid tribute to Busby's scholarly encouragement in a suitably terse, if occasionally florid, Latin letter to his former Head Master, but as with Severne so with Prideaux, awe bordering on fear was blended with gratitude as he evoked his early years of instruction in literary and religious studies, which it would have been an ingratitude to forget, and which had formed in him and his contemporaries an enduring commitment to literature and religion, the graces of which sometimes led to a fear that he himself was not meeting those exacting standards; souls and minds were formed under their reverend master's instruction.[8]

Busby's oriental lectureship and its attendant lectures were more successful than was his proposed mathematical lectureship; it was left to a later Dean of Christ Church, David Gregory, who won his Westminster Scholarship at Christ Church in the closing months of the reign of Queen Anne, to found such a lectureship successfully.[9] But whereas mathematics failed, Hebrew and the comfort of Students and other Christ Church MAs were duly confirmed by the Chapter following Busby's benefaction on 9 June 1667, decreeing that 'the new low room beneath the west end of the Hall to be for euer set apart and applied to the use of the Mathematick and Oriental lectures to be founded by the reurend Dr. Busby; as also the use of the Masters, Students, and others of this house for their publick fires and such like occasions.'[10] Busby did more than merely fund oriental scholarship at Oxford; he also compiled a Hebrew grammar, and alongside their Hebrew studies, he saw to it that boys at Westminster were instructed in Arabic.[11] Busby's benefactions to Christ Church were immediately celebrated in a poem produced by Richard Peters, a Student of the college, in which the Head Master is presented as a virtual monarch, a philosopher-king:

---

[8] Prideaux to Busby, undated, in *Illustrations of the Literary History*, iv. 395-96.
[9] Bill, *Education at Christ Church*, pp. 271-72; 55-9.
[10] Cited in Bill, *Education at Christ Church*, pp. 205-6.
[11] See Mordechai Feingold, 'Oriental Studies' in *The History of the University of Oxford, iv: Seventeenth-century Oxford,* ed. Nicholas Tyacke (Oxford, 1997), 449-503, at pp. 484, 490-93.

Yet though your Wealth flow plentifull and swift,
    We're richer in the Donor than the Gift.
    And while your early merits we review,
    And think what Christ Church challenges in you,
    For that dear Interest we could resign,
    Whatever springs from Quarry or from Mine,
    For here your Greatness with your Youth begun,
    (So men spy Noon-tide in the rising Sun)
    Here were those seeds of Rule and Empire lay'd,
    Which fairly promised, what they since payd,
    Where (as the sacred Infancy of Kings
    To Huts the Right of Sanctuary brings)
    You, Sir, the Muses Interest advance.
    Here you gave proof of how solid merit shines
    When serious Industry with Nature joyns.
    Here your green Age did with unequall'd pace,
    The course of Arts and every knowledge trace:
    Learn'd Matters Laws, her unions and her jars,
    Rounding both Globes and circling with the Starrs.[12]

What gives Busby's Christ Church bust its authority to anyone acquainted with the history of seventeenth-century England is that he is portrayed wearing his cap, for easily the best-known story associated with Busby concerns the celebrated, if sadly apocryphal, occasion when, taking Charles II around the School, Busby explained to his sovereign that he would not remove his cap, his sign of authority, even in His Majesty's presence, because he could not allow his boys 'to believe there was a greater man in the world than himself.'[13] And there never was a greater within the school that he had made his own kingdom. Why and how was this so?

    The answer is authority, both real and imagined, and with authority wielded during one of the most difficult periods in English – indeed, in British - history, and exercised at the very heart of the nation's political, as well as its ecclesiastical, being. Power and authority are different things, and raw power was what was wrested from the authority of King and Church when the Commonwealth was inaugurated early in Busby's

---

[12] Richard Peters, *Poems* (Oxford, 1667), pp. 6-7.
[13] Russell Barker, *Memoir of Busby,* p. 51.

unusually long and firmly authoritative career as headmaster of Westminster School. Power invariably seeks to assume authority, and the newly-established Commonwealth sought to do just that by securing from its citizens a 'solemn engagement' to abide by their accession to office and presumed (and by the 'Engagement' legitimated) authority; historians of Westminster School were troubled by the fact that Busby, of all people, might well have so engaged, and some of them sought, understandably perhaps, to deny that he ever did so.[14] The evidence that he successfully avoided making the Engagement is, to say the least, exiguous, but then it was a necessary sacrifice for him to make were the school to survive in the form that it did. As more than one contemporary observed, the King's Scholars at Westminster remained the King's Scholars when there was no king; when Busby escorted the restored Charles II around the school, he had earned the right to keep his cap on his head as he had kept the school exactly as any monarch would have wanted it to be kept. True, he had previously accompanied Cromwell's body to its burial in the Abbey (when a rebellious pupil, Robert Uvedale, angrily removed the usurper's escutcheon from his cortège), but he was also there at Charles II's coronation, and also that of James II, whose right to the throne had been strongly contested by the radical Locke, who paid for such perceived political malignancy by being stripped of his Studentship at Christ Church.[15]

Busby was a survivor, not a time-server, a man of principles circumspectly held, a politician of no mean ability in a time of dissembling and harsh extremism. He was at once an Anglican and an independent, a Royalist who managed to keep his King's Scholars in place during the Commonwealth, and who would ensure that they regained their allotted role during the coronations of the sovereigns who succeeded the restored Charles II. This is no small achievement. How did he do secure it? In no small part the answer is one he was known to loathe: he was a

---

[14] Russell Barker, *Memoir of Busby*, pp. 14-15; John Sargeaunt, *Annals of Westminster School* (London, 1898), pp. 83-9, is realistic and honest, but see also Lawrence E. Tanner, *Westminster School* (London, 1934), pp. 12-22; John Dudley Carleton, *Westminster School: a history* (London, 1965), pp. 9-23; J.C.D. Field, *The King's Nurseries: the story of Westminster School* (London, 1987), pp. 32-44. The altogether excellent *ONDB* entry on Busby by C.S. Knighton is properly judicious.

[15] On Uvedale, see Russell Barker, *Memoir of Busby*, pp. 17-18.

consummate actor. And acting is pivotal to his achievement as a Head Master, as at least one of his subordinates knew to his cost. In the one great public controversy of his career, Busby was accused by his Second Master, Edward Bagshawe, of systematically abusing his privileges and position as Head Master, and of undermining Bagshawe's authority by bringing in another master. Crucially, Bagshawe's politics were not Busby's politics, and nor was his Churchmanship remotely akin to that of his immediate superior; himself a former pupil of Busby at Westminster, Bagshawe became a Student of Christ Church whence he was appointed to Westminster in 1656 by John Owen, the intruded Independent Dean of Christ Church, to whose political and religious principles he was very much closer than he was to those of Busby.[16] Instituting proceedings against Busby before the school's Commonwealth governors, Bagshawe reported in his published account of these fraught years that, speaking before the generally sympathetic governors and an understandably angry Busby, 'when I pronounced the word *Actor*, Mr. Busby, without any leave, went out of the Committee Chamber; though I meant innocently for an *Actor* in a *Cause,* and not for an Actor for Cratander.'[17] Bagshawe had, innocently or otherwise, hit a raw and peculiarly sensitive nerve; he had also struck, probably unknowingly, at the source of Busby's not inconsiderable inner authority.

In the 1630s, after a celebrated dramatic success, Busby had seriously considered becoming an actor; that he did not, and turned to school mastering and scholarship instead, did not, however, mean that he had ever ceased to act, only as Bagshawe had unconsciously hinted, it was the part of a pedagogue that he was to play to perfection. The man who had played the eponymous role of *The Royal Slave* at Oxford and subsequently at Hampton Court in 1636 had obliged Bagshawe, in the politically-charged language of the Protectorate, 'to justifie my self, and to bear Witness against Mr. Busby's Oppression, Injustice, and Tyranny.'[18] Richly-personated virtue had turned, in just over twenty years, into alleged abuse.

---

[16] For discussion, see Russell Barker, *Memoir of Busby*, pp. 55-76, and Sargeaunt, *Annals of Westminster School,* pp. 85-9.

[17] Edward Bagshawe, *A True and Perfect Narrative of the Differences Between Mr. Busby and of Mr. Bagshawe, The first and second Masters of Westminster-School* (London, 1659), p. 23.

[18] Bagshawe, *True and Perfect Narrative*, p. 32.

As was customary, the Students of Christ Church had, on August 30th 1636, acted a play in the college Hall in the presence of the sovereign in his capacity as hereditary Visitor of Christ Church. Charles I and Henrietta Maria were treated to a play written especially for them by William Cartwright (1611-43), himself a Student of Christ Church and a former King's Scholar at Westminster. Cartwright's career has many parallels with that of Busby, his senior at school and university; and in common with Busby, Cartwright had a strong sense of his institutional entitlements: as a lay Student of Christ Church, Cartwright had earlier appealed to the royal Visitor in November 1629, when the Dean and Chapter had planned to abolish the 'Westminster Supper'; wisely, he subsequently took holy orders, preaching the 'victory' sermon after Edgehill and becoming succentor – that is, assistant to the precentor - in the cathedral in 1642, when he also became the university 'Reader in Metaphysic'; he became Junior Proctor in 1643, shortly before his untimely death, a victim of the "camp disease", then doing the rounds of the city. [19] He had literally been loyal unto death.

The Royal Slave was a lavish spectacle; the music was supplied by Henry Lawes, the sets and costumes were designed by Inigo Jones, and the part of Cratander, the eponymous royal slave, was played by Busby.[20] The plot is fairly if occasionally frenziedly absurd: a group of Ephesians are captured and mistreated by the king of Persia and his retinue; according to Persian religious rites, the virtuous captive Cratander is then isolated from his companions in order to be made king for three days prior to what will be his ritual execution by a priest, but things fall out differently: despite the intercessions of both the king and the queen (who has fallen in love with him), Cratander is led to the sacrificial altar by the chief priest but, at that very moment, a temporary eclipse of the sun is immediately interpreted as a heavenly portent, and the royal slave is consequently released and returned to act as a virtuous philosopher-king in his native Ephesus. The plot was derived from an incident described by Dio Chrysostom, and as its mid-twentieth century editor observed, the play was 'saturated with the doctrines of a sentimentalized and sophisticated Neoplatonism' of a sort then widespread in court and literary

---

[19] See the 'Life of William Cartwright' prefaced by his editor, G. Blakemore Evans, to *The Plays and Poems of William Cartwright* (Madison, Wisconsin, 1951), at pp. 9, 11n, 15-20.
[20] Evans, *Plays and Poems*, pp. 172-75, 177-79.

culture.[21] But even more remarkable than the plot in terms of Busby's future career is the almost prophetic character of much that is said both of and by Cratander. Much that is emblematic can be recovered from those words, just as its evocation by Bagshawe led to his deprivation of office at Westminster School: the royal slave had won his freedom, and he could accordingly act the part of tyrant as consummately as he could that of priest and man of virtue.

Cratander's very first appearance in the play performed before Charles I might be taken as a description of Busby's later apocryphal meeting with Charles II: 'See, there comes one/Arm'd with a serious and Majestique look,/As if he'd read Philosophy to a king.' A fellow Ephesian, Philotus, however, observes of Cratander's rule that 'we live not under a King, but a Pedagogue: he's insufferable.'[22] Similarly, warnings abound as to the nature of royal government, so that Cratander observes in a way prophetic of Charles I's future, 'And if a King do but stumble, 'tis a Precipice.' And more troublingly for Busby's Restoration apologists, Cratander, facing the execution attendant on ceasing to be 'the royal slave', resolutely states that: 'An Oath's the same in Persia, as in Greece: And bindes alike in either.'[23] It seems likely that, all disseverations to the contrary notwithstanding, Busby did take the solemn engagement to the Protectorate; as with Cratander, so with Busby, he 'Speakes well, and like a good Common-wealth's man.'[24] Scrutiny of the records of the governors of Westminster School during the Commonwealth and Protectorate makes it clear that the royalist Busby had to use a long spoon when dining with men of very different principles from his own: among their number were regicides, and all were republicans: John Bradshaw, Lord President of the Council; Edmund Ludlow; William Say; Thomas Chaloner; Thomas Scott; Gilbert Millington; Henry Marten; Sir Henry Vane; Isaac Pennington; Thomas Lister; Henry Scobell; and, more occasionally, the fiercely republican Algernon Sidney and Sir James Harrington, the author of a classic text in classical republican theory, *The Commonwealth of Oceana* (1656).[25] Whatever the nature of Busby's temporising might have

---

[21] Evans, *Plays and Poems*, pp. 172, 187-88.

[22] William Cartwright, *The Royal Slave*, in Evans, *Plays and Poems*, pp. 203, 224.

[23] Cartwright, *The Royal Slave*, pp. 217, 234.

[24] Cartwright, *The Royal Slave*, p. 224.

[25] State Papers, 28/292. I am grateful to Dr David Scott for alerting me to these records and consequently to the Republican Governors of Westminster School

been exactly, however, what the Persian King Arsamenes declares of the providential salvation of Cratander might well have been declared of him by Busby's devoted Anglican admirers as the Restoration drove into oblivion some of the many suspect actions of the Commonwealth and Protectorate era: ''tis some God,/Some God reserves thee into greater works/ For us, and for thy Country.' The Platonist politics voiced by the king at the conclusion of the play seem prophetic of the reputation Busby was rapidly to gain from his long governorship of Westminster School:

'Thy faith hath been/
    So firme and try'd,/
    thy moderation/
    So stay'd, that in a just reward I must My selfe conduct thee into Greece, and there/
    Continue thee a King; but what was meant/ For sport and mirth, may prove a serious honour;/
    And thy happy Dayes passe o'ere into a long/
    And happy government; to be rul'd by thee/
    Will be as freedome to them; 'twill not be/
    Accounted slavery to admit a Prince/
    Chosen from out themselves: thy Ventures there/
    May shine, as in their proper Spheare. Let others/
    When they make warre, have this ignoble end/
    To gaine 'em Slaves. Arsamenes gaines a Friend.'[26]

To the republican Bagshawe, however, to have had to submit to Busby 'concludes nothing but the merit of a Passive Obedience.'[27]

---

during the Interregnum. A full list of governors for these years is given in Russell Barker, *Memoir of Busby*, pp. 9-10. On the varieties of English Republicanism involved, see a series of connected essays by Blair Worden: 'Marchamont Nedham and the beginnings of English republicanism, 1649-1656', 'James Harrington and the *Commonwealth of Oceana*, 1656', 'Harrington's "Oceana": origins and aftermath, 1651-1660', 'and 'Republicanism and the Restoration, 1660-1683', in David Wootton ed., *Republicanism, Liberty, and Commercial Society, 1649-1776* (Stanford, California, 1994), pp. 45-81, 82-110, 111-38, 139-93.

[26] Cartwright, *The Royal Slave*, p. 250.
[27] Bagshawe, *True and Perfect Narrative*, p. 23.

Three of Busby's greatest pupils were at Westminster School during the troubled 1640s, when the political consequences of doctrines of passive obedience were beginning to be felt nationally; two followed their preceptor to Westminster Scholarships at Christ Church, and the third to one reserved at Trinity College, Cambridge. The Cambridge scholar was John Dryden, who trusted his old schoolmaster enough subsequently to send his two sons to Westminster; two letters to Busby from Dryden about his sons survive, and both are quietly rather telling. Writing in 1682 about his younger son, John, who eventually secured but did not take up a place at Christ Church, the poet noted how illness had obliged him to be taken away from school briefly, adding that he 'is always gratefully acknowledging your fatherly kindness to him'; he added in relation to his elder son, Charles who later followed his father to Trinity College, that he was 'of virtuous and pious inclinations'; he closed his short note by observing of both of them, 'that they can promise to themselves no farther share of my indulgence than while they carry themselves with that reverence to you, and that honesty to all others, as becomes them.' Dryden was obliged to intercede on their behalf again in 1683, just as his wife, Lady Elizabeth, had done in 1682, when she had pointedly reminded Busby of his promise to allow her sickly son 'to have one night in a week' away from the school at her house 'in consideration of both his heath and cleanliness', adding in a premonitory way, 'you know, Sir, that promises made to women, and especially mothers, will never fail to be called upon; and therefore I will add no more, but that I am, at this time, your remembrancer'.[28] Both of Dryden's sons followed their father into Catholicism, and this was the aspect of their lives of which their former Head Master would have most disapproved; but as Dr Johnson would subsequently state the case, their father had let Busby down in an even more particular manner:

It will be difficult to prove that Dryden ever made any great advances in literature. As having distinguished himself at Westminster under the tuition of Busby, who advanced his scholars to a height of knowledge very rarely attained in grammar-schools, he resided afterwards at Cambridge, it is not to be supposed that his skill in the ancient languages

---

[28] John Dryden to Busby, in *Illustrations of Literary History*, iv. 398-99; Lady Elizabeth Dryden to Busby, ibid., 399-400.

was deficient, compared with that of common students, but his sholastick acquisitions seem not proportionate to his opportunities and abilities.[29]

In this regard, Dryden slipped intellectually at Trinity College, unlike his school contemporaries at Christ Church, who advanced considerably on the famously firm foundations laid by Busby.

Of John Locke and Busby there is no need to say more, as he is the subject of a separate chapter in this volume, but Locke would move well beyond Busby intellectually and politically, whereas his Westminster and Christ Church contemporary, the scholarly divine Robert South (1634-1717), remained recognisably a favoured Busby protégé. South's first appearance of public note is revealing, and was referred to elliptically much later in a sermon he had planned to deliver to past and present members of his old school. Conjuring up the day of Charles I's execution in Whitehall, which occurred when South was merely a boy of fourteen, he apostrophised Westminster School thus:

> But chiefly, and in the last Place, let your kind and generous Influence upon all Occasions descend upon this Royal and Illustrious School, the Happy Place of your Education. A School, which neither disposes Men to Division in Church, nor Sedition in State, tho' too often found the readiest Way (for *Churchmen* especially) to Thrive by; but Trains up her Sons and Scholars to an Invincible Loyalty to their Prince, and a strict, impartial Conformity to the Church. A School so Untaintedly Loyal, that I can truly and knowingly aver, that in the very worst of times (in which it was my lot to be a Member of it) we really were *King's Scholars*, as well as *called so*. Nay, upon that very Day, that Black and Eternally Infamous Day of the King's Murder, I my self Heard, and am now a Witness, that the King was publickly Pray'd for in this School, but an Hour or two (at most) before his Sacred head was struck off. And this Loyal Genius always continued amongst us, and grew up with us; which made that Noted Coryphaeus [John Owen] of the Independent Faction, (and some time after, *viz.* 1651, promoted by Cromwell's Interest to the Deanery of Christ Church in Oxford) often say, *That it would never be well with the Nation, till this School was suppressed; for*

---

[29] Samuel Johnson 'John Dryden' in Roger Lonsdale ed., *The Lives of the Poets* (4 vols., Oxford, 2006), ii.. 121.

that it naturally bred Men up to an Opposition to the Government.[30]

It was claimed by his memoirist in 1717 that it was South himself who had, as a boy, offered up the Latin prayers at Westminster School for King Charles on January 30th, 1649.[31] In Charles I's end was South's beginning.

But Robert South had his own reason to try to forget the 1650s, just as much as had Busby. In 1654, following the Protector's naval victories against the Dutch, John Owen, in his capacity not only as Dean of Christ Church, but also as Vice-Chancellor of Oxford University, oversaw a short volume of commemorative verse, to which South contributed a Virgilian paean, full of classically-enunciated blandishment of Cromwell, replete with a pun on his name, as he is resolved into both a bringer and a symbol of peace, an olive branch ('Nomine Pacifico gestas insignia Pacis/ Blandaque; per titulus serpit Oliva tuos.')[32] Locke provided no fewer than two poems; a short Latin verse with allusions to Augustus and Julius Casear, and a longer English poem ending with an image of Cromwell's achievement as a bringer of universal concord through empire:

> Our ships are now more beneficiall growne,
>> Since they bring home no spoiles but what's their owne.
>> Unto those branchless Pines our forward spring
>> Owes better fruit, than Autumn's wont to bring:
>> Which gives not only gemms and Indian ore,
>> But adde at once whole Nations to our store:
>> Nay if to make a World's but to compose
>> The difference of things, and make them close
>> In mutual amitie; and cause Peace to creep
>> Out of the jarring Chaos of the deep:
>> Our ships doe this, so that while others take
>> Their course about the World, Ours a World make.[33]

---

[30]Robert South, *Twelve Sermons Preached at Several Times and upon several occasions* (8 vols., 1692-1717), v. 48.

[31] 'Memoirs of the Life and Writings of Dr. Robert South', in *Posthumous Works of the Late Reverend Robert South, D.D.* (London, 1717), pp. 1-144, at p.4.

[32] Robert South, untitled poem, in *Musarum Oxoniensium* (Oxford, 1654), pp. 40-1.

[33] John Locke, untitled poems, in *Musarum Oxoniensium*, pp. 45, 94-5.

South and Locke used their classical training under Busby to make peace, however ambivalently, with the Protectorate; they were trained survivors, treating the 1650s as a new Augustan age as adroitly had their Roman predecessors in the early years of the revolutionary, if autocratic, Principate. More characteristically, Edward Bagshawe, still resident at Christ Church before his unhappy time as Busby's deputy, provided a Latin and an English poem, the latter an instance of the sectarian identification of Cromwell as a direct intervention by providence in England's politics (Bagshawe, as befitted a man of his religious and political principles, would end his life a Dissenting minister to a London conventicle in the 1671, his erstwhile Christ Church patron, Dr Owen, providing him with his epitaph)[34]:

> But that we durst try dangers in the Sea,
>   And in all Elements ayme at Victorie;
> To your Examples due, *Great Sir*, whose Soule
> Full of its Native Fire without Controule
> Breaks through all nets, as if it had been sent
> From Heaven, to be like it, an Instrument
> Of such a Providence, that we confesse
> Who shall compare it, will but make it lesse.
> For thus you must following ages tell
> You are *Your Selfe*; without a *Parallel.*[35]

Christ Church, and Oxford, under Owen had conformed to the new order, obliging South, Locke, and like-minded loyalists to the old regime to lead an underground life, whereas the likes of Bagshawe could feel the 1650s to be the grand climacteric of puritan politics.[36] Likewise, a politic Busby maintained the regime at Westminster School as readily as he could in the unpropitious circumstances, sometimes bridging its interests with those of Christ Church as in his testimonial for a man embarked on the same educational journey he had himself taken some twenty years before:

---

[34] Russell Barker, *Memoir of Busby*, pp. 75-6; Sargeaunt, *Annals of Westminster School,* p. 88.

[35] Edward Bagshawe, untitled poems, in *Musarum Oxoniensium*, pp. 18-19, 63-4.

[36] See Blair Worden, 'Politics, piety, and learning: Cromwellian Oxford' in *God's Instruments: political conduct in the England of Oliver Cromwell* (Oxford, 2012), pp. 91-193.

Certificate by Rich. Busby that Jas. Carkes, B.A., student of Christ Church, Oxford, is of the same standing as those Westminster scholars who take the M.A. degree this Act, 1658, being elected at the same time with them, and senior to most of them, only hindered from residence by the tenuity of his fortunes, which compelled him to reside in Westminster college for a maintenance, and to wait 5 terms for admission to the student's place to which he was elected. He studied diligently during his absence, his proficiency is equal to those who resided, and since his admission, he has proved himself, both in manner and bearing, fit for a degree, and his deprival of it would hazard his credit and fortunes.[37]

The history of the commonwealth of learning during the Commonwealth is a rich and complex one.

Survival during the Interregnum was followed by glory at the Restoration, and luminaries of the soon-to-be restored Church of England – led by the bishop of Chichester and John Cosin, a future bishop of Durham – immediately attested his loyalty, certifying to Charles II on June 20th, 1660, that Busby had faithfully governed Westminster School 'by training up his Scholars in ye Rights of true Religion, & Loyalty', and yet more importantly 'by his Charitable relief of the Oppressed & those who suffer'd for Conscience sake, by his most Exemplary Life for Virtue, Goodness & honesty, being a Constant true Subject to his Majestie & most Obedient Son of this Church of England.'[38] Busby would prove an exemplary Churchman at the Restoration, even playing his part, as a patron of Hebrew studies, in converting a rabbi to Christianity, as witness the:

Petition of Jacobo Ben Rabbi Samuel Augusto, a Jew born of the tribe of Benjamin, professor of the Hebrew, Chaldee, and Syriac tongues, to the King. I have been in England 5 years, and instructed many Divinity doctors and ministers in these tongues; they have endeavoured to convert me, but I was long stumbled because we cannot make out of the Old Testament the word Son of God out of Shiloh; but a divine has lately convinced me from

---

[37] SP, 18/181, f. 134.
[38] SP, 29/4, f. 134.

Prov. xxx. *v.* 4. I have since read the New Testament, and believe in its miracles. I used not to eat any meat in a Christian's house, and the like strictness I used in Oxford and Cambridge, and in Dr Busby's house, and the colleges to which I resorted for 2 years. I beg you to be my witness in order to my baptism, and I shall pray for your return from your progress, with your most illustrious Princess.[39]

Busby was also a canny politician, regularly levering influence at the Palace of Westminster in order to secure admission of well-connected pupils, although his temperament did not always do his cause favours, as when the school lost a prospective pupil to Magdalen College School in Oxford, and hence Magdalen College gaining a demy and Christ Church losing a potential scholar. As William Morgan recorded the matter in a letter to a secretary of state:

In France I was by an old good friend of Dr. Clarke's, the President of Magdalen, Oxford, recommended to him to put in a little son of mine for a demy. It is the same, although to such a morose person, as Dr. Busby was ever known to be, you foresaw well the letter you honoured me with in the child's behalf for King's scholar at Westminster would not so readily take its desired effect. As soon as I perceived their usual too long delays, I removed him thence to Mr. Collins, an ingenious person, and master of Magdalen School, where I think as having never fancied anything else but books he improves himself, in order, I well hope, for a demy the next election in July there. The President told me he had only a single vote, the rest, I think he said, were most in the Fellows, but I should not have the least doubt, if, specially now in my old friend Sir L. Jenkins' absence from England, you would oblige me by writing half-a-dozen lines to the President, to communicate to them to set the child now on the roll, else he cannot be then elected, and I am assured he is a better scholar than one or two who are, I hear, already on the roll since Christmas, as having made their exercises for them, and that you would send it to my good friend Dr. Halton, which my cousin Morgan of Tredegar, your fellow member, who has been a little sick of late,

---

[39] SP 29/448, f. 157.

shall thank you for. I had troubled you with this small concern
before I left London, but was denied the happiness of paying you
my duty at Whitehall, you being that day gone to Council at
Hampton Court.[40]

But this was an exceptional case; more typically, the courtier Charles
Bertie likewise wrote to Secretary Williamson entreating him to use his
interest with Busby on behalf of Henry Steed, one of the King's Scholars
of Westminster, so that Steed might be elected for Oxford by the Dean of
Christ Church at the next election.[41] The roll continued to reflect great
success for Busby and his school: he had laid the grounds for Westminster
School's scholastic and social supremacy, one that lasted well into the
eighteenth century.

In the eighteenth century Westminster School became a centre of
learning and politeness; under Busby it had been one of learning, fear of
punishment, and caustic wit. In a deeply-felt epigram dating from 1711,
the contrast was drawn with a former pupil of Busby, and a successor as
Head Master, Robert Freind (1667-1751), a former King's Scholar and
Student of Christ Church, where his portrait in Hall looks across at that of
Busby:

Ye sons of Westminster who still retain
Your ancient dread of Busby's awful reign,
Forget at length your fears, your panic end:
The monarch of this place is now a Freind.[42]

Busby's enthusiasm for corporal punishment is unfortunately notorious
even by the vicious standards of the seventeenth century, and it was a
persistent and special feature of Bagshawe's complaints; in making his
case to the governors, Bagshawe observed that 'Your Honours would
have me only submit to, Mr. Busby would have me kiss the Road.'
Busby, he continued, 'hath often complained to me, and seemed to take it
ill, that I did not use the Rod enough.' Bagshawe was so repulsed by the
indignity of the birch and Busby's insistence on its efficacy that he
'heartily' wished 'that there were an assistant in Whipping rather than in

---

[40] SP 29/379, f. 8.
[41] SP 29/369, f. 278.
[42] *Commemoration of Busby*, p. 29.

Teaching'; he had seen such 'sad examples of Cruelty in this kind, that I believe I could make your Honours weep at the report of them.' Busby's nephew, John, an assistant at the school 'a Worthless and an Infamous person', abused 'the Liberty of Whipping to such an Excess and Extravagance of Severity, that I do not grieve for the Practise, but I blush to think of the Cause of it': scandalously, it was never reported, and Bagshawe opined that 'it were better the School should perish, than such an Execrable Use of Whipping should again be made.'[43]

Physical violence was echoed directly and persistently in verbal roughness; Busby was a caustic wit: witness two instances celebrated by his Victorian biographer, G.F. Russell Barker, in 1895:

> "Will your permit me, giant, to pass to my seat?" said an Irish baronet one day in a coffee-house. "Certainly, pigmy," said the Doctor. "Sir," foamed the Irishman, "I alluded to the vastness of your intellect." "And I, sir", quietly replied Busby, "to the size of your own."[44]

But this was nothing compared with Busby's exchange with a scion of an old recusant family:

> The famous Father Petre who had been educated under Busby at Westminster, met him one day in St James's Park. Petre accosted his old master, but Busby declared that he could not recognize him in that dress, and Petre had to introduce himself. "But, sir," said Busby, "you were of another faith when you were under me; how dared you change it?" "The Lord had need of me," replied the priest. "The Lord had need of you, sir!" retorted Busby, "why, I have read the Scriptures as much as any man; and I never knew that the Lord had need of anything but once, and then it was an ass."[45]

Not for nothing was it assumed that Busby, who published little but elegantly effective grammars of the Greek, Latin, and Hebrew tongues,

---

[43] Bagshawe, *True and Perfect Narrative*, pp. 18-20.
[44] Russell Barker, *Memoir of Busby*, p. 51.
[45] Russell Barker, *Memoir of Busby*, pp. 51-2.

was the author of a poem entitled 'A Warning to ye Protestant Peers from their best of Friends the Jesuits.'[46]

It would, however, be a gross distortion of Busby's intellect and character to end this account by emphasising the caustic and violent side of his intellect and nature; as his survival during the Commonwealth demonstrates, Busby was capable of meeting the highest demands of diplomacy and tact, and his legacies to the poor of Westminster and Wells and to his native Lincolnshire parish illustrate his profoundly charitable convictions and sense of Christian commitment.[47] He was, above all, a man of consummate liberality of intellect; not merely accurate, but also catholic. It was Busby who saw the merits of Henry Stubbe (1632-76), born like himself into poverty in Lincolnshire, recommending him to Sir Henry Vane as the beneficiary of his charity, and encouraging the republican baronet to finance Stubbe's transition to Christ Church, where he became a Student, losing this position because of his own republicanism in 1660. Busby valued Stubbe's extraordinary abilities as a linguist, and the undergraduate Stubbe repaid such support by dedicating *Horae Subsecivae* (his 1651 Greek paraphrase of the Old Testament stories of Jonah and Susannah and the elders), to Busby.[48] Scriptural Commonwealth classicism promoted by a young radical might seem an unlikely product of Busby's Westminster and loyalist Christ Church, but catholicity of taste and intellect marked out the best of Busby's protégés. But Busby was first and foremost an orthodox conformist, and it was therefore entirely fitting that the last work to be dedicated to him should have been the work of a clerical schoolmaster in Woodstock and Witney, Francis Gregory (1623-1707), who had progressed from Westminster School to Trinity College, Cambridge in 1641, before serving a happier time as an usher to Busby at Westminster than did Bagshawe, his near

---

[46] Russell Barker, *Memoir of Busby, p. 49.*

[47] Busby's will and codicils are given as an appendix to Russell Barker, *Memoirs of Busby*, pp. 129-47.

[48] 'Ornatissimo Doctissomque Viro Mro Busby, Illustrissimae Scholae Westmonasteriensis Archidipascalo dignissimo, suoque Praecptori ac Maecenati unice colendo': Hnery Stubbe, *Horae Subsecivae: seu Prophetiae Jonae et Historiae Susannae Paraphrasis Graeca Veribus Heroicis* (London, 1651), A3r. On Stubbe's controversial career, see James R. Jacob, *Henry Stubbe, radical Protestantism and the early Enlightenment* (Cambridge, 1983); the *ODNB* entry on Stubbe by Mordechai Feingold is exemplary.

successor in that office. In the year of Busby's death, Gregory acknowledged his indebtedness to him in a defence of orthodoxy against the Socinian heresies of the time, notions not without their influence on John Locke.[49] As the title of his tract demonstrates, Gregory's was at once a learned and a dogmatic work, and thus very much to Busby's taste and habits of mind and religious disposition: *The Doctrine of the Glorious Trinity, not explained, but asserted.*

Gregory's dedication is fulsome yet accurate: he declared that there was scarcely a man in the world who had done more good than Busby, noting particularly, with becoming modesty, that 'To You doth the Church of England owe great store of the choicest Divines; and it is no Fault of Yours, hat I my self am none of that happy Number.' Bagshawe's successor-but-one revered that dissenting opinion, when Gregory concluded his encomium with the observation that: 'more Scholars, well grounded in the Principles of Morality, Piety, and Learning, have been trained up under Your happy Government, than were ever bred by any one Master, in any one School, since the World began.'[50]Under Busby, Westminster School appropriately became the nursery of the most orthodox of bishops; in this respect, the acme of his later pupils was George Hooper (1640-1727), bishop of Bath and Wells, orientalist and mathematician, and a former Student of Christ Church, of whom Busby allegedly said that 'he was the best scholar, the finest gentleman, and would make the completest bishop that was ever educated at Westminster.'[51] John Locke may have become the most celebrated of Busby's pupils, but his direct contemporary, the pugnacious controversialist divine Robert South, was much closer to Busby in mind and spirit, not least in asperity in his exercises in controversy and party spirit. Busby's legacy informed South's dedication to a volume of his sermons to Robert Freind, purely and simply, if resoundingly, in his

---

[49] For an instance of the influential imputation of Socinian tendencies to Locke, inferred both from the *Essay Concerning Human Understanding* and *Christianity Not* Mysterious, see Edward Stillingfleet, *A Discourse in Vindication of the Doctrine of the Trinity* (London, 1697), pp. 231-76.

[50] Francis Gregory, *The Doctrine of the Glorious Trinity, not explained but asserted* (London, 1695), A3r-, A4v.

[51] Russell Barker, *Memoir of Busby*, p. 24 note; *Commemoration*, p. 26.

capacity as Head Master of Westminster School, 'that Renowned SEMINARY OF LEARNING, LOYALTY, and RELIGION.'[52]

The bicentenary of Busby's death was piously celebrated with an exhibition at Westminster School in 1895; at the installation of a bust, the Captain of the School read a speech, 'Laudes Ricardo Busbei', in rather than less than lapidary, because distinctly laudatory, Latin. 'What could be more pleasurable work', he asked rhetorically in praising Busby, 'to the Westminster man in this two hundredth year?' ('Quae res iam ducentesimo anno nostris fuit curae, quo quidem opera esse gratius Westmonasteriensi homini?') The legend and the legacy were both ritually evoked and simultaneously instantiated, as the Captain celebrated the peaceful government of the school exercised by Busby in times of turbulence, and closing his praise with a declaration that the prophetic deities and members of Westminster school, parliament, and the church, all witnessed the greatness of Busby alongside two centuries of witness by its many parliamentarians, poets, philosophers, orators, priests - the best men of the republic – as was proclaimed by the walls of the most celebrated temple of all (Westminster Abbey):

> 'Iam quid Camenae nostrae, quid senatus, ecclesia, populus omnis, debuerint Busbeio, legenti optime de republici meriti, vociferantur etiam hi nostri muri et fanum omnium celeberrimum'

What was said of Busby in the fustian of 1895 can continue securely to be said of him and his considerable legacy in our altogether more demotic age.

---

[52] South, *Twelve Sermons*, v. A1r. Although, Francis Gregory his predecessor by ten years at Westminster, regretted that South's satirical tone inadvertently tended to undermine his learned defences of Trinitarian orthodoxy: Gregory, *Doctrine of the Glorious Trinity*, p. 9.

John Locke

Sarah Mortimer[1]

No way that I follow against the protests of my conscience will
ever bring me to the mansions of the blest
(Locke 2010: 21)

---

[1] I am grateful to Jon Parkin and David Scott for their comments on an earlier
draft of this chapter.

John Locke has long been seen as one of the heroes of English liberalism, celebrated for his defence of the individual's right to pursue their own happiness and to challenge prevailing opinion. But his strong support for individual freedom rested on even deeper principles, particularly his sense of the obligations and duties which all human beings owe to God and which mean that our earthly loyalties can only ever be provisional. Indeed, the very possibility of 'loyal dissent' stemmed, for Locke, from his religious commitments and from his conviction that God had given human beings laws which must guide their actions and their relationships. Following these laws may mean dissenting from the prevailing government or the established church, for each person must take responsibility for their own life, their duty to God and their own salvation. As a philosopher, political theorist and advocate of toleration, Locke sought to explain our freedom, our obligations to God and our more limited obligations to each other. His writings opened up space for a kind of dissent which remained loyal to what he saw as the most fundamental truths, both human and divine.

Locke's ideas were formed in a period of dramatic political and religious change. Born shortly before the English Civil War, he was a seventeen year-old pupil at Westminster in 1649 when Charles I was executed, and he lived to see not only the Restoration of monarchy in 1660 but also the overthrow of James II in the Glorious Revolution of 1688-1689. As Locke was all too well aware, these political events were driven in large part by religious tensions and by clashing convictions about the will of God. His experience of the instability created both by divergent opinions and by the efforts of authoritarian rulers to clamp down on any dissent convinced him that it must be possible to discover a better way to manage human relationships. His writings reflected his own particular context but they proved extremely influential, and were embraced with particular enthusiasm during the American Revolution. Today they remain an important part of English and American political culture, with Locke often remembered as a spokesman for liberty.

Although Locke is rightly placed within a liberal tradition, he was as concerned with duty as he was with freedom. Throughout his life he remained convinced that men and women were created by God and placed on earth to do his will. God 'demands of us that the conduct of our life should be in accordance with his will' (Locke 1954: 151); there is no scope for dissent when it comes to divine commands. Indeed, it is because our primary duty must always be to obey the laws which God has given to us that we can never commit to doing whatever a sovereign or a priest tells us. We must always remember that we are, first and foremost, the creatures of God, obliged to obey him by the very fact of our creation. As this suggests, Locke's moral and political thinking rests upon distinctively religious foundations and much recent discussion of the Locke's writing by contemporary political theorists and commentators has concerned the extent to which his arguments are still appropriate in our secular world (see especially Dunn 1969 and 2003; and Waldron 2002). But whether we share Locke's religion or not, his efforts to unravel the limits of both loyalty and dissent can still be stimulating and even inspirational.

At the heart of Locke's thinking was his effort to understand the relationship between the individual and the communities of which he or she forms part. That concern may well have arisen while he was at Westminster School in the 1640s, for the close relationship between the different but overlapping communities of School and Abbey cannot have escaped his notice.[2] No less significant was his progression in 1652 to Christ Church, Oxford, founded as both a college and as a cathedral and in which lay and ecclesiastical activities were deeply intertwined. But these activities were heavily disrupted by the civil war and its aftermath; most obviously, Christ Church endured a succession of Deans who were foisted upon it by the regimes in London. Locke came up just after the arrival of a new Dean, John Owen, a famous Calvinist preacher and one of Oliver Cromwell's favourite chaplains. Owen's efforts to reform the wider university in a Puritan direction met with resistance and opposition within Oxford, while creating controversy at a national level. Throughout the 1650s, Oxford University experienced upheaval and dislocation as the different regimes tried to place their own men in positions of power and trust. Only the Restoration of the monarchy in 1660 held out the possibility of some stability for a while, and the chance to rebuild the shattered communal bonds within Oxford and the wider nation.

The Restoration settlement enacted a particular view of church and monarchy. It was one in which ceremony and ritual were important, and dissent was to be suppressed as far as possible. Individual opinions about the legitimacy of particular acts or practices were seen as highly destabilising, and Charles II's Parliaments did their best to make sure that everyone toed the Anglican line. Discontent remained, however, and at

---

[2] For Locke's life see Dunn 2002.

Christ Church, Locke experienced at first hand the divisions that could arise from different views of religious worship. One of his fellow Students, Edward Bagshaw, was so unhappy about the new requirements, including the wearing of white surplices in the cathedral, that he and his supporters stole as many of the surplices as they could and cast them into the sewers. Bagshaw claimed that men should worship as they believed the scriptures commanded – and there was nothing about surplices in either the Old or the New Testament. He refused to accept that the magistrate could command men to perform any 'religious' act or practice that they could not find in the Bible.

Locke's first substantial pieces of writing (printed in Locke 1997: 3-78) were a response to Bagshaw, whose views Locke feared would lead to anarchy as each person interpreted the Bible in his own way. Instead Locke argued that the magistrate must be able to decide in matters 'indifferent', that is, in matters where the Bible offers no specific guidance – like whether to kneel at communion or wear a surplice. The need for civil peace and order was paramount in Locke's mind at this point, and he feared that any concessions towards individual conscience of the kind that Bagshaw demanded would reopen the wounds of the Civil War and prevent the new settlement from achieving its purpose. The manuscript was never published, however, and soon Locke came to believe that peace was in fact best secured by limiting magisterial power over religion.

In responding to Bagshaw, Locke had made a strong distinction between that which God had decided and that which he had left open to human discretion, but Locke quickly realised that such a line was very difficult to draw. He explored these issues further in a series of lectures on the *Law of Nature*, given to undergraduates at Christ Church. Here he sought to establish just how human beings could come to know what God required of them, and his answer was that they did so through the use of reason and the experience of their senses. Through these means, they could apprehend and appreciate a moral law governing the world, and this law underpinned all human societies and civil laws. Because humans could perceive that this law came from the God who had created them, they could also understand that they were obliged by it; their obligation to obey the divine and natural law stemmed from God's rights over human beings as their creator and therefore their lord. Such a view was quite unusual for the time, especially because Locke rejected the suggestion that human beings had 'innate ideas' of God and morality. Instead, Locke thought that men and women came into the world without any such formed ideas – they had to exercise their reason in order to work out for themselves the existence of God and his commands for their lives (see Locke 1954).

Locke's investigations into moral knowledge and natural law were shaped by his other activities during the 1660s. He was fascinated by new advances in medicine and science, spending much of his time with medics and with Robert Boyle, whose new experimental method promised to advance the cause of natural philosophy. In this company, Locke came to the view that a lot of our knowledge is in fact deeply uncertain, and that it was essential to work out just exactly what could be known fully and what was simply hypothetical. The paradigmatic discipline for establishing certainty was mathematics; the properties of a triangle, for example, could be known with absolute certainty because they followed from the nature of a triangle itself. Locke began to speculate whether the axioms governing mathematics had any parallel in the moral sphere. Was morality like maths, capable of real certainty? Or was it like medicine, where diagnosis and treatment were only ever probable?

Before Locke could come to any firm conclusions, his medical skills brought him into contact with Lord Ashley (1621-83) – a man whose impact on Locke would be profound. Ashley was Chancellor of the Exchequer from 1661 to 1672, and was well known for his opposition to some of the more stridently Anglican policies of the government and willing to allow some degree of religious dissent. By this time Locke had his own doubts about the stringent requirements of the Anglican Church, doubts that were especially troubling because it was a condition of his Studentship at Christ Church that he should be ordained. In 1667 Ashley offered him the opportunity to move to Exeter House, Ashley's London residence, and managed to obtain a dispensation for him so that he could retain his Studentship without ordination. From then on, Locke's energies were devoted to engaging with the vexed issues of political loyalty and religious dissent.

It was the question of religious toleration and uniformity of worship which again caused Locke to put pen to paper in the first year he spent with Ashley. By this point, a growing number of people were unhappy with the restrictive nature of the Restoration Church Settlement, and several schemes for the toleration of dissenters outside the Church or the 'comprehension' of a range of different opinions within it were being floated. Although these proposals found some support, hostility was a more common reaction. It was widely felt that England was a Christian kingdom, whose people ought to be united in their religious as well as their civil practices and that Charles II, as Supreme Governor, must rule over both church and state. On this reasoning, a dissenter who refused to worship in the established church deserved not only religious but also civil penalties – and any scheme to mitigate these was regarded as ill conceived at best, and at worst as treasonous.

Locke's views, circulated in manuscript and later published as the *Essay Concerning Toleration*, were not so much a direct engagement with the specifics of this controversy as an attempt to step back and assess the scope and limits of the civil ruler's power. By now, as this *Essay* shows, Locke's position had changed quite radically. Here he insisted that the magistrate's authority extended only to the actions that were necessary to preserve peace and security – and this had nothing to do with divine worship. The 'power & authority of the magistrate is … for the good, preservation & peace of men', Locke wrote, and the only reason why people were willing to give one man any power over them was so that he could preserve them in peace (Locke 2006: 269). The magistrate's control, therefore, extended as far as necessary to secure such peace, but beliefs and opinions which were 'purely speculative' remained beyond his sphere of authority. Among such opinions Locke included belief in the Trinity, in the Catholic doctrine of transubstantiation and even in the existence of the Antipodes – none of which beliefs, Locke thought, had any bearing on our social life. Peace could be secured whatever people felt about the Trinity or Australia, Locke thought, and thus the magistrate ought not to concern himself with such matters (Locke 2006: 271-2).

Just as speculative beliefs lay outside the magistrate's authority, so did purely religious ceremonies and worship. These practices, Locke argued, had nothing to do with the civil community, they were between the individual believer and God. Indeed, he now saw 'the way to salvation' as 'by the voluntary & secret choise of the mind' (Locke 2006: 273) and so he thought it was worse than useless to try to force anyone to worship in a way which they did not feel would be pleasing to God. Furthermore, anyone who sincerely believed that God wanted them to worship in a particular way was hardly going to be dissuaded by any earthly arguments or punishments, for the believer would feel that their eternal salvation was at stake. On these grounds, coercion in matters of religion was pointless, for it would not change people's minds, and it was illegitimate, because the magistrate's authority did not extend this far. Here in this *Essay* we can see the development of Locke's theory of toleration, a theory that would show how religious dissent need not be disloyal.

Locke's ideas were not formed in a vacuum, for questions of natural law and magisterial power were much discussed in the tense decade of the 1660s. But Locke's inspiration seems to have come, in large part, from thinkers who were not directly part of the English debate but who were engaged in a parallel effort to explain how people could live together in a civil society and to show how that society differed from the Church. Chief among these were the Catholic writers who had revived the ideas of St Thomas Aquinas, and especially the great Spanish theologian Francisco Suarez (1548-1617). In Suarez's key works of the 1610s he explained that to understand the state we need to think about the purpose which it fulfils within the wider divine plan, and that purpose was, for him, the attaining of natural or earthly happiness. If we turn to the Church, we see that it exists for a higher purpose, to enable humans to reach spiritual or supernatural blessedness. Looked at this way, Suarez thought we could distinguish between the different kinds of authorities wielded by the state and the church, because we could see that each existed for a different end (this argument is outlined most clearly in Suarez 1614). This kind of teleological thinking, analysing the powers and duties of people and institutions by examining the purposes for which they exist, always appealed to Locke and he, like the Catholics, became increasingly convinced that the state and the Church must be distinct because they had very different ends and goals.

Suarez's argument was designed to support papal power, on the grounds that spiritual ends were superior to earthly ones, but some Protestants hoped they could adapt and reshape it to fit with their own agenda. The most important of these Protestant writers was the Dutch lawyer and theologian Hugo Grotius (1583-1645), who believed that by distinguishing clearly between Christianity and natural law it would be possible to prevent some of the conflict and warfare raging among his contemporaries (see Grotius 2005). Grotius believed that the natural law obliged individual human beings to come together into communities because these would enable them to achieve the peace and prosperity which they desired. But this natural sociability had nothing to do with

Christianity or the church, on Grotius's reading. Instead, he thought that men and women would and should want, voluntarily, to follow the laws and commands of Christ in the hope of attaining eternal life. These two purposes, peace and eternal life, were different and parallel; for Grotius it was not the case that the state was inferior to the church. Furthermore, Grotius's own view of Christianity was individualistic rather than communal, he thought that what mattered was a person's own faith and their own commitment to living according to Jesus's principles. But Grotius was never entirely clear about quite how religion and civil life fitted together, and one way of thinking about Locke's work is as an exercise in trying to resolve this conundrum.

Locke's solution in the *Essay on Toleration* was circulated among his friends, though it is difficult to tell what impact it might have had. It was a work of theory, standing at one remove from the contemporary political debate about the mechanics of toleration and comprehension, and may have seemed too academic and disengaged to affect the course of the debate. Whatever Locke and his readers thought, plans for church reform were shelved and the Anglican Church retained its civil as well as religious authority. Indeed, the conversion of James, Duke of York, the heir to the throne, to Roman Catholicism in the late 1660s only intensified demands for penalties against those who refused to join the Anglican Church. Locke's *Essay* lay in a drawer, but he never forgot the issues it raised. They were in the back of his mind as he continued to wrestle with his philosophical investigations into knowledge, truth and human social life.

At Exeter House Locke had plenty of opportunities to discuss philosophical issues, but in 1671 a discussion with some friends made a particularly deep impression on him. The subject was the principles of morality and revealed religion, and how they could be justified. Locke suggested that the best way forwards would be to 'examine our own Abilities, and see, what Objects our Understandings were, or were not fitted to deal with' (Locke 1975: 7). In other words, Locke wanted to explore how human beings came to have knowledge, and how reliable or certain that knowledge might be in different areas of human understanding. Most of all – and here he was reprising some of the themes of the *Essays on the Law of Nature* – he wanted to show that the rules of morality could be demonstrated with certainty, using reason and sense experience. He hoped that by studying the way human beings came to

69

form ideas and to join them together into complex chains of reasoning, he could help his fellow men to differentiate clearly between the true and certain knowledge they had of some principles, like mathematics and morality, and the more unstable, probable knowledge they had of natural philosophy or even Christian revelation.

Although Locke was fascinated and perplexed by these issues, he could not spend his whole time on them. His patron Ashley, now the Earl of Shaftesbury, was becoming increasingly concerned about the future of Britain, especially if the Catholic convert James, Duke of York were to succeed Charles II. Both Charles and James were seeking to strengthen the monarchy and to weaken sources of opposition in Parliament and in the country as a whole. They were great admirers of Louis XIV of France, by now the most mighty king in Europe, and it was his martial prowess as well as his political skills that appealed to them. Shaftesbury feared that the Stuarts favoured coercion over co-operation, and that Britain would slide into the kind of absolutist rule now becoming evident in France. Shaftesbury's opposition to the policies of the court was made clear in a long pamphlet widely known to have come from his circle, and in which Locke very probably had a hand. Entitled *A Letter from a person of Quality to his Friend in the Country* (1675), it denounced those who had, since the Restoration, conspired to make 'the Government absolute and Arbitrary', and to base it on the divine right of kings and bishops (Locke 2006: quotation from 337). It was a strident indictment of the direction of political travel since 1660s, which Shaftesbury saw as leading to despotic rule underpinned by a powerful episcopate - a situation that he feared would only get worse under James. The *Letter* caused a public storm and Locke found it prudent to depart for France, ostensibly in order to improve his health but perhaps also to escape the rising political temperature.

When Locke returned to England in 1679, the country was gripped by the 'Exclusion Crisis', a period of political upheaval from 1679 to 1681 in which Shaftesbury and his allies attempted to exclude James from the succession to the throne. Charles was so horrified by Shaftesbury's mobilisation of the forces of popular anti-popery that he had the Earl arrested and imprisoned in the summer of 1681. Although Shaftesbury was released later in the year, his life was still in danger – especially after the government discovered an assassination plot against Charles and James in which many of the earl's friends were implicated, causing him to flee to the relative safety of the Netherlands, where he died in 1683. By this time, fear at the prospect of a Catholic king had sparked an intense political and religious conflict which threatened to reopen the wounds of the Civil War. It was in this context that Locke wrote the works for which is today best known, the *Two Treatises on Government*. The radical views expressed in these works were controversial, verging on the treasonous, and it is not surprising that they were not published until 1689, when the political landscape was very different. But if we see them in their true context, then Locke's bravery and audacity become evident.

In these works, Locke set out to explain the origins and nature of government, making clear that no king could command the complete and total obedience of his subjects. Dissent from the prevailing political trends of the day was not only legitimate in many cases, but could even be necessary, where the ruler was frustrating the very ends and purposes for which civil society existed. Indeed, where the ruler was acting in a tyrannical way and threatening to destroy the commonwealth he was supposed to serve, then that commonwealth was dissolved and Locke argued that the people had the right and duty to find a new ruler.

In arguing that resistance was sometimes justified, that loyalty to the commonwealth and to divine laws might sometimes mean opposition to the prevailing ruler, Locke was stepping onto very controversial ground. His contemporaries, having seen the disruption and chaos of the Civil Wars at first hand, prized obedience to the ruler very highly. Some saw the king as divinely appointed and ordained, some even suggested that he was the direct descendant of Adam, the first man, and so had a fatherly authority over all his people. But perhaps most notorious of all was Thomas Hobbes's argument, according to which absolute and sovereign power was the only antidote to the brutish life of humans in their natural condition. To Hobbes, men without government, in a 'state of nature', could never be at peace with each other but would be constantly in fear of conflict and violence. Faced with this situation, their only hope of security and a comfortable life was to set up a sovereign whose power must be 'as absolute as men can possibly make it'. The obvious implication, in the 1680s, was that Shaftesbury's campaign for Exclusion could only lead to war, disorder and the anarchy of the state of nature.

Locke needed to show, therefore, that human beings were not simply faced with a choice between chaos or monarchy, that the natural condition of human beings was not so bad as Hobbes had suggested. If sovereign power were not necessary for peace and security, if human beings were able to live in some kind of settled condition even without a king to keep order, then he could suggest that defying the king need not lead to anarchy. Locke always assumed that men were able to live together peacefully because God had given them natural laws to govern their behaviour, and that a king who violated these laws forfeited his right to rule. But to make these claims persuasive in the 1680s, Locke found he needed to step back and consider in more detail the central features of civil society, particularly the nature of human beings and the purposes of government.

According to Locke, human beings were created by God and given particular abilities and responsibilities. 'God having made man, ... put him under strong obligations of necessity, convenience and inclination to drive him into society, as well as fitted him with understanding and language to continue and enjoy it.' (Locke 1988: 318-9) God did not make human beings as atomistic individuals, but he gave them both a desire to live with others and the ability to work out the rules and structures necessary to facilitate society. These rules were the natural law – a set of principles independent of any particular time and place or society, and which constitute the building blocks of communal existence. While men and women would have many different, legitimate opinions about what was enjoyable or pleasurable, they would all be able to accept these fundamental, natural obligations. We have seen how Locke had long been interested in the concept of natural law, and keen to assert that human beings could figure out for themselves, from reason and sense experience, what the law of nature demanded of them. Now Locke explained that God not only gave human beings the abilities to work out the law of nature, but also the means to uphold it by punishing those who broke it. Even without a sovereign, therefore, humans were subject to clear rules and there were sanctions for those who did not obey them.

The condition of nature was, for Locke, one of equality (at least for adult males); no man had any authority over another. To explain the origins of government and civil society, therefore, it was necessary to show how hierarchy emerged and how one person came to have power over his fellow men. Locke's answer was simple: it was through consent. A man had to agree with his fellow men 'to joyn and unite into a Community, for their comfortable, safe and peaceable living' (Locke 1988: 331) in order to establish a commonwealth, and it was through this agreement that he accepted the power and authority of the commonwealth's ruler over him. Locke thought that men had very good reasons to give such consent and to set up a ruler, of which the most compelling were that ruler's ability to organise punishment more effectively and to act as a judge of final appeal. Indeed, Locke elsewhere defined a civil society as a group of men united in having recourse to a single judge who can settle disputes and thus preserve peace. As this formula suggests, when a man agrees to join a society and to obey a ruler, he does not oblige himself to follow that ruler slavishly, nor to give up his own judgement and opinions. All that he needs to do is to accept the decision of the ruler in controversial matters, because this is necessary to attain the ends for which civil government is established. Locke believed that people would continue to disagree about many matters outside the natural law, but private dissent was acceptable so long as it did not frustrate the purposes of the society. Furthermore, a ruler who refused to allow dissent was straying well beyond the limits of his authority.

Locke insisted that the role of government was limited; for him, human beings can, on their own, form opinions, build relationships, and even own property. Indeed, Locke sometimes suggested that the central function of government was to protect the property which men owned independently of the sovereign's decisions. This point was important because Hobbes had argued in his *Leviathan* (1651) that property depended upon civil law, and civil law depended upon a sovereign; in a state of nature no one had anything which they could meaningfully call their own. For Hobbes, each individual had the same right as any other to the apples on a tree or the corn in a field, it was only the sovereign who could decide who should 'own' these (and who could then back up that claim of ownership in his courts). To counter Hobbes's argument, Locke needed to show that men and women could in fact own property independently of the sovereign, and he did so by explaining that when they 'mixed their labour' with the materials provided by nature, the products of their labour became their own. By tending the tree, or ploughing the field and sowing the corn, a person gained a right to the harvest, and that right was guaranteed by natural law. Moreover, such ownership was underpinned by divine law because it is God who gives us the ability and inclination to put the natural world to our own use; for Locke, the sovereign's decisions and laws cannot override these divine and natural principles. If a ruler steps out of the boundaries of his authority by seizing his subjects' property (which is just as bad as trying to force their beliefs), then he can hardly expect the consent of the people and his authority may be forfeit. In this situation, a new sovereign may be necessary.

The implications of Locke's account are clear enough, and when the *Two Treatises* was published in 1689 it was easy to read the text as a defence of the Glorious Revolution. By then, Charles II was dead and his brother, James, had been forced from the throne when his daughter Mary and her husband William of Orange invaded England in defence not only of Protestantism but also its constitution and liberties. It was Locke, therefore, who had provided what would become the most famous justification of this change of ruler. But his intention was not so much to give theoretical backing to the new elite as to explore the scope and limits of obedience more broadly, and to show how the laws of nature provide a framework for life in a commonwealth. These laws enabled human beings to develop their potential while allowing for diversity and difference of opinions; they showed how government could improve upon the natural human condition. And, importantly, they did not demand complete unity of mind and will, as Hobbes's understanding of natural laws had required. Instead, they offered a way of resolving disputes through the setting up of an authoritative judge, while respecting the fundamental equality of mankind.

Locke probably finished the *Two Treatises* by 1683, by which time the worsening political climate prompted him to depart for the Netherlands as Shaftesbury had done before him. There he joined a circle of English exiles, but could do little to prevent the succession of James II in 1685. In the Netherlands, his attention turned to other matters, including medicine – he attended the autopsy of a lion – but also, and most importantly, religious toleration. In the same year as James acceded to the throne, Louis XIV of France revoked the Edict of Nantes which had guaranteed protection to the Protestant minority, the Huguenots, forcing them to convert or flee the country. Many French Protestants went to the Netherlands, and Locke and his friends were clearly touched by their plight. In response, Locke penned a Latin *Letter Concerning Toleration*, designed as a contribution not only to the English debate over the scope of state power in religious matters but as a wider, properly theoretical account of the value and necessity of (limited) toleration.

The argument of the *Letter* is shaped by Locke's distinctive, teleological approach to the question. He began by asking what the purpose of a commonwealth was and answered, drawing on the *Two Treatises*, that it existed to secure peace and preserve the property of those within it. It was, therefore, entirely distinct from a church, which fulfilled a quite different function. A church was 'a free and voluntary association of people coming together of their own accord to offer public worship to God' (Locke 2010: 9). Locke stressed that worship had to be freely offered, and that each person must decide for themselves what kind of worship was most acceptable to God. Underpinning his account is the thought that human beings would always have different views of what God demands, and that no one could trust the judgement of another when it came to matters of salvation. Worship had to be sincere, and thus it would be diverse. Yet this diversity of religious practice need not lead to conflict or sedition, because it did not affect the core purpose of the commonwealth. Where ceremonies or rituals did endanger the public welfare then they should be stopped, but otherwise the magistrate should allow and encourage a range of churches.

Locke's point was that political and religious allegiance should be both distinct and complementary; a good citizen could reject the magistrate's way of worshipping God while remaining loyal in all civil matters. This was an unusually tolerant position to take in the 1680s, when so many of his contemporaries believed that dissenters from the state church would necessarily be opponents of the government and of the social order. But even Locke's account of toleration had its limits, and he flatly refused to accept that Roman Catholics or atheists should be included within it. Catholics were unacceptable because their religion was not simply spiritual – they owed temporal or civil loyalty to the papacy, and their secular allegiance to the magistrate would always be compromised by this tie. Atheists, meanwhile, fell outside the boundaries of Locke's argument because they did not seek toleration for their own public worship of God at all. Indeed, they failed in what Locke saw as the human duty to acknowledge and worship God.

In the *Letter Concerning Toleration*, many of the assumptions which structured Locke's thought are evident. Human beings are created by God to live together in civil societies which maintain peace and order, and to worship God publically in churches. These two sets of duties come from the same source, God himself, and they cannot therefore clash or conflict, as long as they are understood correctly. All human beings lie under the same duties and they are all, fundamentally, equal in the sight of God. No one can renounce their duty to live in society or to worship God, although God allows human a wide degree of latitude to decide how to shape their lives, to pursue happiness and property, and to explore the nature of the world around them. The boundaries of loyalty and dissent within the human world are set by the divine and natural laws which come from God, laws which enable men and women to achieve their full potential alone and in society. What frustrates that potential and subverts the true law is the heavy handed, arbitrary exercise of authority in civil or religious matters. As Locke saw it, rulers like James II and Louis XIV were seeking to go beyond the powers given to them under the natural law, and the result was tyranny and the dishonouring of God.

Locke was once seen as the founding father of liberalism, a political philosophy centred upon the autonomous individual who seeks freedom to pursue wealth and happiness. It will, however, be clear that any account of Locke which ignores the role of God, and the laws and inclination he gives to human beings, fails to capture the true sense of his writing. As historians and political theorists have become increasingly aware of his Christian commitments, they have wondered whether his political views can be detached from those commitments and salvaged for our modern, secular world, or whether Locke's entire intellectual enterprise is in fact so dependent upon his religious beliefs that we have to take or reject the package as a whole. The latter opinion is becoming more common, for the heart of Locke's account of human life and human freedom is a deep commitment to laws and values beyond the individual and their transient preferences. It is the existence of divinely sanctioned and natural laws which can give shape and purpose to our lives, individually and collectively, and it is these laws which, for Locke, can justify our opposition to the arbitrary exercise of authority. They ground our deepest allegiances and they open up a legitimate space for the expression of loyal dissent.

James W. P. Campbell

Other chapters in this book focus on single characters: this chapter deals with two contemporaries who knew each other well, shared many of the same interests and worked closely together. Both made outstanding contributions in the apparently separate worlds of architecture and science. Despite this commonality, their experiences of school and, indeed, of life, could hardly have been more different. Both figures show clearly how life is modelled partly by the vagaries of chance and circumstance. But their lives also demonstrate how a combination of hard work and genuine merit can lead to success whatever your background, given the opportunity.

Robert Hooke's place in a book on Westminster School is without question. He was one of its most brilliant creations and his time there under the formidable Richard Busby was undoubtedly transformative: Westminster made Hooke. Wren's situation is less clear. As we shall see, although his name is linked to Westminster School, and he almost certainly attended at some point, there are no clear records to support this and it seems likely that he was there for only a short period when circumstances at home were particularly precarious. If that is the case, it seems likely it was also directly under the Royalist Busby's protection. It was almost certainly no coincidence in this regard that Wren and Hooke were both sons of Royalist clergymen.

Robert Hooke's background was relatively humble. He was born on July 18th 1635 in Freshwater on the Isle of Wight.[1] His father was a curate who ran the local school. Robert was the youngest of two boys and two girls.[2] A sickly child, he was not expected to make much of his life and his father vaguely hoped that he might become a watchmaker or limner. He showed considerable artistic ability and was good with his hands, creating a clock as a child that, even though it was made of wood, worked "tolerably well". He also built himself a toy boat "about a yard long, ...[with]... Rigging of Ropes, Pullies, Mast, &C. with a contrivance to make it fire off small guns, as it was sailing across a Haven of pretty breadth."[3] Models of ships and clocks tell us something of Hooke's character. He was self-motivated, good at making things, demonstrating a keen intelligence, combined with a deeply inquisitive nature, all characteristics he shared with the young Wren.

---

[1] R. Waller (ed.), *The Posthumous Works of Robert Hooke* (London: Waller, 1705), p.ii.

[2] The best accounts of Hooke's early life are Stephen Inwood, *The Man Who Knew Too Much* (London: Macmillan, 2002) and Lisa Jardine, *The Curious Life of Robert Hooke* (London: Harper Collins, 2003). For a bibliography, see these works and M. Hunter and S. Schaffer, *Robert Hooke: New Studies* (Woodbridge: Boydell, 1989), pp.295-305.

[3] Waller, *op.cit.,* p.ii.

Christopher Wren's background was distinctly more privileged than Hooke's.[4] His mother had inherited money. His father was a well-connected Oxford don, who had followed the familiar path from academia to the clergy with a couple of livings.[5] The young Wren was born on October 20th 1632 (he was nearly three years older than Hooke) in East Knowle in Wiltshire where his father was rector.[6] Within a couple of years his father had been appointed to replace his brother, Matthew Wren, as Dean of Windsor and Registrar of the Order of the Garter. As a boy, Wren was bought up in the Deanery at Windsor Castle, the rectory at East Knowle being used as a second home. He was the only surviving son in a family of girls. He was, like Hooke, a somewhat sickly child. This may explain why he was initially educated at home, although it could simply have been the Dean's preference. What is certain is that he had a series of remarkable tutors, starting while still at Windsor, with his father and the curate William Shepheard, who acted as the chapter librarian and taught Latin to the choristers. According to John Aubrey, Wren was taught in this period 'Grammar [Latin] and School-learning' and this 'continued all his minority under his father's eye, and the tuition of his curate Mr William Shepeard'.[7]

---

[4] There are a large number of biographies of Wren. J.A. Bennett, *The Mathematical science of Christopher Wren* (Cambridge: Cambridge University Press, 1982) remains one of the most accurate. The most recent are A. Tinniswood, *His Imagination so Fertile* (London: Jonathan Cape, 2001) and Lisa Jardine, *On a Grander Scale: the Outstanding Career of Sir Christopher Wren* (London: Harper Collins, 2002).

[5] The best account of Wren's early years is C.S.L. Davies, 'The Youth and Education of Christopher Wren', *English Historical Review,* vol.123, no.501 (April 2008), pp.300-327, which corrects a number of errors in previous accounts, including Jardine's. See also Bennett, above. For Wren's father see *Oxford Dictionary of National Biography* (60 vols., Oxford, 2004) see C.S.L Davies 'Christopher Wren (1589-1658), Dean of Windsor, His Family and Connections', *Southern History,* xxvii (2005), pp.24-47.

[6] Aubrey stated that Wren was born in 1631 (John Aubrey, *Brief Lives* (Woodbridge, Boydell, 1982) edited by Richard Barber, p.331) but this was a mistake: another son, also called Christopher, was born in 1631, and died soon after, see A. Tinniswood, *His Invention so Fertile* (London: Jonathan Cape, 2001), p.3. Wren was named after him.

[7] British Library, Add. MS 25071, fols. 27v, 29v, 123 v., cited in C.S.L. Davies, 'The Youth and Education of Christopher Wren', p.303.

Thus both Wren and Hooke had fathers who were experienced at teaching and encouraged their sons to learn. Both boys shared a fascination from an early age with mechanical devices and intellectual ideas, which would never go away, and both were deeply affected by the Civil War.

The young Wren's comfortable upbringing in Windsor was brought to an abrupt halt when in May 1643 the Parliamentarians took over the Castle and the family was thrown out of their home. Wren was 11 years old and suddenly life must have seemed very precarious.[8] The family appears to have moved briefly back to East Knowle. They then moved in with Wren's brother-in-law, William Holder who was rector of Bletchingdon. Holder had started teaching Wren in Windsor as early as 1643.[9] He treated Wren as if he were his own child and 'gave him his first instructions in geometry and arithmetic'.[10] Wren proved an excellent mathematician. He was fascinated by sundials, building a number of them including one that reflected light from a window onto the ceiling and was richly decorated.[11] Among other things, he made for his father a *panorganum astronomicon* (pasteboard model of the solar system), built a 'pneumatick engine' and drew pictures of a sign language for the deaf.[12]

The idea that Wren went to Westminster is based on the statement in his biography *Parentalia* that 'for some short Time before his Admission to University he was placed under Dr Busby at Westminster School'.[13] There is no reason to doubt this, but the timing is unclear.[14] Wren's father was arrested in May 1645, released on 29 August and rearrested in 1646,

---

[8] For an account of this period see C.S.L. Davies, 'The Youth and Education of Christopher Wren', p.304-6 & n.22. Jardine (2002) places Wren at Westminster in this period (p.41) but Davies convincingly argues against this.

[9] ibid.

[10] John Aubrey *Brief Lives,* ed. Andrew Clark (2 vols. Oxford, 1898), I, 403 cited in C.S.L. Davies, 'The Youth and Education of Christopher Wren', p.305.

[11] Jardine, *op.cit.,* pp.74-75.

[12] Tinniswood, *op. cit.*, p.21, *Parentalia,* p.182. The sign language for the deaf was enclosed in the heirloom copy of *Parentalia* reprinted in facsimile by Gregg Press in 1965, inserted between 193 and 195. For other childhood discoveries see Davies, *op.cit.*

[13] S. Wren, *Parentalia,* p.181.

[14] Jardine argues that he was there from 1641-1646 (p.50-53), but Davies, 'The Youth and Education of Christopher Wren' (pp.304, 306) convincingly disputes this, suggesting the dates discussed here.

this time spending five months in prison in Bristol and Longford Castle before being finally released in July 1646.[15] Oxford surrendered to Parliament and the first Civil War ended in June 1646. It is probably during this time of particular danger and turmoil in 1645-46 that Wren was sent to Westminster to continue his education in relative safety.[16] If this is the case, the time at the school was short-lived (possibly less than a year) and this may explain why no trace is to be found in the school records. He was not formally enrolled and does not appear on the lists of King's Scholars. Presuming this timing is correct, he must have left the school by the end of 1646, when he is known to have passed into the care of the surgeon John Scarborough.[17]

John Scarborough provided the last phase of Wren's education before he went to University. Scarborough was by then in his forties. He had been a Fellow of Gonville and Caius College in Cambridge and a good friend of both Holder (Wren's brother-in-law) and Seth Ward under whom he studied mathematics. Ejected from Cambridge by the Parliamentarians, he had moved to Oxford and had been persuaded by William Harvey to become his assistant, receiving a medical doctorate with his help. Wren probably started as Scarborough's assistant in Oxford in 1646, moving with him in 1648 to London where Scarborough became a Fellow of the Royal College of Physicians and Anatomy Reader to the Barber-Surgeons. In London, Scarborough "lived magnificently, his Table being always accessible to the distressed Royalists and yet more to the Scholars ejected out of either of the Universities for adhering to the King's Cause".[18] He was in the perfect position to tutor Wren on mathematics and introduce him to the very latest ideas on anatomy, perhaps even getting the young man to assist him with lectures and dissections.[19]

---

[15] Davies, "Dean Wren", pp. 34-35.

[16] Davies, 'The Youth and Education of Christopher Wren', p. 306.

[17] For Wren and Scarborough, see Davies, "The Youth and Education of Christopher Wren", pp. 309-10.

[18] Walter Pope quoted in Davies, "The Youth and Education of Christopher Wren", p. 310.

[19] The evidence for and against Wren being involved in Scarborough's demonstrations is discussed in Davies, "The Youth and Education of Christopher Wren", p. 310 and J.A. Bennett, *Mathematical Science,* p.79. Even if he wasn't directly involved there is little doubt that Scarborough would have introduced him to Harvey's ideas.

Scarborough was at the centre of a group of men who met in London in the mid-1640s to discuss scientific theories and conduct experiments. This group was centred on John Wilkins. Wilkins became Warden of Wadham College, Oxford and through him young Wren came to enter Wadham in late 1649 or early 1650.[20] With his Royalist connections Wren was barred from scholarships and occupied the position of fellow-commoner instead. University was however to provide him with a place of safety and it was in Oxford that he first encountered Hooke.

The Civil War arrived a little later in the Isle of Wight but no less dramatically than it had in Windsor. In November 1647, Charles I escaped from Hampton Court where he was being held prisoner and headed south, seeking refuge from Parliamentary forces. It was here he made his last stand as King, arriving secretly in Carisbrooke on 13 November. Up to this point the island had remained largely unaffected by the Civil War but now it found itself the centre of attention. The islanders supported the King and thus found themselves subject to considerable penalties after he surrendered. Hooke's father made his Will on 23 September 1648. He died less than a month later and was buried on 18 October. It has been speculated that he took his own life.[21] Before his death he seems to have made arrangements for his son to leave the island. He left him £40 and another £10 from his grandmother, as well as a stout chest and his books.[22] Hooke was thirteen years old. His likely escort was the Reverend Cardell Goodman, the vicar of the church where his father was curate and an executor to the Will. Hooke was destined for London. Aubrey says that he was apprenticed to the painter Sir Peter Lely:

> ...with whom he was initially upon trial; who liked him very well, but Mr Hooke quickly perceived what was to be done, so, thought he, 'why cannot I do this myself and keep my hundred pounds'[23]

Whatever his reasons, rather than training to be a painter, Hooke went to Westminster instead. There is a strong possibility that the Cardell

---

[20] *Parentalia* say that Wren went up to Oxford in 1646 when he was 14 (p.182), but Davies corrects this using records in the college (Davies, Youth, p. 311-14).

[21] Jardine, *Curious Life*, pp. 47-52.

[22] Jardine, *op.cit.*, p.53; Inwood, *op cit.* p.8.

[23] John Aubrey, *Brief Lives* (Woodbridge, Boydell, 1982) edited by Richard Barber, p.167

Goodman, an Old Westminster himself, had recommended him. Hooke
was neither a King's Scholar nor does he seem to have lodged in the
school itself.[24] He seems to have stayed directly with Richard Busby.
Again the best source for his school days is Aubrey:

> There he learned to play twenty lessons [pieces?] on the organ. He
> there in one week's time made himself master of the first six
> books of Euclid, to the admiration of Mr Busby (now Doctor of
> Theology), who introduced [it to] him. At school here he was very
> mechanical and (amongst other things) he invented thirty different
> ways of flying, which I have not only heard him say but also Dr
> Wilkins (at Wadham College at that time), who gave him his
> Mathematical Magic, which did him a great kindness. He was
> never a King's Scholar and I have heard Sir Richard Knight (who
> was his schoolfellow) say that he seldom saw him in the school.[25]

In this short passage we learn something of Hooke's ingenuity and
education. Busby was renowned for his harsh discipline but Hooke
remained in contact with Busby throughout his life and it is obvious that
there existed a genuine affection between the two of them. For Hooke,
Busby seems to have been a surrogate father figure, a source of protection
and inspiration in a difficult world. Busby no doubt enjoyed having such a
diligent, self-motivated and so obviously brilliant student.

It was while he was at Westminster that Hooke began to exhibit the
symptoms of the medical condition that he suffered from for the rest of his
life. It is now thought to have been *Scheuermann's Kyphosis*. Nodules
form in the discs between the vertebrae turning them into wedges, twisting
and contorting the spine. The result is a stoop or twisting of the back.[26]
Hooke's condition got worse throughout his life so that people remarked
in late middle age he was a sorry sight with his huge head, thin crooked
body and angular features. Hooke blamed the condition on too much time
spent working bent over a lathe making things at Westminster.[27] He was

[24] On Goodman see Jardine, *op.cit.*, pp. 54-56.
[25] John Aubrey, *Brief Lives* (Woodbridge, Boydell, 1982) edited by Richard
Barber, p.167.
[26] For this diagnosis see Inwood, *The Man Who Knew Too Much,* pp.10-11.
[27] For Richard Waller's description of Hooke and of the story of the lathe see
Waller, *op. cit.*, p.xxvi and Jardine, *Curous Life*, p.63.

probably correct that such pastimes made his condition worse or at least more painful, but they were probably not the cause. Hooke's awkward appearance, coupled with his acute awareness of his relatively low social position no doubt partly explains his defensiveness, which was to mark his social relations in later years, most notably, of course, in his famous long-running arguments with Isaac Newton.

Hooke's slightly ambiguous remarks about learning the organ (did he learn the organ in twenty lessons or learn to play twenty pieces?) are important. Separated from the rest of the school, perhaps to shield him because of his Royalist connections, Hooke was not a Kings Scholar. Being such would have given him the opportunity of a place at Christ Church, Oxford. Nor was his bequest enough to enable him to finance both school and a university education. However among his many talents, Hooke was clearly musical and he was thus admitted to Christ Church as a Choral Scholar, which gave him a place in the college and a small stipend. He was listed as a "servitor" of Mr Goodman. This may well have been the Cardell Goodman who brought him to London, and who had himself been to Christ Church and may have still been keeping a watchful eye over his progress.[28] No doubt Busby also played a part and Hooke was soon working as an assistant for the notable anatomist Dr Thomas Willis.

Hooke went up to Oxford in 1653. Wren had been there since Hooke arrived in Westminster in 1649. Thus their paths could never have crossed at school but it was a background they shared and would no doubt have been a topic of conversation when they met at University. Once in Oxford, they both fell into the circle of John Wilkins.

In the 1640s a group of academics had been meeting in London at Jonathan Goddard's house in Wood Street or at Gresham College (a place which would later feature highly in the lives of both Wren and Hooke). They included John Wallis, John Wilkins, Jonathan Goddard, Samuel Foster, Scarborourgh (Wren's tutor) and Theodore Haak. They met to discuss the latest ideas in science including astronomy, anatomy and physics. Wallis, Wilkins and Goddard moved to posts in Oxford under the

---

[28] If that is the case 'servitor' was merely a term of convenience to indicate that Goodman was paying. Alternatively Hooke was acting as a servant for another student (the usual use of the word servitor) although no Goodman has been traced in the university at this time (see Jardine, *op.cit.,* p.65, and Michael Cooper *A More Beautiful city: Robert Hooke and The Rebuilding of London after the Great Fire* (Thrupp: Sutton, 2003) p.20.

Protectorate, the others continuing to meet in London and being supplemented by John Ward, Ralph Bathurst, Thomas Willis and William Petty. Wilkins became Warden of Wadham College and the Master's Lodgings became the new home of the Oxford group and a focus for experimental science at the time. As Wilkins had been instrumental in securing Wren a place at Wadham, he was associated with the group from his arrival. Wren took his BA in 1651. The Fellowships of Wadham were closed to him as he was not a scholar and so he changed college at this point, finding a Fellowship, presumably with the help of Wilkins and others, at All Soul's in November 1653. He took his MA in December of the same year.[29]

It was during this period, when he was regularly attending the meetings in Wilkins's rooms, that we get more reports of his scientific activities. *Parentalia*, the biography of Wren compiled by his son and published by his grandson, contains a list of no fewer 53 items that Wren worked on in this period including investigations into "whether the Earth moves"; a Weather-wheel, a Weather clock, perpetual motion, a double writing instrument, a balance to weigh without weights, new ways of printing, new ways of sailing, methods to "stay long underwater", new ciphers, an artificial eye and new designs tending to strength, convenience and beauty in building.[30]

This list gives an idea of the breadth of interests of the group. It omits the various anatomical experiments and dissections that Wren had already undertaken with Scarborough who had worked closely with Harvey on the circulation of blood. It was these experiments that led to Wren's own on the intravenous injection.[31] It is strange to think that Wren, who is known to us today almost entirely as an architect, was at this stage one of the country's leading anatomists and a pioneer in a technique we take so much for granted. In later life Wren would state that he would have preferred to have been a physician had the King not diverted him into architecture.[32] This was no doubt an exaggeration made to suit the

---

[29] For the London group and Wren at Oxford see Bennett, *op.cit.,* p.16-17; Davies, *op.cit*, p.310-16; Jardine, *Grander Scale,* pp.111-112.

[30] S. Wren, *Parentalia,* pp. 198-99.

[31] Bennett, *op.cit.*, pp.77-78;

[32] Michael Hunter, 'The making of Christopher Wren', *London Journal*, 16 (1991), p. 101.

moment but Wren was fascinated with the working of the body and continued to carry out anatomical work in the Royal Society.

Wren was also present to report the famous case of Nan Greene. Greene had been sentenced to death for infanticide. She had been hanged and her cadaver given for dissection. It was only when Thomas Willis and William Petty got her on the operating table that they realised that she was not dead. The story surrounding the 'miracle of her resurrection' caused a stir at the time and her revivers successfully petitioned for her pardon, becoming minor celebrities in the process. Petty was appointed as the Tomlins Reader in Anatomy by the University as a result.[33] Perhaps the most important of Wren's investigations in this period, however, were astronomical, in particular in observing the rings of Saturn. It was this that was lead to his later appointments in astronomy.

Hooke joined Wilkins's circle in 1653. He passed from working for Willis to become the laboratory assistant of the Honorable Robert Boyle at Wilkins's suggestion. Boyle, an independent scholar of means and very keen experimental scientist, set up his laboratory next to University College in Oxford High Street. [34] Here Hooke was responsible among other things for making and operating the vacuum pumps so critical for his experiments, which led of course to "Boyle's Law". As he was working for Boyle, he was also heavily involved in Wilkins's group.

Wren's time at Oxford provided more useful connections. Wilkins married Cromwell's sister in 1656 and Wren suddenly found himself in the circle of the Lord Protector. It was through this and other connections that he was put forward for the Chair of Astronomy at Gresham College, which he took up on 7 August 1657, presenting his work on the rings of Saturn as his inaugural address.[35]

Gresham College marked Wren's return to London and would later provide a home for Hooke too. The College had been founded in 1597 in accordance with the will of Sir Thomas Gresham (1519-1579) to provide free public lectures. There were Professorships in Astronomy, Divinity, Geometry, Law, Music, Physic and Rhetoric. Lawrence Rooke was at the time occupying the Chair of Astronomy, but moved to the Chair of Geometry which had recently become vacant to make way for Wren. As well as salaries for the professors, Gresham had left his house in

---

[33] For Nan Greene and Petty see Jardine, *Grander Scale*, p.117.
[34] Jardine, *Curious Life*, p.66-72.
[35] Davies, "The Youth and Education of Christopher Wren", p.320.

Bishopsgate which closely resembled an Oxbridge College, with chambers ranged around a central courtyard. The Professors were provided with free board and lodgings. Wren retained his Fellowship and rooms in All Soul's but now divided his time between London and Oxford. As Gresham Professor, Wren turned to a detailed study of Kepler and the mathematical problems surrounding the principles of planets moving in ellipses. Here the mathematical training he had received early on from Holder and others and his own mathematical ability came to the fore. He made a major breakthrough in 1658 admired by mathematicians throughout Europe by rectifying the cycloid (the arc traced by a point on a wheel rolling along a line), found a geometrical solution to Kepler's problem and produced a solution to a problem posed under the pseudonym 'Jean de Monfert' to derive the length of a chord across an ellipse from given dimensions.[36]

Gresham was the centre of academic life in London. The chambers of Wren and Lawrence Rooke became a meeting place for the scientists. The King was restored in 1660 and it was in that year, on 28 November, after one of Wren's lectures, that the members of the group that regularly gathered there formed the Royal Society (a title that they subsequently managed to ratify by Royal Charter of July 1662). Within a few months of the Restoration, Wren had secured an audience to present the King with the treasures of the Order of the Garter which his late father had managed to hide, thereby securing his Royalist credentials. The following year he was to be rewarded with the Savilian Professorship in Oxford during the general shuffling of academic positions that occurred at the Restoration to remove those who had been placed in positions in the Interregnum. Wren thus resigned the Gresham Professorship and moved back to Oxford but remained part of the new Royal Society. He retained rooms in All Soul's and then Wadham although as a Professor he could no longer officially be a Fellow.[37]

Hooke too was heavily involved in the new Royal Society, acting as its curator and organising experiments for its meetings. This was initially

---

[36] See J. Ward, *Lives of the Professors of Gresham College* (London, John Moore, 1740), p. 97.

[37] He finally moved out of college accommodation in 1669 when he was made Surveyor of the King's Works, a post that came with a house in London and enabled him to marry, see Davies, "The Youth and Education of Christopher Wren", p.320-21.

difficult as he was still employed by Boyle and had to divide his time between Boyle's houses in Oxford, London and Dorset. He was officially appointed Curator of Experiments in 1662 and elected a full Fellow [member] of the Society in 1663, and by December 1663 the Society had arranged rooms for him in Gresham College and asked him to live there four days a week to prepare experiments for the members and look after its growing collections of objects and apparatus.[38] In September 1664 he finally moved into Gresham College. He had been put up in June for the vacant post of Professor of Geometry but been defeated thanks to corruption among the electors.[39] This was challenged and the following year corrected, giving Hooke the post that he was to hold for the rest of his life. Gresham now became his permanent home. His rooms, although larger than an Oxbridge College set, were not palatial but Hooke[40] adapted them to his purposes and they were more than adequate to his needs.[41]

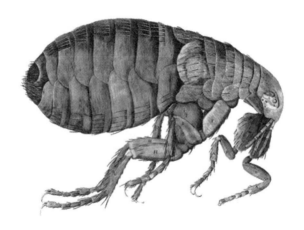

[38] S. Inwood, *The Man Who Knew Too Much*, pp.30-31.
[39] S. Inwood, *The Man Who Knew Too Much* (Basingstoke: Macmillan, 2002), pp.31-32; M. Cooper, *A More Beautiful City,* p.37; M. Cooper, 'Hooke's Career' in J. Bennett, M. Cooper, M. Hunter, & L. Jardine, *London's Leonardo: the Life and Work of Robert Hooke* (Oxford: OUP, 2003), pp.22-23.
[40] There is no surviving portrait of Hooke. The image is that of a flea from *Microgaphia.*
[41] M. Cooper, *A More Beautiful City,* pp.66-72.

The twelve men who met in Laurence Rooke's rooms to found the Royal Society after Wren's lecture on 28 November 1660 were William Ball, Robert Boyle, William Brouckner, Alexander Bruce, Jonathan Goddard, Abraham Hill, Sir Robert Moray, Paul Neile, William Petty, Lawrence Rooke, Wren and John Wilkins.[42] Rooke was the then Gresham Professor of Geometry, Petty was the Gresham Professor of Music and Goddard was the Gresham Professor of Physic. The importance of this organisation in encouraging the growth of experimental science in England in this early period can hardly be over stated.[43] Its journal, *Philosophical Transactions*, established in 1665, was the first scientific journal in the world. Wren and Hooke were both central in its early gestation and development. The breadth and range of scientific pursuits that Wren and Hooke had been involved in were now expanded and deepened.

Both Wren and Hooke were actively involved in developing scientific instruments. Wren designed a double writing machine (a form of pantograph).[44] He had begun a book of observations through microscopes but he was rapidly becoming too busy so he passed it to Hooke.[45] It appeared under the name *Micrographia* and was an immediate success. Wren and Hooke worked together on developing a weather clock, a machine that recorded on paper discs the temperature and barometric pressure against time.[46] Hooke meanwhile, as well as the vacuum pumps already mentioned continued to work on other apparatus, perfecting mirrors for lighting microscopic specimens, adding micrometers to telescopes, and adding telescopic sights to quadrants and micrometers to sextants and quadrants.[47] While Wren continued his fascination with sundials, Hooke was working on clocks large and small, making important

---

[42] The tale is well told in A. Tinniswood, *His Invention so Fertile,* pp.70-71.

[43] It is important to understand that while the Society's meetings made few discoveries, they encouraged its members to produce great advances outside it. On its structure and contribution see M. Hunter, *Establishing the New Science* (Woodbridge: Boydell, 1989), pp. 1-41.

[44] Bennett, *Mathematical science,* pp. 8, 114-5.

[45] R. Hooke, *Micrographia* (London: Martyn, 1665), preface; Bennett, *op.cit.,* pp. 73-74.

[46] Bennett, *op. cit.,* pp.83-86.

[47] J. Bennett, 'Hooke's Instruments for Astronomy and Navigation', in in M. Hunter & S. Schaffer (eds.), *Robert Hooke; New Studies* (Woodbridge: Boydell, 1989), pp.21-32.

contributions in horology.[48] He may not have invented it, but he introduced the spirit level into Britain. He invented and tested a diving helmet supplied with air from the surface, sending a diver down in the Thames.[49] He tested the speed of falling bodies dropped from a great height and carried out many experiments on pendulums.[50]

Perhaps the most striking discovery was the inverse square law of gravitation. Both Wren and Hooke discussed the fact that they both thought gravity obeyed the inverse square law long before Newton produced *principia* but neither could solve the mathematical problems involved. Newton could, but only by inventing calculus.[51] Newton's much repeated phrase "if I have seen further it is by standing on the shoulders of giants" was directed at Hooke, though possibly not without sarcasm.[52]

Today all schoolboys remember Robert Hooke for Hooke's Law, a fundamental principle that underlies much of mechanical engineering.[53] Hooke's Law, however, was only one of a huge number of inventions, improvements and ideas that emanated from this brilliant scientist in the last decades of the seventeenth century. Hooke never ceased building apparatus, testing ideas and publishing the results. While Wren was happy for others to takes his ideas and build on them and cared little for publication or fame, Hooke was careful to publish and guarded his ideas jealously, fiercely defending them against people he saw as stealing his glory. Profit may also have been a motive, although it was not science but surveying and architecture, which were to provide all the money he required.

---

[48] Michael Wright, 'Robert Hooke's Longitude Timekeeper' in *Robert Hooke; New Studies,* pp.63-118.

[49] R. Hooke, *Micrographia* (London: Martyn, 1665) pp.139-40; Inwood, *op.cit.,* p.42.

[50] Cooper, *A More Beautiful City ,* pp.54-64.

[51] The best rendition of the story, which is complex, is R. Westfall, *Never at Rest: a Biography of Isaac Newton* (Cambridge: CUP, 1980), pp.401-404.

[52] Letter from Newton to Hooke dated 15 February 1675 [1676 new calendar], in the Historical Society of Pennsylvania, Simon Gratz Collection, [0250A], MS 12/11, 37. For image of original see www. http://digitallibrary.hsp.org/index.php/ Detail/Object/Show/object_id/9285.

[53] First explained in Robert Hooke, *Lectures De Potentia Restitutiva, or of Spring Explaining the Power of Springing Bodies* (London: John Martyn, 1678). See Cooper, *A More Beautiful City,* pp.49-53.

Today it is common for people to discuss and worry over Wren's transition from science to architecture. It is important to realise that Wren and Hooke recognised no such distinction: for them and their contemporaries architecture was a branch of practical mathematics in much the same way as we might describe engineering.[54] Indeed surveying, architecture (civil architecture) and engineering (military architecture or mechanics) were all seen as branches of practical mathematics. In 1661 the King offered Wren the position of Surveyor of Tangiers (which Wren refused) on the understanding that such a position involved surveying that required a competent mathematician. At Wadham, Wren had already offered "new designs tending to strength, convenience and beauty in building".[55] Wren's involvement in practical design which began with University architectural commissions was thus just a natural extension of his mathematical interests. His first design was for Pembroke College, Cambridge where he produced a modest and elegant chapel for his uncle, Bishop Matthew Wren who was later buried there.[56] The Sheldonian Theatre followed. It was a much grander building on more familiar ground, and again was a commission acquired through connections.[57] However nothing at this point suggests that Wren would turn entirely to architecture. It was just one aspect of his scientific endeavours and Wren never gave up science. The shift was not an intellectual one, but one of appointment. Up to 1673 Wren's primary post remained his Savilian Chair in Oxford, which he relinquished reluctantly.[58] After that date his salary came entirely from outside the University. The events that led to this change and Hooke's involvement in architecture are easy to identify.

Gresham College was closed in 1665 and the members decamped to the country, many joining the King in Oxford until the plague arrived there too.[59] Wren then left Oxford for Paris, taking the opportunity while the University was closed to see the architecture and visit French

---

[54] For a discussion see Bennett, *op.cit,* passim. but especially pp.87-93; Campbell, *op.cit.*, pp.11-16.
[55] See above note 30 above.
[56] A.V. Grimstone, *Building Pembroke Chapel: Wren, Pearce and Scott* (Cambridge: Pembroke, 2009)
[57] A. Geraghty, *The Sheldonian Theatre* (London: Yale University Press, 2013).
[58] He resigned on the day he was knighted, 14 November 1673 (see Jardine, *Grander Scale*, p.283.
[59] Jardine, *Curious Life,* p. 70.

scientists.[60] He returned to England in 1666 full of ideas and armed with a large number of engravings of buildings.[61] Before he left for France Wren had been advising on the repair of St Paul's Cathedral.[62] The great gothic cathedral was in a very sad state. Cromwell's troops had used it as stables and it had been left to fall apart. At the Restoration Wren was appointed one of the Commissioners to investigate its repair. Returning from France Wren drew up an elaborate plan for replacing the existing tower with a magnificent dome, the first in England, as the centrepiece for a rejuvenated London. On Monday 27 August a meeting was held at St Paul's and according to John Evelyn those present enthusiastically agreed to follow Wren's design. It was never to be. Less than a week later, on Saturday 1 September the Great Fire started in a baker's shop in Pudding Lane. In the devastation that followed 13,200 houses were destroyed. The economic heart of England was reduced to smouldering rubble and tens of thousands of people cowered in makeshift tents in the fields outside London.

In the ensuing days Wren drew up plans for rebuilding London and presented them to the King. Hooke presented his to the Royal Society. Neither plan was accepted, largely because speed was of the essence, but both Wren and Hooke were appointed to a group of six charged with overseeing the rebuilding of the City. They helped draw up the new building regulations that were to determine the shape of London for the next two centuries and they devised the method of rebuilding. Each owner was to be required to rebuild their own plot at their own expense. Before they could start they needed to have a survey done to establish their boundaries (very often lines of buildings had been destroyed in the Fire and roads were to be widened). These surveys were to be carried out by surveyors appointed by the City, one of whom was Robert Hooke. Over the next decade Hooke surveyed literally thousands of plots, a job which could easily have been full time but Hooke managed to fit around his numerous other commitments.[63]

---

[60] Jardine, *Grander Scale*, pp.239-247; Bennett, *Mathematical Science*, pp.90-91.
[61] S. Wren, *Parentalia*, p.262.
[62] For the story of Wren, St Paul's before and after the Great Fire see Campbell, *op.cit.*, pp. 16-34.
[63] For a full description of the processes and numbers see Cooper, *A More Beautiful City*, pp. 129-163.

The Fire had destroyed 87 parish churches. A Commission was formed to oversee their rebuilding and in the end fifty were built with money from a tax on coal. Wren was put in charge of their construction. St Paul's too had been badly damaged and Wren was called upon to advise on its repair. He advised replacement but the church refused and a plan was devised for a new roof over the nave. Before it could be enacted the building began to collapse and Wren was summoned from Oxford to oversee its safe demolition.[64] In 1668 he became Surveyor of the Cathedral and began to plan its rebuilding. Again funding came from the Coal Tax but at such a slow rate that the building progressed at a snail's pace taking over forty years to complete. Wren planned and oversaw its construction from beginning to end, guiding the project through five deans, four bishops, and six monarchs.[65] In 1669, the King made Wren the Surveyor of the King's Works. He was now in charge of the maintenance of all the Royal Palaces (barring the Tower of London and Windsor Castle). The Surveyorship came with a substantial house in Whitehall, yet even at this stage it is clear that Wren valued his academic career more than this prestigious new post and he retained his Professorship in Oxford until 1673, appointing a Deputy to carry out his lectures.[66] During all this period he was very active in the Royal Society, regularly attending its meetings and becoming President in 1680/81.[67]

Once established as Surveyor for the King's Works, architectural projects increasingly came Wren's way. Some of them, such as his work at Hampton Court Palace, Winchester Palace and Kensington were a part of his remit. Others such as Chelsea Hospital and Greenwich grew out of it. The sheer number of projects that Wren undertook is staggering and he was by far the most prolific architect of his day. Of course he did not manage this alone: he ran a complex organisation, delegating work to trusted assistants. He ran not one but three physical offices. One was at St Paul's. The old cloister next to the church had been rebuilt to accommodate a substantial office and workshops with the Great Model for the Cathedral on display to the public in the Chapter House. Here Wren kept a team of draughtsmen working exclusively on the cathedral and had

---

[64] *Wren Society* (Oxford: OUP, 1923-1943), 20vols., vol. XIII, p.46.

[65] For lists see Campbell, *op.cit.,* pp.60-63.

[66] Tinniswood, *op.cit.,*p.180.

[67] For Presidency and how it led to Chelsea Hospital see Tinniswood, pp.254-265.

his own room with a drawing board and a map above the fireplace.[68] A separate office in Whitehall looked specifically after the City Churches, while a third office adjoining his house looked after the other projects. This delegation of work was key to Wren's success and in many ways he was the first person in England to run what we would recognise today as an architect's practice. Two assistants were key to Wren's success: Robert Hooke and Nicholas Hawksmoor. Hawksmoor was to appear in the 1680s but for the earlier period Hooke was pivotal.[69]

Hooke kept a regular diary in the 1670s, 80s and 90s which is an invaluable source for his activities in this period.[70] It shows the sheer range of his interests. While he was carrying out his surveying tasks and working for Wren, he was preparing demonstrations and building apparatus for the Royal Society meetings and carrying out his own scientific experiments. But it would be wrong to imagine that Hooke worked long hours alone as some sort of solitary obsessive. Between all his activities he found time to meet his friends and colleagues, to talk to craftsmen in taverns and converse with scientific acquaintances in coffee shops and to spend time with scientific instrument makers and in bookshops. Hooke was not a lonely creature but a deeply sociable man who needed company and enjoyed conversation and debate. Amongst all this activity he found time to draw plans for Wren and to act as his eyes and ears on building sites around the City while Wren was busy in Whitehall or elsewhere. He and Wren designed the Monument to the Great Fire which they jointly used unsuccessfully as a zenith telescope (it

---

[68] Campbell, *op.cit.*, pp.42-52.

[69] For Hooke's part in assisting Wren, see Cooper, *A More Beautiful City*, pp.188-192; On all Wren's draughtsmen and location of the offices see introduction to Geraghty, *The Architectural Drawings of Christopher Wren at All Soul's College, Oxford* (London: Lund Humphries, 2007), pp.8-13.

[70] Felicity Henderson, 'Unpublished Material From The Memorandum Book Of Robert Hooke, Guildhall Library Ms 1758' Notes Rec. R. Soc. (2007) 61, 129–175, publishes March –July 1672 and January 1681- May 1683. Henry W. Robinson and Walter Adams, The diary of Robert Hooke, M.A. F.R.S. 1672–1680 (London: Taylor & Francis, 1935) covers the period 1672-1680; R. T. Gunther, *Early science in Oxford*, vol. X (The life and work of Robert Hooke) (Oxford: Gunther, 1935) covers the periods 1 November 1688 to 9 March 1690 and 6 December 1692 to 8 August 1693.

moved too much in the wind to take reliable observations).[71] They were also involved in the construction of the Fleet Canal, a project that was both expensive and in the longer term rather an embarrassment.[72]

Wren's status as one of England's most well-known architects is entirely justified. His place in architectural history is well-established and many of his works survive.[73] Hooke has not been so lucky.[74] His Royal College of Physicians (1672-78) in Warwick Lane consisted of a noble courtyard and an anatomy theatre behind. The theatre was demolished in 1866 and the remainder was destroyed by fire in 1879. His Merchant Taylor's School (1674-75) was demolished in 1875, and the grand town house he built in Bloomsbury for the courtier and diplomat Ralph Montagu in 1675-79 on the site currently occupied by the British Museum was gutted by fire in 1686 shortly after it was completed. His Haberdasher Aske's Hospital (1690) in Hoxton, a huge building with a great central portico, was demolished to make way for new buildings in 1826. All these would have been well-known to Londoners of his time. However the building that everyone knew was Bethlehem Hospital (Bedlam) which was on the north side of London Wall backing on to Moorfields which were public gardens stretching over what is currently Finsbury Circus and Finsbury Square. Here Hooke designed a huge palace consisting of two great wings and a central block with a high lantern. The building was remarkable for its style and of course for its use as the largest lunatic asylum in London. It was in every respect an extraordinary building, but it too was demolished in 1810 as it had become structurally unsafe. A few of his designs remain. In London the churches he was most involved in with Wren are St Benet's, St Paul's Wharf and St Edmund the King. Outside

---

[71] Jardine, On a Grander Scale, pp.xii, xiii, 275, 318-21, 424; Jardine identifies the wrong staircase at St Paul's, see J. Campbell, *Building St Paul's* (London: Thames and Hudson, 2005), p. 145-150. It is correct in Bennett, *Mathematical Science*, p.42. Hooke was probably responsible for the whole design. On this and the nature of their relationship, see Matthew Walker, 'The Limits Of Collaboration: Robert Hooke, Christopher Wren And The Designing Of The Monument To The Great Fire Of London', *Notes Rec. R. Soc.* (2011) 65, 121–143.

[72] See Cooper, *A More Beautiful City*, pp.164-173; T. Reddaway, *The Rebuilding of London after the Fire* (London: Arnold, 1940), pp. 200-243.

[73] For a list see H.Colvin, *A Biographical Dictionary of British Architects* (London: Yale, 2008) 4th edn, pp.1156-1165.

[74] Colvin, *op.cit.*, pp.532-536.

London, Escot House burnt down, but his almshouses at Buntingford for Seth Ward survive. Ragley Hall has been altered out of all recognition and Shenfield Place has been made into a care home but Ramsbury Manor survives largely intact. But perhaps his best building is the delightful church he designed at Willen in Buckinghamshire for his old Head Master Richard Busby c.1680, [75] and, of course, the Ionic portico and steps he added leading up to the 'School' and Busby's library at Westminster which he completed c.1680-82.[76]

Reading Hooke's diaries, one cannot help but be surprised by how anyone had the energy to do so much. Hooke was always rushing from one engagement to the next. He went out with friends and colleagues and then toiled long into the night. He was a hypochondriac and recorded his ailments as carefully as he recorded the weather (meteorology was another of the obsessions which he shared with Wren). He used his own body to try out experimental remedies, in the process often making himself ill.[77] Gradually the pace of life wore out his frail body. His mobility became worse and he grew increasingly thin. His physical appearance became increasingly shocking to his friends and he finally passed away in his rooms on 3 March 1703.[78]

In his later years Hooke cared little what he wore and his rooms were in disarray. Outwardly he gave the impression of someone who was struggling to make ends meet, so it was all the more surprising when after his death the locked chest at the end of his bed was opened. It may well have been the very chest his father had left him as a child. Much to the surprise of all those present it was found to contain a fortune in coins, which Hooke had diligently salted away from a lifetime of activity. Hooke left the world a very rich man. He was buried in the church of St Helen's Bishopsgate.

Wren outlived Hooke twenty years. He was still an active architect in his eighties, but gradually his posts were taken from him.[79] He lived to see St Paul's completed and he retired to Hampton Court, retaining a house in St James's which was probably occupied by his son. It was on a visit to

---

[75] M. Batten, 'The Architecture of Robert Hooke', *Walpole Society*, xxv (1936-7), pp.96-97.
[76] See Geraghty *op.cit.* dwg no.365.
[77] See Jardine, *Curious Life,* pp. 230-34, 304-5.
[78] Inwood, *op cit.*, pp.436-439.
[79] Campbell, *op.cit.,* p.165; Colvin, *op.cit.,* pp.1154.

London that he caught a chill. He went for a nap after lunch and when his servant tried to raise him he realised he was dead.[80] He was buried in St Paul's Cathedral.

After Hooke's death the Royal Society was forced to vacate Gresham College and remove its possessions from Hooke's rooms.[81] The only portrait of Hooke seems to have been lost in the process.[82] However the Society itself continued to flourish. Its motto "Take nothing on trust" could equally have applied to Wren and Hooke. It was only with Hooke's diligence and hard work that the Society flourished in those early years. It was Hooke, Wren and Halley that challenged Newton to write *Principia* and it was only in the context of the Royal Society that such conversations could have arisen. Both men sat at the heart of events and navigated their way through the troubled politics of the period unscathed. We tend to associate Wren with architecture, and Hooke with Hooke's Law, but to do so is to do an injustice to both men whose breadth of achievement was truly extraordinary. They continually challenged the status quo. The end result was everything we take for granted today in terms of technology and science. If you want their monument, look around you.[83]

---

[80] Campbell, *op.cit,* pp.165-66; Wren Society, XVIII, pp.181-85.
[81] Inwood, *op cit.*, pp.436-439.
[82] *ibid.*
[83] Wren's epitaph: *Lector, si monumentum requiris circumspice.*

William Murray

Dominic Grieve[1]

William Murray, first Earl of Mansfield (1705-1793), is one of Westminster's most eminent jurists. His career, which spanned over fifty years, saw him rise to the office of Lord Chief Justice

---

[1] I wish to acknowledge my indebtedness in particular in writing, this to the recent biography of Lord Mansfield "Justice in the Age of Reason" by Norman Poser and to the entry in the DNB by James Oldham.

and placed him at the heart of the Georgian social and political establishment which he reflected in many aspects of his life. But he was not born into it. On the contrary, Murray started out as an outsider and the role played by the school in facilitating his success within it, was crucial to shaping his future and enabling him to make the exceptional contribution to English jurisprudence, which is his principal legacy.

Murray was born on 2nd March 1705, at Scone Abbey, near Perth, the ancestral home of his parents, the fourth son of fourteen children of David Murray, fifth Viscount Stormont (d. 1731), and of his wife, Marjory, the only child of David Scott of Scotsarvet.

The fortunes of the Murray family had been intimately linked to that of the Stuart dynasty, James VI and I having raised them to the Scottish nobility as reward for their loyal services. In the context of 1705, however, that loyalty had relegated them to being Jacobite outsiders flirting with treason. After the Union of the parliaments in 1707, Stormont travelled throughout Scotland to raise support for a rebellion. He was a signatory to a memorial to Louis XIV asking for help to reclaim the throne for the Old Pretender. In the rising of 1715, he attended a meeting with fellow rebels at the outset, but then prudently kept his head down in what was a doomed enterprise. But he was sentenced to a year's imprisonment and fined £500, after failing to come to Edinburgh to answer for his actions. His second son, Murray's brother James, was deeply implicated in the rebellion. A Tory MP under Queen Anne, he travelled to France where he became the Pretender's chief secretary, remaining in exile for the rest of his life. Murray's sister, Marjory, married Colonel John Hay who was present at the 1715 rising and was later made Earl of Inverness by the Pretender. He and his wife likewise led a life of exile at the Stuart court at St Germain and later in Rome. When the Young Pretender came to Scotland in the "'45", Murray's mother, long widowed, made him welcome at Scone.

This Jacobite connection was to have a profound impact on Murray. There is ample evidence that his own youthful enthusiasm was to share in a romantic Jacobite allegiance. When studying at Oxford he visited his brother in Paris. There is also a surviving letter to John Hay in exile, desiring him "to make tender of my duty and loyalty to the King-a very small present but all I have to offer." Later in life these youthful inclinations were either abandoned or, of necessity, suppressed. The consequences returned at times, however, to haunt him and may explain the caution he was seen by contemporaries as exercising in his own political career.

Murray started his studies at Perth Grammar School, an establishment principally devoted to preparing boys of diverse social backgrounds for the Church and which gave him a thorough grounding in Latin and English Grammar. Initially, he travelled there daily from Scone but, from the age of eight, his parents' removal to another property at Camlogan in the Borders, brought family life to an end and left him lodging with the headmaster. It was after the "'15" that a decision was taken to send him to Westminster. It was already clear that his intellect, powers of application and maturity of behaviour marked him out. His father consulted his brother, James, in exile. The choice of school was almost certainly carefully calculated. James Murray had a long standing friendship with another avowed Jacobite, Francis Atterbury, Bishop of Rochester and Dean of Westminster, who was later to go into exile himself. The school had managed to maintain a position of pre-eminence in educating the sons of the governing class of Great Britain although it was also known for the Jacobite sympaties of its Head Master Robert Freind. Sending him there would allow for the possibility of one member of the Murray family maintaining some influence at the heart of the British establishment.

Thus in 1718, Murray, at the age of 13, travelled to Westminster from Scotland by horseback, on a pony given to him by his father, never to return. The journey took seven weeks and included a farewell stop with his parents at Camlogan. There is no evidence he ever saw them again and not a single letter between them survives. He does not appear to have ever returned to Scotland. Samuel Johnson was much later to remark of this circumstance, "Much can be made of a Scot, if caught young".

On arrival in London Murray contacted John Wemyss, a Scottish apothecary who was known to his parents. He arranged for Murray to lodge with George Tollett who ran a house for Westminster boys in Dean's Yard. The accounts show him being provided, amongst other things, with a sword, two wigs and pocket money and his school fees-all billed to his parents. But within the year he had been elected a King's Scholar.

Murray flourished at Westminster. He excelled at Classics and at oratory. He made the lifelong friendships which were to help shape his career. These included Andrew Stone, later secretary to his patron, the Duke of Newcastle; Thomas Clarke, who became Master of the Rolls in

1754; and Thomas Newton and James Johnson, later bishops of Bristol and Gloucester respectively.

He also impressed older people. A school friend called Vernon took him home to meet his father, a City merchant, and thus started a friendship with the family. When Vernon died at an early age, the father treated Murray as a son, standing in as a parent at his wedding and later leaving him an estate of 500 acres in the Midlands. When Murray was inclining away from a career in law because of the cost involved, it was the financial intervention of Lord Foley, the father of another school friend that made it possible. He provided him with £200 per annum as support for his legal education.

Murray's talents as a classicist meant that he was able to tutor younger children by the age of 16. These included the two sons of the Earl of Kinnoull. The Kinnoulls, who were an influential Tory family, took him under their wing and he stayed with them during vacations. It was Lady Kinnoull, who, on asking Murray what was the theme of the homework he was doing, was surprised to receive the reply "What is that to you?" When she remonstrated with him for his unexpected rudeness he responded "indeed my Lady, I can only answer once more: "What is that to you?" as the subject of the Latin essay was "Quid ad te pertinent?". It was this mixture of self possession, intelligence, polite manners and precocious humour that attracted attention.

Throughout his life Murray kept an interest in the school. He was a Busby Trustee from 1741 until his death. He was involved in choosing Head Masters and attended reunions of Old Westminsters. It is clear that he saw it as the foundation of his fortunes.

Murray next proceeded to Christ Church, Oxford, where he matriculated in June 1723. He pursued his classical studies with diligence and appears to have avoided the dissipated living that characterised undergraduate life at the time. In 1727 he beat his contemporary and future political opponent, William Pitt the Elder in a Latin poetry competition on the death of George 1. He was admitted to Lincoln's Inn when at Oxford and was called to the Bar in 1730, but we know little of how he was taught and it is very likely that he was largely self taught, reading widely, although he did some pupillage with a Catholic Jacobite. He read particularly in the field of jurisprudence where his classical education took him to Roman law and the pandects of Justinian. He also practised oratory and was coached by Alexander Pope, the poet, who had become a close friend and whose literary and Tory circle he enjoyed. Pope made him practise in front of a mirror. That summer he proceeded on a Grand Tour with another Westminster friend, Charles Sackville, Earl of Middlesex. He then set himself up in chambers in the Temple.

The progress of Murray's career at the Bar, reflected his ability as an academic student of law, and his winning manner as an advocate but also his networking skills. His early cases largely came from Scotland and required him to appear in front of the House of Lords. It gave him a grounding in Scots Law that was to be of great importance to him later. He also appeared before the Commissioners of the Board of Trade in the lengthy dispute between the Penns and Lord Baltimore over the boundaries of Maryland. The first case in which he made a mark was when he appeared before, first the House of Lords and then the House of Commons, to argue against the retributory bill brought against the City of Edinburgh for its failure to protect Captain Porteous from being lynched by a mob, outraged at his reprieve following a conviction for opening fire on a tumult and killing eight demonstrators, without having first read out the Riot Act. The bill passed but with greatly attenuated penalties and the City presented him with a gold box in token of its appreciation. The case established his reputation and he was thereafter in receipt of lucrative work.

Murray worked extremely hard in the preparation of his cases and made the presentation look easy. The poet William Cowper commented that Murray "was wonderfully handsome and would expound upon the intricacies of the law, or recapitulate both matter and evidence of a cause.....with an intelligent smile on his features, that bespoke plainly the perfect ease with which he did it." An observer wrote: "Often when the audience part of the court of King's bench would begin to thin from the expectation of no material business coming on, no sooner was the cry given of "Murray being up", than the crowds would run back so as not only to fill the court, but all the avenues leading to it."

It was not surprising, therefore that his practice grew rapidly. A key role as junior counsel for William Sloper, accused by Theophilus Cibber of adultery with his wife, cemented his reputation in a matter that caused sensation at the time. Murray was able to show that Cibber had connived at and arranged the affair. After this work poured in. Murray's self confidence is illustrated by the way he dealt with one of his most difficult clients, Sarah Churchill, Duchess of Marlborough. She sent him the huge retainer of a thousand guineas, which he returned to her, less five guineas, which he said was his usual retainer fee.

On 20th September 1738, Murray, at thirty three, married Lady Elizabeth (Betty) Finch at Raby Castle in Durham, the home of Betty's sister, Henrietta, Duchess of Cleveland. His bride was the daughter of Daniel Finch, seventh Earl of Winchelsea and second Earl of Nottingham and of his second wife Anne, the daughter of Viscount Hatton, and was a year older than him. The fortunes of her family and their rise to prominence in government in the previous two centuries were steeped in the practise of the Law. But it was also a marriage of like-minded companions, their courtship at least in part conducted in the literary circle of Pope, the poet Christopher Smart and Henry St. John, Viscount Bolingbroke. Although childless, they shared a clearly happy and harmonious marriage for forty six years until her death in 1784. The marriage also helped open the door for him to participate in the political life of the country.

Murray's connections through marriage were, however, only one part of the reason for his progress. His friendship from school with Andrew Stone who had become secretary to the Duke of Newcastle, drew him into Newcastle's political circle which also included the Lord Chancellor, Hardwicke, with whom Murray had developed a friendship through the Law. Murray had become a neighbour of Newcastle's, as he had taken up residence after marriage in a house in Lincoln's Inn Fields. In November 1742, Newcastle, desirous of securing Murray's services in government appointed him Solicitor General, despite his social connections with the Tory opposition and two days later, Murray was elected to the Commons as MP for Boroughbridge, a seat Newcastle controlled. In 1743 he was made a Bencher of Lincoln's Inn in recognition of his new status.

In the Commons, Murray quickly made his mark. He had already impressed the House when appearing in front of it as an advocate on behalf of the merchants and sea captains, complaining of the conduct of the Spanish authorities towards them which led directly to the War of Jenkin's Ear. Now he deployed his advocacy on behalf of the government, as its principal Commons spokesman, sparring with William Pitt, as he defended its handling of the War of the Spanish Succession. But his key role was in providing advice to his colleagues and working closely with the Attorney General, Sir Dudley Ryder. Together they conducted the prosecutions of the leaders of the 1745 rising as well as determining when prosecutions were not required. This was done in a manner that was commended for its firmness and moderation. As the accused were mostly connected with Murray's family by blood or political alliance this gave rise to more than one allusion to his past. Lord Lovat, on trial for his life and shortly to be beheaded for treason, commented to the court after Murray had successfully argued against his request to adjourn proceedings that: "I heard him (Murray) with pleasure, though it was against me. I have the honour to be his relation, though perhaps he neither knows it, nor values it. I wish that his being born in the North may not hinder him from the preferment that his merit and learning deserves."

There was little sign at the time of any such hindrance. Murray made himself indispensable, providing legal opinions on issues of domestic and international law, the drafting of bills for presentation in Parliament and giving political and private advice to Newcastle who was a man who valued and needed such assistance. There is little evidence of any partisan ideology present in Murray's work, save that he argued forcefully for policies to promote the growth of commerce and against trade restrictions, even to the point of opposing the prohibition on British insurers insuring enemy ships in time of war. He helped produce a memorandum for the government to submit to Prussia, which was successful in persuading that country to accept the principles of the courts of Admiralty of England, as to the handling of violations by neutral ships of their duty of neutrality and the grounds for the seizure of their cargo.

In 1753, however, Murray was confronted by the past in a manner that looked as if it might destroy his career. He was accused by the Recorder of Newcastle on Tyne, Christopher Fawcett, of toasting the Old Pretender with James Johnson (just appointed bishop of Gloucester) and Andrew Stone (now sub-governor to the Prince of Wales) at Vernon's father's house in the City "some years before". All the protagonists had been at Westminster together and the allegations have the flavour of modern stories of past substance abuse by politicians. The Secretary for War Henry Fox, was moved in defence of Murray to admit to King George II that he himself had transgressed in this way when at Oxford, thereby earning Murray's eternal gratitude. A Cabinet committee was set up to examine the matter and Murray appeared before it to deny the accusation. The Cabinet committee was then attacked in the Lords as acting as a Star Chamber and there were demands for a full examination of the issues in Parliament. But the matter then fizzled out, there being no public outcry but considerable condemnation of the accusers. Many were cynically realistic about the issue. Lord Chesterfield wrote of Murray and Stone's denial of ever having been Jacobites: "This seems extraordinary, considering that they were of Jacobite families, bred up at Westminster School and sent from thence to Oxford, the seat of Jacobitism. All I can say to this last particular is what Ariosto says of Angelica, who after having travelled all over the world tête-a-tête with her lover, professed herself an untouched virgin."

The outcome probably affected Murray personally much more than was warranted. The issue continued to make him uncomfortable for the rest of his career. It left him more cautious politically than ever and constantly keen to show his loyalty to the Hanoverian Crown. But it did not prevent him being made Attorney General on Ryder's elevation to Lord Chief Justice in 1754. On Ryder's death two years later, Murray was elevated to the peerage and created Lord Mansfield, called to the degree of sergeant-at-law and sworn in as Chief Justice of the King's Bench. His choice of title reflecting his indebtedness to Newcastle whose family had a long association with the town.

Murray, or Mansfield, as he must now be called, sat on the bench as Chief Justice for thirty two years. He was as diligent and hard working as a judge as he had been as a barrister. His court sat very long hours and he once threatened to sit on Good Friday, until a barrister in the case suggested with good humour that he would be the first judge to do this since Pontius Pilate. He cut through its business and frowned on long winded advocacy. He refused to countenance the then accepted practise that a case might be argued several times before judgment was given. But his reputation as a lawyer and his cordial nature ensured that he was both liked and respected by most of those who appeared in front of him. Mansfield insisted that junior barristers should not be prevented from having their motions before him heard because of the court's business being monopolised by senior counsel and changed his court's procedure so that this did not happen. He was generally liked by his fellow judges. As time went by his reputation became so dominant that other judges may have felt that they lived under his shadow. But it is noteworthy that in his first twenty years on the bench there were only two recorded occasions when other judges sitting with him dissented from his opinion.

His greatest contribution to the development of the law lay in the field of commerce, an area of interest for him which he had already displayed as a parliamentarian. The country was undergoing a rapid period of change with great increases in both manufacture and trade. But the law was hedged about with restrictions on the way commerce was conducted; some of them archaic relics of the later Middle Ages. There was also an absence of consistent rules for the resolution of commercial law disputes.

Helped by his deep knowledge of Roman Law and the civil law traditions of continental Europe and Scotland, Mansfield looked to supplement the common law with civil law principles to create an English Law Merchant that provided consistent and predictable norms for mutually enforceable contractual obligations. As he put it in the insurance case of *Milles v Fletcher* in 1779 "The great object in every branch of the law, but especially in mercantile law, is certainty and that the grounds of the decision be precisely known."

We can see this illustrated in the case of *Carter v Boehmin* 1766. Mansfield established the fundamental principle of "good faith" in all insurance contracts. The case concerned the insurance of a fort in India against its being taken by the French. In finding for the insured, he held that there was need for an insured to place before the insurer any special facts that the insurer does not know and that a failure to do so was a fraud that voided the contract, a rule that still survives in many Common Law jurisdictions, but has just been abolished in its original form in England.

Another example of his approach was to seek to construe strictly the application of any statute that inhibited commerce, so as to negate its effect. When in 1773 English lace makers sought to enforce a law that fined any person who brought foreign made lace into the country (*Dyson v Villiers*), he restricted its scope to items for resale, saying he could not conceive that Parliament intended that a gentleman returning from abroad be stripped stark naked and be subject to a penalty. A similar attitude can be seen in other cases involving claims to trade monopolies. He was also very reluctant to find that a necessary business, even if environmentally unpleasant, was a nuisance, as this would restrict trade. Similarly he defined attempts at creating labour organisations to negotiate collectively on wages and conditions as conspiracies. In *R v Eccles* he said "every man may work at what price he pleases, but a combination not to work under certain prices is an indictable offence"; a rule which was not abrogated until the early 20th century.

Another area where he substantially developed the Law was in the field of intellectual property. He encouraged juries to provide strong common law protection to ideas by trademarking. In the case of *Millar v Taylor* in 1769 he argued in a judgment in which the court was split, that the common law allowed for perpetual copyright, a decision overturned in the Lords five years later. He believed strongly that patent and intellectual property rights were advantageous to the commercial well being of the nation.

Mansfield also developed the law to give greater rights to women who, once married, lost their legal status to enter into contracts. In a series of judgments, he enlarged the previously narrow exception that allowed a married woman to sue or be sued, only if her husband was out of the country never to return. He extended this to cases where there was a formal separation (*Rinsted v Lady Lanesborough* 1783). This not only gave justice to a creditor by allowing a woman to be held liable for her debts in such circumstances, but also enabled her to obtain credit, which might be essential for her welfare.

In certain areas Mansfield's attempts to shift the law were unsuccessful. In the 1765 case of *Pillans and Rose v Van Mierop*, he sought radical alteration of the law of contract by removing the need for consideration on the grounds that it was "an ancient notion... for the sake of evidence only", which could be disregarded if there was other good evidence of agreement. This was overturned in the next decade by the House of Lords. The same fate befell his attempt to give effect to the clear intention of a testator, in breach of the long established rule that intention was irrelevant and that that intention could only be construed from the words of a Will itself.

Today, Mansfield is best remembered for his judgment in the case of *Somerset v Stewart* in 1772. Stewart was a Scottish merchant in Massachusetts. In 1769 he brought his slave, James Somerset, to England. He was befriended by abolitionists and escaped his servitude only to be recaptured and placed on a ship to be taken to Jamaica and sold. The challenge brought by abolitionists to his detention under a writ of Habeas Corpus and Stewart's defence on the grounds that Somerset was his property to dispose of as he pleased, became a cause celebre and one of the defining cases on the legality of slavery in English law.

Mansfield's approach was entirely legalistic. He appears to have been embarrassed by the implications of the case for a slave trade that was underpinning mercantile prosperity and had brought an estimated 15,000 slaves into the country. He was also mindful that slavery was lawful by statute in many of the British colonies and he made clear that the contract for the sale of a slave abroad was enforceable in English courts. He sought to encourage a settlement that would avoid a judgment. He uncharacteristically allowed the case to be adjourned. But at the end his decision was governed by the law and not the interests of slaves or slave owners. It was also crystal clear. He said that "...the state of slavery is of such a nature that it is incapable of being introduced on any reasons moral or political; but only by positive law. Whatever inconveniences, therefore, may follow from the decision, I cannot say this case is allowed or approved by the law of England; and therefore the black must be discharged."

The judgment did not end slavery as it did not declare illegal an entire system of bondage created by colonial legislatures. On other occasions Mansfield dealt with contractual disputes involving slavery with apparent disregard for its humanitarian implications. But the Somerset judgement provided a mechanism that could be invoked to secure a slave's release if he was in Great Britain and by the time of Mansfield's death it was seen by many, including Mansfield himself, as a key decision in challenging its general legitimacy. Mansfield was no abolitionist but his decision showed complete professional integrity in interpreting and applying the Law without fear or favour.

Mansfield did, however, display a deep belief in religious toleration which may have originated both in his Jacobitism and his youthful friendship for Pope who suffered discrimination for his Catholicism. He consistently interpreted statutes restricting religious freedom so narrowly that his directions to juries had the clear intention of making the law inoperable. Between 1766 and 1770 he heard six prosecutions of Catholic priests for saying mass, a crime punishable by life imprisonment. None was successful. In one, *R v Webb*, he directed the jury that "These penal laws were not meant to be enforced except at proper seasons, where there is a necessity for it; or more properly were not meant to be enforced at all, but were merely made in terrorem."

He was equally supportive of dissenters. In 1767 he ruled that the City of London's practice of deliberately electing dissenters as sheriff and then fining them £400 if they refused to serve as they had then to conform to Anglican rites of worship was in breach of the Corporations and Toleration Acts.

Mansfield paid a considerable price for his enlightened stance. In June 1780, when he was 75, popular opposition to the relaxation of the Penal laws against Catholics turned to violence in what became known as the Gordon Riots. Mansfield had to be rescued when he was beset by the mob as he made his way to Parliament. Several days later his London residence on Bedford Square was a special target of the rioters. He and his wife had to escape as the house was sacked and set on fire, destroying its contents which included his library with signed works by Pope and Swift, and his personal archive. The total loss of the content was estimated at £35,000. Mansfield characteristically turned down an offer of government compensation and took pride in the reasons for his being the object of the mob's anger.

Equally characteristically Mansfield saw no conflict of interest in sitting as judge in the subsequent trials of many of the ringleaders, although public comment at the time highlighted this as a potential issue, in the case of the treason trial of the alleged instigator of the riots, Lord George Gordon, who was acquitted by the jury. To modern eyes this conduct would be seen as damaging to any assessment of his character. At the time, however it fell well within the acceptable. It is inescapable that his impartiality can be questioned in his handling of cases concerning the security of the state, or involving members of the aristocracy with whom he had some association. He gave extremely sympathetic treatment to the Duchess of Kingston when she was indicted for bigamy in 1775 and did his utmost, unsuccessfully, to try to get the case against her dropped. The Duchess had a close connection to his mentor Newcastle. His speech as a member of the House of Lords in 1769, considering the appeal of Archibald Douglas from the dismissal of his claim to the Douglas estates by the Court of Session, on the grounds that he was not the son of his mother Lady Jane Douglas, ignored entirely the evidence and appealed to his fellow peers' emotions, urging them that Lady Douglas, a woman of high birth could not have sought to perpetrate such a fraud. As the evidence of the fraud was very strong and Lady Douglas had been married to an exiled Jacobite, it is difficult to escape the view that Mansfield had reverted to being an advocate rather than acting as a judge. Campbell, Mansfield's 19th century biographer, judged his speech as "very inferior to his usual judicial efforts" and his behaviour attracted adverse comment at the time.

The final area in which Mansfield's influence was considerable, was in respect of freedom of the Press. Here he showed himself to be very conservative in his views. He upheld the right of the government to control the Press through the criminal charge of seditious libel and insisted that it was for the judge not the jury to decide whether or not a particular statement was libellous, a principle that was criticised at the time and was eventually changed after his retirement by Charles Fox's Libel Act of 1792.

This issue arose in the case of John Wilkes, the radical politician and editor of *The North Briton*, whose edition number 45 in 1763, notoriously attacked the government of Lord Grenville. Mansfield became involved in a series of courtroom confrontations with him, in which it was plain that he saw himself as under a duty to uphold the government in his role as a judge rather than promote freedom of expression. He sentenced Wilkes to outlawry when he escaped abroad and thus incurred the enmity of radical opinion. But on Wilkes' return and surrender to the court for trial in 1768, the outlawry was reversed on a technicality and he had earlier found in Wilkes favour on the issue of the validity of the general warrant used to seize his papers The issues were in any event not personal. Later, when Wilkes had been Lord Mayor of London and achieved greater respectability and when Mansfield was retired, Wilkes made him a gift of books. Mansfield described him as "the pleasantest companion, the politest gentleman and the best scholar he knew".

Contrary to Montesquieu's belief that Britain enjoyed the separation of powers, it was a feature of Mansfield's tenure of office that it engaged him directly in politics. As Lord Chief Justice he acted twice as Chancellor of the Exchequer in 1757 and 1767, as it was customary for the Chief Justice to fill that post when it was vacant. In 1770 and 1783 he acted as speaker of the House of Lords, while the great seal was in commission, as the office of Lord Chancellor was vacant. His appointment to the Privy Council on being made Lord Chief Justice placed him at the heart of the political system. He served for over twenty years in Cabinet without portfolio with the title of "Cabinet Councillor Extraordinary" and was the informal adviser of several Prime Ministers and of both King George II and George III.

In these roles Mansfield was very active. Within a year of appointment as Chief Justice he was instrumental, by acting as a wise intermediary, in helping create the successful Newcastle-Pitt wartime ministry that led Britain to victory in the Seven Years War. He was also deft in helping to rescue Newcastle from the damage to his reputation for the loss of Minorca, although he was much criticised by some for doing this at the expense of any possibility of reprieve for Admiral Byng who was shot for cowardice in relation to its loss.

Thereafter he was heavily involved as an adviser to successive administrations, managing to remain in Cabinet, despite the change in administration to that of the Earl of Bute in 1762, a survival that attracted to him opprobrium as a trimmer with no principles. The truth was that he lacked any strong political convictions but was skilled at government. As Prime Ministers succeeded each other rapidly in the 1760's he was a source of stability. When Lord North had formed his long running administration in 1770, he declined the offer of being made Lord Chancellor but chose to continue a role as an "eminence grise", with direct access to the King. In this role he wielded both influence and patronage, frequently intervening to secure appointments for those he favoured.

During the crisis over the American colonies and the subsequent war of independence, Mansfield consistently supported the view that the demands of the colonists were incompatible with the principles of parliamentary sovereignty. He argued strongly against the repeal of the Stamp Act despite the sense of injustice it engendered in America. His customary mixture of pragmatism and astuteness failed him and he contributed to the rising tension, describing the Boston Tea Party as an act of high treason. As Chief Justice he used the laws of seditious libel to suppress opposition to the war. At the start of the war his firm support of the King's views earned him elevation to an earldom with a special remainder to his nephew's wife and her sons as he was childless. But by 1779 the war was going badly. There were disagreements in Cabinet and he withdrew from its meetings. He had become very unpopular as a politician. It marked the effective end of his role in top level politics. But his political failure did not translate into animus against those who had been responsible for it. When the American revolutionary and diplomat, John Adams, was in London in 1783, Mansfield went out of his way to be helpful. Adams commented of him, "His politics in American affairs I had always detested. But now I found more politeness and good humour in him than in Richmond, Camden, Burke or Fox", all of whom had been supporters of the colonists.

Mansfield's favourite toast was "old books and young friends" and it aptly reflected his love of learning and of convivial company. His principal recreational pursuits were riding, walking, playing cards and visiting and entertaining his friends.

In 1754, after fifteen years of married life living in London, Mansfield was able to purchase Kenwood House in Hampstead, from the Earl of Bute. Elegantly brought up to date by the Adam brothers and surrounded by landscaped grounds and with its own dairy it provided a perfect setting both for entertainment and as a bucolic retreat. It was the delight of Lady Mansfield who took a close interest in its management. She was herself at the centre of a circle of highly educated women with a range of cultural interests and was fully involved in the hospitality they jointly extended there and at their London home and which was clearly much valued by those who experienced it.

Kenwood also provided a framework for developing a life with his extended family. By the 1760's two of his great nieces, Elizabeth and Anne Murray, were in residence at Kenwood. They were joined by Dido Elizabeth Belle, the mixed race daughter of his nephew, the naval officer, John Lindsay, and a black slave in the West Indies. She enjoyed an intermediate status in the household, neither quite a full family member nor a servant. It is, however, clear that Mansfield was very fond of her and made provision for her in his Will.

Mansfield was very much of his epoch in promoting his family. He exercised his influence unremittingly in favour of his nephew and heir, Lord Stormont. He helped him in his career as a diplomat, despite Stormont's talents being judged by many to be rather limited. He also showed great partiality to one, Thomas Mills, who was rumoured to be either his illegitimate son or nephew or indeed the son of the Old Pretender. Despite Mills' serious character flaws, Mansfield secured for him a commission in the Army and later, a lucrative sinecure and a knighthood as Receiver General of Quebec. When he fell into debt Mansfield secured him another lucrative post in India with the help of Warren Hastings.

Mansfield himself managed his finances with consummate acumen. Starting with little he made a great fortune from his practice at the Bar, from his salary as Lord Chief Justice and the emoluments of that office, including the sale of offices in his gift and court fees. His chief Clerk, John Way, also doubled as his financial agent. His fortune was largely invested in mortgages many of them granted to members of the nobility. A valuation of his assets in 1789, put them at half a million pounds.

As well as his support for Westminster School he was an active trustee of the British Museum and a governor of the Charterhouse. It is noteworthy that he provided a great deal of advice, personal and financial, to his many friends. He was seen by them as a pillar of wisdom and reliability.

By 1786, Mansfield, a widower and over 80, found it increasingly difficult to sit as a judge. In recognition of both his services and the high status he had achieved by his work and age, he was given a second earldom of Mansfield with remainder to his nephew. He tendered his resignation that year, but did not leave office until two years later, probably because he was intent on influencing who succeeded him. He then lived in retirement at Kenwood, increasingly infirm but in full possession of his intellectual powers. His visitors found him preoccupied with the French Revolution. He was concerned as to its consequences and shocked by its barbarity.

He died on the 20th March 1793. The entire Bar and judiciary wanted to attend the funeral, but he had left instructions that it should be private. He had also stated that "from the love I bear to the place of my early education, I wish it to be in Westminster Abbey". This was duly done, the Captain of the King's Scholars attending, to honour his memory in Latin verse. He was buried there alongside his wife. In due course a vast monument was put up to him, financed by the legacy, for that purpose, of a grateful client from his days at the Bar.

Mansfield's own legacy as a jurist has been long lasting. His judgments continue to be cited in courts in every common law jurisdiction. For in his jurisprudence, his learning transcended the age in which he lived and the mores it encompassed and produced ideas rooted in principles that had the capacity to endure. As he said himself when arguing a case as a barrister in 1744: "As the usages of society alter, the law must adapt itself to the various situations of mankind".

On his monument there is the usual wordy Georgian epitaph about his accomplishments. But there is also a short inscription that looks like a Westminster School epigram:

"Here Murray, long enough his country's pride,
Is now no more than Tully or than Hyde."

"Foretold by Alexander Pope and fulfilled in the year 1793."

I suspect that this would have pleased him the most.

Charles Wesley

Leslie Griffiths

When Charles Wesley arrived at Westminster School in 1716, he'd not quite reached the age of nine. Yet he came formidably well equipped for the intellectual road that lay ahead of him. His father, Samuel, was the Rector of Epworth – a boggy parish on the Isle of Axelholm in Lincolnshire. His wife, Susanna, had borne him 19 children only ten of whom survived infancy. There were three boys and seven girls. The oldest son was named for his father. He was 19 years older than Charles and, at the time of the youngest brother's birth, he was already at Christ Church, Oxford, after completing his studies at Westminster. The remaining son, destined to be the most famous of them all, was John. He was almost 5 years older than Charles and, unlike the other two boys, he went to Charterhouse. Both parents were the children of clergymen who'd been ejected from their parishes in 1662 for refusing to give their assent to the Act of Uniformity. But both Samuel and Susanna had found their way back into the established church. They were high church Tories with some sympathy for the Stuarts. The father had accepted the inevitability of a change of dynasty after the death of William III but Susanna was obdurate in her loyalty to "the king over the water." She seems to have been a closet Jacobite and, in line with this, there has been some speculation about her reasons for naming her last child as she did.

Like all his siblings, Charles was home-educated by his mother. Her pedagogical methods, together with her steely discipline and determination, ensured that all her children could face the world well prepared for its demands. Especially the boys. She began their education when they reached the age of five. They were expected to learn the alphabet on their very first day of schooling. Soon they were reading the scriptures, singing the psalms, listening to edifying stories, taking an interest in what was happening around them. Long before their formal education began, their mother had seen to it that she'd broken their wills; only then, she believed, could she be sure of success. She set aside a special one-to-one time for each of her offspring. Charles was "Saturday's child." In these sessions, she would see to it that the children could handle adult conversation. It was expected of them that they should obey instructions, speak kindly to one another and forgive each other graciously.

By the time Charles was ready to go away to school, his brother Samuel had completed his studies at Oxford and was well established as an Usher at Westminster. Not only that, but he'd recently married the daughter of the Reverend John Berry who kept a boarding-house for Westminster (town) boys. So Samuel and his new wife Ursula could accommodate the younger brother and keep a close eye on him too.

Charles Wesley arrived at Westminster in 1716 at a turning point in the nation's history. The Elector of Hanover, George I, had just come to the throne and this ushered in a Whig ascendancy within the political order of the day. The ecclesiastical realm, meanwhile, was dominated by bishops of an erastian disposition who became the spiritual arm of the social and political order, ready to tolerate and carry out its decisions. So the Stuarts, the Tories and the High Church party were all pushed to the sidelines. The Jacobite rebellion of 1715, an uprising intended to kill the new regime at birth, offered proof that there were significant groups of people who were deeply resentful at the passing away of the old order.

Westminster – the parliament, the Abbey and the school – were particularly affected by these developments. Thomas Spratt was Bishop of Rochester and Dean of Westminster from the early 1680s till his death in 1713. His tenure had begun in the reign of James II, gone through the Glorious Revolution and survived until the eve of Queen Anne's death. He'd had to be Janus-faced to survive these changes. His successor in both roles, Francis Atterbury, was nowhere near as subtle or pragmatic. He'd already nailed his colours to the mast in the way he'd defended Henry Sacheverell in the disturbances following his November 5th sermon of 1710. Indeed, it was he who wrote Sacheverell's much-admired speech delivered in his defence at the bar of the House of Commons. Though he'd sworn the oath of allegiance to William and Mary in 1689, he joined others who plotted the return of the Stuarts. There is some likelihood that, but for Queen Anne's sudden death in 1714, these activists might have secured their objectives and restored what they considered "legitimate" rule. In the event, Atterbury was arrested, imprisoned in the Tower, tried, stripped of all office, and banished to exile in France. Suspicion reigned on all hands, nowhere more than at Westminster.

There was no way the nine year old Charles Wesley could remain on the margins of this tumult. His brother Samuel had been closely related to the political events that played themselves out at the very heart of the school. He'd enjoyed the patronage of both Thomas Spratt and Francis Atterbury. Spratt had ordained his father and, perhaps for that reason, chose him as a reading companion, a role he didn't really like; he felt suffocated by the attentions of the Bishop, describing him as his *inimicus amicus* (his unfriendly friend). It was very different with Atterbury, however. Here was a man who fostered his gifts and offered him real friendship. Samuel remained loyal to Atterbury throughout his troubles and, indeed, after his condemnation; he defended him publicly and wrote to him in exile. It's hardly surprising that he was widely suspected of sharing Atterbury's views.

John and Charles Wesley were just children when all these events were unfolding. Their older brother's position, however, was only too obvious. And it led to his losing all chance of preferment – in the school and in the Church. When Dr Nicoll became Head Master in 1733, Wesley (by then the First Usher) had high hopes of stepping into his shoes as Under Master. He'd played a significant role in establishing St George's Hospital at Hyde Park corner, the first public institution of this kind and yet, despite his efforts within and beyond the school, he was passed over. This filled him with a bitterness which he nursed to the end of his life. He left Westminster to become headmaster of Blundell's School in Tiverton where he remained until his death in 1740.

The fact that Charles Wesley spent several years living with his oldest sibling is too often forgotten by those seeking to evaluate the qualities of the younger man. After four years under his brother's roof, Charles entered St Peter's College as a King's Scholar. He was then 13 years of age and, four years later, became Captain of the School. His whole career at the school saw him close to Samuel "whose fine scholarship, poetic genius and Christian feeling made him a fit guide and counsellor for his younger brother." So wrote John Telford, one of the earliest biographers of Charles Wesley. I believe that much of what happened in Charles' later life can best be explained by the intimate relationship with his oldest brother during his formative years at Westminster School.

Charles Wesley forged friendships whilst at school which were to last him the whole of his life. The most significant of these was with William Murray. Murray had come to London from Perth where he'd attended the local grammar school for a couple of years. His family had had strong dealings with the Jacobites and this was not a propitious time for them. What's more, Murray spoke with a pronounced Scottish accent and was therefore subject to much taunting and mockery. On one occasion this led to a fight on the Green within the Cloisters when, surrounded by a large crowd of cheering and jeering boys, Charles Wesley stepped in to defend Murray. He fought off those seeking to down the newcomer. There were to be other such battles to fight and win and Charles was always ready. The two boys became firm friends. Their subsequent lives went off in radically different directions but, curiously, both of them went on to play a significant part in preparing public opinion for the great cause of abolishing the institution of slavery. And they became neighbours towards the end of their lives and called on each other frequently.

In 1735, almost a decade after leaving Westminster, Charles Wesley travelled to Georgia as secretary to General Oglethorpe the first governor of the colony. He remained there for just over a year before being sent back to London with despatches from Oglethorpe. Illness prevented his ever returning but he never forgot the time he spent there. An article in the founding charter of the colony specifically forbade slavery – for fear that runaway slaves might seek refuge in the Spanish-controlled territory of Florida. Within fifteen years however, after the military defeat of the Spanish, slavery was legalised in Georgia though it was as he travelled through the Carolinas on his way to London that Wesley had direct experience of the institution. What he saw made him an inveterate opponent of slavery. The descriptions in his journal still make grim reading.

> [Journal August 2nd 1736] I had observed much, and heard more, of the cruelty of masters towards their Negroes; but now I received an authentic account of some horrid instances thereof. The giving a child a slave of its own age to tyrannize over, to beat and abuse out of sport, was, I myself saw, a common practice. ... A gentleman I often met [would] first nail up a negro by the ears, then order him to be whipped in the severest manner, and then to have scalding water thrown over him, so that the poor creature could not stir for four months after. Another much-applauded punishment is drawing their slaves' teeth. One Colonel Lynch is universally known to have cut off a poor negro's legs; and to kill several of them every year by his barbarities. ...[Another man, a teacher in Charlestown, once] whipped a she-slave so long that she fell down at his feet for dead. When, by the help of a physician, she was so far recovered as to show signs of life, he repeated the whipping with equal rigour, and concluded with dropping hot sealing-wax upon her flesh. Her crime was over-filling a tea cup.

This direct experience made him and his brother John implacable opponents of slavery. John wrote his *Thoughts upon Slavery* in 1774 and, from his death bed in 1791, penned his very last letter to William

Wilberforce urging him to pit all his energies in the struggle to put an end to what he called "this execrable villainy."

It's interesting to note the way William Murray too became a significant player in the campaign to abolish slavery. In 1756, he was made Lord Chief Justice and ennobled as Baron (later Earl of) Mansfield. In James Somersett's case in 1772, he ruled in favour of the discharge of a black slave who'd escaped his American master whilst on a trading voyage to England. The slave was captured and pressed aboard a British ship by people intent on selling him back into slavery when the ship arrived in Jamaica. [Slavery is] "so odious," he wrote, "that nothing can be suffered to support it but positive law. Whatever inconveniences may, therefore, follow from a decision, I cannot say this case is allowed or approved by the law of England; and therefore the black [man] must be discharged." He remained uncertain how the law might be enforced and this led him, in his will, to specify that his great niece, a mulatto named Dido Elizabeth Belle, should be considered a free woman. She was the illegitimate daughter of his nephew; she'd been born into slavery in the West Indies and remained technically a slave though she lived with the nephew and his wife for 30 years. This was a simple but significant step towards creating an atmosphere within which efforts to abolish the slave trade (and indeed slavery itself) could be furthered.

Wesley and Murray became near neighbours towards the end of their lives, one living in Chesterfield Street and the other in Bloomsbury Square. They'd frequently walk over to each other's house and continue their friendship over a glass of wine. When Murray's house was sacked and his library burned by a mob during the Gordon riots in 1780, Charles Wesley was among the first to comfort him and offer him solace. The twilight years of both men offer a charming picture of a lifelong friendship.

Other schoolboy friendships produced a more variegated pattern of ongoing relationships. Once Charles Wesley embarked on his evangelistic career, his lifestyle hardly lent itself to much social inter-action with his old friends. Take Richard Robinson, for example. He and Wesley left Westminster for Christ Church together in 1726. They'd held leading roles in the Latin play produced at the school in their final year. It was Terence's *Andria*, an intricate little play about love and social class where an impossible situation eventually gets sorted out by the discovery that a peasant girl was all along the daughter of someone of noble birth.

Shakespeare resorted to this kind of plot again and again. Richard Robinson played the part of an Athenian nobleman named Chremes while Charles Wesley acted a slave named Davus. Chremes is imprisoned within the attitudes of his social set while Davus is free to roam, to pick up information wherever he can and to act on it creatively. Looking back on these roles and at subsequent events in the lives of Robinson and Wesley, this theatrical moment seems to have anticipated the social roles they were eventually to play in real life.

After their time at Oxford, they went their separate ways. But their paths crossed from time to time and the friendship they'd had for each other soon blossomed again. By 1748, Charles and John Wesley were itinerant preachers breathing life and shape into the emerging Methodist movement. In July of that year, while Charles Wesley was preaching in an orchard near Bristol, a coach drew up and those sitting in it listened attentively to his sermon and sang the hymns. One of them, Sir William Bunbury, hailed Wesley as an old school friend and they had a good conversation. The party returned to the preaching on successive days and, on the last occasion, they brought Richard Robinson with them. The two former thespians, both now ordained clergymen, seemed glad to see each other but were soon locked into a theological argument. Robinson told Wesley that he had refused to believe many of the scandalous things he had heard about Charles and John Wesley but that his greatest surprise had been to hear that they employed laymen. "It is your fault, my lord," Charles is reported to have said. "My fault, Mr Wesley?" "Yes, my lord, yours and your brethren's." "How so, sir?" said Dr Robinson. "Why, my lord, you hold your peace, and so the stones cry out." The friends took a turn around the field in silence. Then Dr Robinson said, "But I hear they are unlearned men." "Very true, my lord; in general they are so; so the dumb ass rebukes the prophet." Wesley declared that when God called anyone to preach the gospel and his calling became evident by repeated conversions then he wouldn't ever dare reject such a person. They talked with great candour and obvious affection for each other.

Robinson, soon after this meeting, headed for Ireland. Through the influence of two Lords - Holderness and Sandwich (both laymen) and two Dukes - Dorset and Northumberland (both laymen), he was soon enjoying his own very different experience of itinerant ministry as he became successively Bishop of Killala (1751), Leighlin-Ferns (1758) and Kildare (1761) before his final translation to the archiepiscopacy of Armagh as

Primate of All Ireland in 1765. Had the two school chums met after this astronomical rise to power, I'd like to imagine that Charles Wesley might, with wicked irony, have pointed to the role of lay people in effecting the prelate's advancement in life. Robinson turned out to be a very able and committed leader; he was soon transforming Armagh from "a collection of mud cabins to a handsome town." John Wesley visited Armagh in 1787 and found the city strikingly endowed with fine buildings but, quoting the Latin poet Horace, he offered a wry comment on the prelate's continuing obsession with his building projects. A piece of marble, suggested Wesley, should serve as a *memento mori*. He should be thinking of the tomb that he'd soon need rather than yet another palace waiting to be built.

Charles Wesley would have bumped into a dozen or so Westminster schoolmates in Oxford. He was away from the influence of his family for the first time in his life and his undergraduate days took on a surprising pattern. He seems to have enjoyed the company of a school contemporary called Stephen Lushington, something of a smart, elegant, indolent young man, not averse to losing money at cards, failing to put in an appearance at the beginning of term and susceptible to female charm. Charles seems to have had thoughts of copying the Lushington example, finding it difficult to work, only too easy to play. He was, for a while, bewitched by a young actress and only drew back in alarm when the young lady's mother sought to press him into marriage. It was that experience, together with the arrival of his brother John to take up a fellowship at Lincoln College, that forced Charles to take stock of his position and to re-connect with the lifestyle he'd enjoyed before his arrival at Oxford.

The influence of the school and the network of friends and acquaintances (good and not-so-good) it offered Wesley should not be underestimated. Bishops, politicians, top lawyers, country squires, educators, aristocrats, - all retained fond memories of Wesley and he, in turn, was always glad to encounter any of them as he travelled hither and yon. But his life was about to veer off into a direction radically different from any of theirs. And it's to that we must now turn.

Charles Wesley was undoubtedly chastened by the worldly life he'd been living and the near miss occasioned by his flirtation with the actress. He resolved to give greater attention to his spiritual life. With a small group of friends at Christ Church he formed what came to be known as the "Holy Club." At first, they met together to pray and read the

Scriptures; soon they added hymn singing to these activities. Wesley, with his greater erudition, was concerned as far as possible to revive the traditions of the Apostolic Church. This meant, as far as they understood it, regular reception of the sacrament, so sadly neglected by their contemporaries, the nourishment of the interior spiritual life by regular devotional readings, and the acceptance of religious discipline through fasting, almsgiving and a renunciation of worldly pleasures. One of their number decided to visit a condemned prisoner in the Oxford prison. Soon Wesley and his associates were making regular visits to the Castle and the other Oxford prison, the Bocardo, the chief inmates of which were poor debtors. They took services and administered Communion, conversed with and comforted the prisoners, distributing pious tracts, giving alms, clothing and fuel. They also gave some teaching their children. They took immense pains to help the poor prisoners, interesting themselves in the legal aspects of some of their cases. Charles Wesley retained an active interest in the visitation of prisoners for much of the rest of his life. Members of the Holy Club frequently ran the gauntlet of the sarcasm and jibes of fellow students. And, no doubt Wesley and his friends displayed a degree of priggishness too. They were soon being called "Methodists," a term used either as a badge of honour or else opprobrium as fitted the case. Charles Wesley is often described (and with due reason) as "the first Methodist." His older brother John, however, soon took over the running of the Holy Club; it was a tool that suited his purpose and, under his astute and brilliant leadership, it spread Methodism throughout the university.

Mention has already been made of Charles Wesley's voyage to the newly established colony of Georgia as General Oglethorpe's secretary. His older brother John also went but with a priestly brief – to offer spiritual oversight to the British colonists and, he trusted, to convert the native people to Christianity. The mission of both brothers was thwarted. Charles' health did not allow him to continue in his role and John's zeal was too much for anyone's taste. Both brothers could look back at their American adventure with a sense of utter failure. Nor was that all. They'd met a group of Moravians whose faith had impressed them mightily. It seemed to be of a different order from theirs. Each of the brothers came to see himself as, in John's descriptive phrase, "an almost Christian." Soon, both these ordained Anglican clergymen were seeking the sense of assurance they'd seen in the Moravians, a missing factor in their own spiritual make-up - the disposition of the soul and the open-ness of the heart, that would allow the Holy Spirit to flood their inner beings with a new understanding of their mission and a release of pent-up energy to go about God's business.

And it came with a bang in 1738. Charles was overwhelmed by a religious experience that carried his faith onto a different level. That was on May 21st of that year. Three days later, his brother John entered into a similar experience. "I felt my heart strangely warmed," he wrote famously in his journal, "I felt I did trust in Christ, in Christ alone, for salvation; and an assurance was given me that he had taken away *my* sins, even *mine*, and saved me from the law of sin and death." Charles recorded his experience in verse. It's from this moment that we begin to see his poetic genius emerge. "And can it be," he wrote, "that I should gain an interest in the Saviour's blood?" Later in the same hymn he answers his own question resoundingly: "My chains fell off," he wrote, "my heart was free; I rose, went forth, and followed thee."

The Methodist movement was well and truly launched and John and Charles Wesley together now threw themselves into the work of, as they put it, spreading scriptural holiness throughout the land. First, they separated from the Moravians. Whilst they had admired the tenacity and assurance of these evangelical Christians, they could not agree with their doctrine of "stillness." The Moravians held no truck for any activity that purported to add to the faith granted them by God: – prayer, fasting, almsgiving, attendance at Holy Communion, all were rejected. For the Wesleys this was nonsense, the "means of grace" were simple acts which could help to focus a believer on the need to grow in faith, or dispose a non-believer towards the claims of faith. This parting of friends led to the Methodists acquiring a place of their own – a disused ruin, a one-time government munitions factory situated near Moorgate, right by the City of London. This building, the "Foundery" as it was called, became the headquarters from which John and Charles Wesley took their revival across the land.

The tireless energy with which they undertook their work still beggars belief. They criss-crossed the country from Newcastle in the North East to the furthest corners of Cornwall in the South West. In London, they addressed huge crowds in the open air at Kennington and Moorfields. They travelled through Yorkshire and the Midlands, into Wales and into Ireland. They preached three, four and five times a day, indoors and out of doors. Increasingly, they were banned from Anglican pulpits, widely reviled for their "enthusiasm." Their exhortations reached swathes of the population who rarely attended church services – tin miners in Cornwall, coal miners in and around Bristol, foundrymen and metal workers in Staffordshire and so many others. As John Wesley put it, they had "submitted to become more vile" by leaving the precincts of the Church and taking their activities into the streets and market places, into the fields and along the highway. The clergy accused them of abandoning the ordered liturgical life of the Church of England. Others accused them of being "Jesuits, seducers, bringers in of the Pretender." They were attacked and persecuted by mobs while the constabulary and magistracy were organised to deny them the freedom to preach at will. One example must suffice. In May 1743 Charles Wesley, in the company of a band of hymn-singing Methodists, walked from Wednesbury in Staffordshire to Walsall in the company of a band of hymn-singing Methodists. He found his opponents lying in wait for him:

> "The street was full of fierce Ephesian beasts (the principal man setting them on), who roared and shouted, and threw stones incessantly. Many struck without hurting me. I besought them in calm love to be reconciled to God in Christ. While I was departing, a stream of ruffians was suffered to bear me from the steps. I rose, and having given the blessing, was beat down again. So the third time, when we had returned thanks to the God of our salvation. I then, from the steps, bade them depart in peace, and walked quietly back through the thickest rioters. They reviled us, but had no commission to touch a hair of our heads."

Such incidents were numerous. Excrement and dead cats, as well as sticks and stones were thrown. This was a time of turbulence in the country at large. There was widespread fear of another attempt to restore the Stuarts. So these Methodist disturbances were suspected by some to be a deliberate agitation intended to subvert good order and make a Jacobite rebellion more likely to succeed.

Thousands of people responded to the preaching of Charles Wesley and he wore himself out in the work he felt called to do. His marriage in 1749 to Sarah Gwynne saw the couple set up home in Bristol. From this base Charles superintended the Methodist work in the south and west of the country (with occasional forays further afield). Their happy marriage was scarred by the death of a succession of children in infancy. It must have been with some relief that, in 1761, with two young children (their third was yet to be born) they left Bristol for London. The frenetic energy he'd invested in the cause during the 1740s was modulated in the decade following his marriage. Once in London, he stopped itineracy altogether and limited his activities, focusing now on the work being done in the capital city. He also developed a social life, especially in his desire to further the development of his astonishingly gifted children.

He was now able to develop his friendship with Priscilla Rich, the wife of John Rich who'd built the Covent Garden Theatre in the early 1730s. She was converted under his ministry in the mid-1740s and gave up her life as an actress as a consequence of her new-found faith. But she didn't give up her friendships or the network of contacts enjoyed by her husband. And Charles Wesley was able to benefit from these. Mrs Rich had three step daughters. One, Isabella, was married to John Frederick Lampe, a German who'd lived in London since 1725 and who played the bassoon in the Covent Garden Theatre orchestra. He was one of the leading composers of his day. He too was converted under Wesley's preaching and was soon setting his hymns to music. The two men became firm friends. The second step daughter was Cecilia who married Thomas Arne. She was frequently engaged by Handel to sing in his oratorios. Arne was a leading operatic composer of the time. This is the man to whom we owe *Rule Britannia*! And the third step-daughter Charlotte had married John Beard, one of the most eminent of English tenors at that time, for whom Handel composed the tenor parts in the *Messiah* and other oratorios. John Beard was the first London authority to confirm the verdict on the rare talent of Charles Wesley's first son (also called Charles). Mrs Rich had given the youngster (born in 1757) a copy of Handel's songs and Beard gave him Scarlatti's lessons and music by Purcell. Dr Johann Christoph Pepusch also hovered on the edges of this amazing musical circle. He was the organist at the Charterhouse and greatly sought after in royal circles. Mrs Rich's step daughters were all taught by Handel. When the great man quarrelled with the conductors at the Opera House, her husband put his own theatre at his disposal and this was how the paths of Handel and Wesley crossed. They met at the Richs' home in Chelsea and enjoyed their occasional meetings for fourteen years until Handel's death in 1759.

It's worth mentioning at this point an event that occurred in 1826. Samuel Wesley, the second son of Charles and Sarah (another Samuel!), had become one of England's leading musicians. He was an organist and in the forefront of efforts to popularise the music of J. S. Bach in the first decade of the 19th century. Whilst examining some autograph Handel manuscripts in the Cambridge University Library, he discovered a sheet that contained tunes composed by Handel for three of his father's hymns. The friendship between the two men had clearly been practical and productive as well as merely social.

The actor David Garrick was another member of this astonishing circle of friends. They held soirées at Mrs Rich's Chelsea home and also at the Wesleys' home in Marylebone. There were many raised eyebrows amongst the Methodists and John Fletcher, a national leader of the cause, was led to write in 1771:

"You have your enemies, as well as your brother; they complain of your love of music, company, fine people, great folks, and the want of your former zeal and frugality. I need not put you in mind to cut off sinful appearances."

Wesley weathered these storms easily enough. The hymns and poems that he was writing in huge numbers were his best protection against such criticism. Over 6,000 hymns flowed from his pen in a steady succession. When the first official Methodist Hymn Book was compiled in 1780, it contained 525 hymns, most of them culled from 37 short collections that had begun to leave the press in 1739, a few months after his conversion. This Hymn Book was to the earliest generations of Methodists what the Book of Common Prayer was to Anglicans, the breviary or the rosary to Catholics. They sang their faith. "Methodism was born in song" – so declared the opening words of the Preface. Further reading makes its claims clear:

"It …. contains all the important truths of our most holy religion, whether speculative or practical; yea, to illustrate them all, and to prove them both by Scripture and Reason. The hymns … are carefully ranged under proper heads, according to the experience of real Christians, so that this book is in effect *a little body of experimental and practical divinity.*" (my italics).

The beating heart of the book is the section dedicated to "Believers"; here are 283 hymns intended to nurture and strengthen the faith, hope and love of those who have entered the portals of belief. There are ten sub-sets and it may be of interest to list them. These are hymns for believers rejoicing, fighting, praying, watching, working, suffering, groaning for full redemption, brought to the birth, saved and interceding for the world.

What is remarkable about the hymns of Charles Wesley is the number of them that are cheerful, joyous, uplifting, even merry and happy. They combine the cultivation of inward piety with a concern for outward and practical action. These hymns were for use by the body of people brought to faith by the Methodist Revival.

In addition to these "Methodist" hymns, of course, Charles Wesley wrote any number of hymns to resource the classical and traditional festivals of the Church. "Hark! The Herald Angels Sing," "Christ the Lord is risen today," and "Hail the day that sees Him rise" are perfect vehicles for congregational singing at Christmas, Easter and the Ascension. He could turn into verse the complicated doctrine of the Trinity with a brilliance all his own:

> Three uncompounded Persons One,
> One undivided God proclaim:
> In essence, nature, substance one,
> Through all eternity the same.

Amazing! If he'd been alive in the patristic era they'd have made him Pope!

We can see the learning he'd acquired at Westminster pulsing through his verse. There are abundant references to the Church Fathers, especially Ignatius, Tertullian, Jerome, Eusebius, Lactantius and Augustine. Thomas Aquinas and Thomas à Kempis figure, so does the Book of Common Prayer. The Caroline divines and William Law touched and sharpened his thought. Secular literature constitutes another rich seam in his creative output. There are allusions to Horace, Virgil, Caesar, Aesop and Homer; and also to Milton, Dryden, Pope, Prior, Young, Shakespeare, Herbert, Quarles, Walter and Cowley. And everything he wrote is shot through with his intimate knowledge and love of Holy Scripture.

He wrote for every conceivable occasion. There are hymns inspired by his conversion, his marriage, the panic surrounding the 1750 earthquake, the rumours of an invasion from France, the defeat of Prince Charles Edward at Culloden, the Gordon riots, every festival of the Christian church, every doctrine of the Christian faith, striking scenes which came within his view, the deaths of friends, little children, and so much else. We can only allude to them here.

Charles Wesley died in July 1788 and was buried at St Marylebone's parish church.

And so we bring this narrative to a close. We began with Charles Wesley and his older brother Samuel at Westminster School. We end by returning to Westminster, but this time to the Abbey. Dean Arthur Stanley in 1876 ordered an inscription to be cut on a flagstone in the south cloister to remember the four "infant children of Samuel Wesley, brother of John Wesley." Then, touchingly, their names and the dates of their death are given: Nutty 1725, Susanna 1726, Ursula 1727 and Samuel 1731. In fact, Samuel and Ursula Wesley were survived by just one child from the seven they bore. A tragic but not untypical story of that time.

The same Dean Stanley dedicated a carving of John and Charles Wesley by J. Adams-Acton fixed to the wall of the south choir aisle. His wife had died just a short time before and, as he unveiled the tablet, he quoted a verse from one of Charles Wesley's hymns, explaining how deeply he felt its meaning in his present circumstances:

> Come, O Thou traveller unknown,
> Whom still I hold, but cannot see!
> My company before is gone
> And I am left alone with Thee;
> With Thee all night I mean to stay,
> And wrestle till the break of day.

In the words of an early report of this event: "The pathos of the Dean's touching reference to his great bereavement is still fresh in the hearts of those who were in the Chapter House on that memorable morning, when the Old Westminster boy found a fitting memorial in the Abbey he knew and loved so well."

And so this story ends where it began and perhaps now many of us may understand it for the first time.

Warren Hastings

Zareer Masani

W arren Hastings was the first of a long line of British Governors-General in India, ending with Lord Mountbatten and Indian independence in 1947. He was undoubtedly the most curious and learned of them all about Indian culture and, judging by contemporary accounts, the most popular among his Indian subjects. So how was it that he alone of all British officials in India was put on trial for alleged crimes against humanity, in a nine-year-long impeachment in the British Parliament, led by the great Whig orator Edmund Burke? The answer lies in a clash between two very different visions of empire: one respectful of indigenous customs and traditions and crudely labelled "Orientalist", the other inspired by a Whig brand of westernising liberal intervention.

Hastings himself was very much a product of the European Enlightenment, although, unlike his aristocratic successors as Governor-General, he had to work his way up to high office from modest beginnings. Born in 1732 in a family of impoverished minor gentry in Gloucestershire, he went to the local village school with farmers' children. Orphaned at an early age, he was rescued by a benevolent uncle who got him into Westminster in London, then ranked with Eton as the best school in Britain. Here he excelled at the classical education which, according to his eminent biographer, Sir Penderel Moon, gave him "a mind enlarged... by the wisdom, the warnings and the examples of classical antiquity" and ensured that he would become a scholar and a statesman, not a mere merchant or fortune-hunter".

Among his friends and near contemporaries at Westminster were outstanding intellects like the poet William Cowper and the historian Edward Gibbon, two future Prime Ministers, Lords Portland and Shelburne, and his own best friend, Sir Elijah Impey, who would work closely with him in India as the first Chief Justice of a new Supreme Court. Hastings was a particular favourite of the Head Master, Dr. Nicoll, who intended him to go on to Christ Church, Oxford, and distinguish himself "as a scholar or a bishop or as both". But his academic career was cut short at the age of fifteen when his uncle died and his new guardian, a distant relative, decided to withdraw him from school, over the protests of the Head Master, and got him apprenticed to the East India Company.

Hastings first arrived in India in 1750, aged 17, as a writer or clerk in the Company's service at Calcutta. He began on a salary of £5 per annum, with the duties of book-keeping and superintending the warehousing of export goods. He was later sent up-country to the Company's factory at Kasim bazaar, where life was lonely and he "depended for society mainly on the natives of the country". Living "among the country people in a very inferior station", as he put it, gave him the opportunity to study their habits and customs on a footing of equality never open to most British administrators. His cultural curiosity was matched by a talent for languages. He became fluent in Bengali, the regional vernacular, and had a good working knowledge of Urdu and Persian, the languages of the Mughal elite. This early grounding in Indian culture later flowered as Governor-General in his founding of the Asiatic Society of Calcutta, which became the centre for Orientalist scholarship, and his patronage for the revival of Sanskrit and the translation from it of Hindu religious classics like the *Bhagvad Gita*. Hastings's introduction to the first ever English translation of the *Gita* said passages of it were "elevated to a track of sublimity into which our habits of judgement will find it difficult to pursue."

It was Hastings's excellent Indian connections that helped him to emerge unscathed from the violent confrontations of the 1750s between the Company and the Nawab of Bengal, the autonomous viceroy of the now much weakened Mughal emperor at Delhi. After Robert Clive had defeated and deposed a hostile Nawab, he appointed Hastings to the key liaison post of Resident at the court of the new and more docile, British-appointed Nawab. Hastings was only 25, but already recognised as a rising star among the Company's officials in the province of Bengal. He used his position as Resident to support the new Nawab's fragile authority and to restrain the Company's attempts to usurp his rights as "a sovereign prince". He complained that the Nawab was being exposed "to daily affronts such as a spirit superior to that of a worm when trodden on could not have brooked."

When Hastings was promoted to the Governor of Bengal's Council in 1761, he continued to support the Nawab's attempts to curb the illegal, private trading privileges that corrupt Company employees were claiming to evade local taxes and customs duties. He found himself in a minority in Council, with the majority determined that all Company employees and agents must be exempt from the Nawab's authority. "Such a system of government," Hastings protested, "cannot fail to create in the minds of the wretched inhabitants an abhorrence of the English name and authority, and how would it be possible for the Nawab, whilst he hears the cries of his people which he cannot redress, not to wish to free himself from an alliance which subjects him to such indignities?"

Matters came to a head when a new Nawab, the energetic, young Mir Kasim, decided it was time for the worm to turn. He very sensibly abolished all internal customs duties in Bengal and established free trade, thereby denying British traders their unfair advantages. The Company's

Bengal Council, despite Hastings's opposition, retaliated by declaring war on the Nawab. Hastings was accused of being Mir Kasim's "hired solicitor" and hit in the face by an angry fellow Council member. There followed the decisive Battle of Buxar in October 1764, at which the Company's forces defeated the combined armies of a formidable coalition of Indian powers, including the Nawabs of Bengal and Oudh and the Mughal Emperor. This marked the end of any real autonomy, let alone sovereignty, for future Nawabs and the recognition by the defeated Mughal Emperor of the East India Company as the legitimate civil administration of Bengal.

Two months later, "disheartened and disillusioned" by the rejection of his own more conciliatory policies, Hastings resigned his post and returned to England, "being unwilling...to give authority to past measures of which I disapprove". There his Indian career might have ended unnoticed, had he not been compelled by financial near-bankruptcy to seek re-employment by the Company four years later. His earlier pacifism had made him unpopular with Clive, whose influence on the Company's Directors was still considerable. But Clive eventually relented, and Hastings returned to India in 1769, to the relatively minor post of member of the Governor's Council in Madras. It would be fifteen years before he returned to Britain. Along with the fourteen years already spent in Bengal during his first term of Company service, this would make him the longest-serving and most experienced of all colonial governors ever sent out to India.

Within two years of his arrival in Madras, Hastings found himself appointed to the post of Governor of Bengal. The promotion was unsolicited and unexpected, brought about by a change of leadership back home at India House and by the Directors' need for someone they could trust. Two years later, new legislation in Parliament to regulate the Company's chaotic affairs elevated his post to that of Governor-General, with authority over the two subordinate Presidencies of Madras and Bombay.

In many respects, it was a poisoned chalice. "Government in Bengal had completely broken down. It was for Hastings to re-establish it...," wrote his biographer, Penderel Moon, himself an experienced veteran of the "heaven-born" Indian Civil Service. "The company was still a trading organisation: it was for him to adapt it to the functions of a sovereign power." The so-called "Dual System" he inherited, in which policing and criminal law were left to an increasingly impotent Nawab, had been undermined by the arrogant and lawless freebooting of the Company's own servants. When Hastings took over as Governor, one of the worst famines in the history of Bengal had decimated its population, also hitting the Company's revenues and leaving it seriously in debt.

Writing to his still very influential predecessor, Lord Clive, Hastings bravely made it clear that he intended to tackle his dubious legacy "in a different line from that which a different situation of affairs required Your Lordship to pursue." In what reads like a political manifesto, Hastings promised "to cultivate the arts of Peace, to establish a regular Administration of Justice, to reduce the enormous expenses of the Company to fixed bounds, and to prune them as much as possible from remote wars and foreign connections." These policies were necessitated, he wrote, by "the general licentiousness which seems to have prevailed since we took the internal administration...out of the hands of the former [Nawab's] Government and placed them without any fixed system in those of our agents."

Hastings was enough of a pragmatist to recognise that the Nawab's authority, which he had once championed, was by now too far eroded to be restored. The Company, he believed, must therefore assume full control and responsibility for both the criminal and civil administration of Bengal. But it must do so by reviving, as far as possible, the decayed Mughal administration and by avoiding measures "which the original constitution of the Mogul Empire hath not before established and adopted and thereby rendered familiar to the people."

Hastings was particularly keen to confine European institutions and personnel as far as possible to the bounds of Calcutta, the Company's Bengal capital, and to leave the actual collection of revenues and administration of justice to Indian intermediaries. Based on recent experience, he believed that European administrators were more prone to gross abuses of power. "There is a fierceness," he warned, "in the European manners, especially among the lower sort, which is incompatible with the gentle temper of the Bengalee, and gives the former such an ascendant as is scarce supportable even without the additional weight of authority." Faced with Company officials who continued their illegal trading monopolies and corrupt extortions from local landlords, Hastings thought "native oppression was less truculent, more easily punished, more familiar to the people and in every way preferable to the corrupt tyranny of overbearing Englishmen".

In view of his proclaimed respect for Indian sensibilities, it is ironical that the charges on which Hastings was impeached fifteen years later focussed on his alleged persecution and spoliation of his Indian subjects and allies. Edmund Burke's historic, four-day-long opening speech – an unrivalled model of parliamentary invective – accused Hastings of having "gorged his ravenous maw …feeding on the indigent, the dying and ruined", like "the ravenous vulture devouring the carcasses of the dead." "I impeach him in the name of the English nation, whose ancient honour he has sullied," Burke thundered. "I impeach him in the name of the people of India, whose rights he has trodden under foot, and whose country he has turned into a desert."

Burke's apocalyptic view of Hastings's alleged reign of terror later found a more restrained echo in a famous biographical essay by Thomas Macaulay, the great Whig historian and parliamentarian of Victorian times. Macaulay's own experience as the imperial reformer who introduced English education and justice to India predisposed him against what he saw as Hastings's preference for "Oriental despotism". Macaulay concluded that "in the two great elements of all social virtue, in respect for the rights of others, and in sympathy for the sufferings of others, he [Hastings] was deficient."

Hastings's impeachment was the first human rights trial of modern times. Who were the alleged victims of his crimes, and how would we judge him today? First on the list were the Rohillas, Muslim settlers of Afghan descent, who ruled over an autonomous and very prosperous area known as Rohilkhand, on the Himalayan borders of the kingdom of Oudh (Awadh), an independent ally of the Company. Strapped for cash, struggling with demands to remit larger revenues back to the Directors in London, Hastings had rented out a regiment of Company troops to the Nawab of Oudh in return for a handsome subsidy. The charge of war crimes arose when he allowed the Nawab to use these mercenaries to invade and annex the Rohilla lands.

Macaulay echoed Burke's accusations of Hastings looking callously on while Rohilla "villages were burnt, their children butchered, and their women violated". "This picture," Penderel Moon later objected, "is almost entirely imaginary". The Rohilla War was no more violent than any other Indian conflict of its time, and Hastings was quick to warn the Nawab of

Oudh against any excesses. He instructed his Resident at the Nawab's court:

> "Tell him that the English manners are abhorrent of every species of inhumanity and oppression, and enjoin the gentlest treatment of a vanquished enemy. Require and entreat his observance of this principle towards the family of Hafiz [the Rohilla leader who had died in battle]. Tell him…that no part of his conduct will operate so powerfully in winning the affections of the English, as instances of benevolence and feeling for others. If these arguments don't prevail, you may inform him directly that you have my orders to insist upon a proper treatment of the family of Hafiz Rahmat, since in our alliance with him our national character is involved in every act which subjects his own to reproach."

The charge of atrocities and war crimes against the Rohillas, cast as noble victims by Burke, was based on malicious and largely fictitious reports fed back to the British press by Hastings's formidable political nemesis, the Whig politician and columnist, Sir Philip Francis. He was one of a new batch of Council members sent out to Calcutta in 1773, took an instant dislike to Hastings and spent the next decade opposing his every move in Council and sending the most hostile despatches about him back home.

Francis was one of three political nominees appointed to the Bengal Council by the British Crown, not the Company, under the provisions of the new Regulating Act. According to Moon, they "knew nothing of Bengal, had no previous connection with the Company and viewed all its servants with prejudice and suspicion. The chances that they would cooperate loyally with Hastings were obviously small." The new Councillors, who had a majority in Hastings's Council, saw it as their mission "to cleanse the Augean stable" of the corruption and extortion for which the Company's administration was so notorious, and they saw Hastings as the chief representative of Company rule, who must be exposed and driven from office.

The enmity between Hastings and Francis eventually escalated to the point where they fought a duel with pistols, from which Francis emerged defeated and wounded but unrepentant. A more fatal casualty of their battle was a Hindu banker called Raja Nandakumar, a powerful local ally of the Francis faction, whose execution for fraud in 1775 was later regarded by Hastings's accusers as a judicial murder for which he was directly culpable.

Nandakumar, who had held important offices in the Nawab's administration, supplied the Francis faction with allegations that Hastings had accepted bribes from him and the Nawab's powerful stepmother. Although the charge could not be substantiated, Nandakumar now became a centre for opposition to Hastings and rumours against him. "The word went round," writes Moon, "that the new rulers of the provinces believed Hastings to be corrupt and would welcome evidence of his corruption." Such evidence, mostly fabricated, was soon forthcoming. Hastings himself wrote at the time:

> "The trumpet has been sounded, and the whole host of informers will soon crowd to Calcutta with their complaints and ready depositions. Nandakumar holds his darbar in complete state, sends for zamindars [landlords] and their wakils [lawyers], coaxing and threatening them for complaints, which no doubt he will get in abundance, besides what he forges himself."

It was a measure of public support for Hastings among both the Indian notables of Calcutta and the Company's officials that he was able very skilfully to turn the tables on Nandakumar and the Francis faction in Council. Based on evidence from Indian informants, Nandakumar was charged with forgery and arraigned before the newly formed Supreme Court, presided over by Hastings's old Westminster friend and Calcutta ally, Sir Elijah Impey. Though a minor offence under traditional Indian laws, forgery then carried the death penalty under British law. With the encouragement of Hastings and his supporters, the case against Nandakumar was vigorously prosecuted. He was found guilty by a European jury, sentenced to death and hanged soon after.

> "The voices of a thousand informants were silenced in an instant," Macaulay said of this execution. "From that time, whatever difficulties Hastings might have to encounter, he was never molested by accusations from natives of India." Penderel Moon dismisses the accusation by Hastings's impeachers that this was the result of a deliberate conspiracy between the Governor-

General and the Chief Justice. But he concedes that "at the time it was certainly assumed that Nandakumar was hanged because he ventured to attack the Governor-General; and it is hard to dispute that this contemporary assumption was correct."

Macaulay held Hastings directly responsible, but conceded in mitigation that he should be judged by the standards of 18th century India rather than Victorian Britain:

"He was struggling for fortune, honour, liberty, all that makes life valuable. He was beset by rancorous and unprincipled enemies. From his colleagues he could expect no justice. He cannot be blamed for wishing to crush his accusers.... He knew the native character well. He knew in what abundance accusations are certain to flow in against the most innocent inhabitant of India who is under the frown of power."

And yet, one has to acknowledge that Hastings's collusion with the judicial murder of this troublesome Brahmin marked an opportunistic betrayal of his own much proclaimed view that Indians must, as far as possible, be governed according to Indian, not European, laws. Whether or not Hastings planned it, the execution of Nandakumar proved a decisive turning-point in his struggle against his opponents. "Hastings," writes Moon, "went up in popular estimation. He had taken legitimate revenge on a bad man who had gravely injured him. He had done no wrong, and he had been successful. He gained more in respect than he lost in love."

Hastings's finest hour came soon after, during the War of American Independence, when his leadership managed to defeat an anti-British coalition between the French and two dominant regional powers, the Hindu Marathas in Western India and the Muslim warlord Haidar Ali in the South. Though committed like the Directors back home to avoiding military adventures, Hastings was insistent that any show of weakness would be fatal to the Company's standing, "for in no part of the world is the principle of supporting a rising interest and depressing a fallen one more prevalent than in India." Six years of these local wars ended in 1784 with the British as the dominant power in the subcontinent. The alternative, Hastings maintained and historians agree, would have been the loss of the Company's Bombay and Madras Presidencies and possibly even its return to "the humble and undreaded character of trading adventurers."

While these wars may have been essential to the Company's survival, they imposed major new strains on the Governor-General's already overstretched purse-strings, and these financial strains accounted for two major crimes of extortion, of which Hastings later stood accused. The first was his treatment of an independent-minded Hindu nobleman, Raja Chait Singh of Benares.

As feudal lord of Hinduism's most sacred city, the Raja was both immensely wealthy and widely respected. Hastings decided that, as the Company's vassal, Chait Singh was fair game for the extraction of funds badly needed for the war effort. It began with a special levy from him of the relatively modest sum of approximately four million pounds a year in today's money. But he paid reluctantly "after much procrastination and many unreal pleas of poverty". More seriously, he was believed to be in correspondence with the Company's military opponents, the Marathas. And to cap it all, he was cosying up to the hostile Francis faction on Hastings's own Council.

In the autumn of 1780, after the Raja failed to respond to a Company demand to supply a cavalry battalion for defence against the Marathas, a furious Governor-General resolved to teach him a lesson and made the journey up the Ganges to deal with him in person. Chait Singh, we are told, "met him in a very contrite mood…, laid his turban at his feet in token of his complete submission, begged forgiveness and assured him that all his property was at his disposal." But Hastings was not so easily mollified and insisted on a written apology for the Raja's dilatory responses to the Company's demands for money and horsemen. The Raja responded with a polite but firm refusal to accept blame, in a letter which Hastings described as "not only unsatisfactory in substance, but offensive in style".

What followed reflected, even according to Hastings's kindest critics, a serious error of judgement. He sent his sepoys to arrest Chait Singh, whereupon the Raja's far more numerous retainers mounted an armed rescue of him, massacring the inadequate Company troops on guard. Chait Singh fled to join the Marathas, taking much of his treasure with him. It was Hastings who now found himself under virtual siege from the rebels, until reinforcements arrived to rescue him.

The rebellion was suppressed, and the Company took over direct administration of Benares, but Hastings had failed to extract the financial or military aid which had been the purpose of the whole exercise. Penderel Moon concludes that the Governor-General's treatment of the errant Raja "judged even by despotic standards was both severe and unwise; and, judged by his own high standards of courtesy and consideration towards Indian notables, it was deplorable.... The truth is that the fatal temptations of despotic power...were the real cause and must be the partial excuse for his conduct. Those who have actually experienced the temptations of power in the hot climate of India will judge him less harshly than historians."

The same combination of financial exigency and despotic hubris drove Hastings in another episode soon after, which was to win him the most opprobrium back home, because it involved the intimidation of two venerable old princesses allied to the Company, the Begums of Oudh, mother and grandmother of its Nawab. The fertile and wealthy kingdom of Oudh occupied most of what is today's Indian heartland, its most populous state of Uttar Pradesh or UP. Its ruling dynasty, of Persian Shia descent, had been established by the former prime ministers or Wazirs of the Mughal Emperor and were recognised by the Company as a sovereign, independent, allied state bordering Bengal to the north and west.

Oudh was both a valuable buffer against the Marathas and a rich source of financial subsidies paid for the hire of Company troops. But under an extravagant, young Nawab, Asaf-ud-Daula, Oudh had been running up huge debts and descending into administrative and economic chaos. Having chastened the Raja of Benares, Hastings now decided that it was time to rescue the Nawab from his predatory, mainly British creditors, and restore Oudh to the status of a solvent and stable neighbour. It was a formidable challenge because the Nawab, though a great patron of the arts, was renowned for the hedonistic debauchery of his court. His homosexuality and opium addiction made him thoroughly disreputable in contemporary British eyes, and there were dark rumours that he kept a male harem.

Hastings was especially keen to rescue the Nawab from the Company's own military officers, who had been seconded to his forces and were now shamelessly sponging on his generosity and lending him money at exorbitant rates of interest to fund it. "Every Englishman in Oudh," Hastings wrote, "was possessed of an independent and sovereign authority. They learned...to claim the revenue of lacs[1] as their right, though they could gamble away more than two lacs (I allude to a known fact) at a sitting." Nevertheless, Asaf's biggest debts were to the Company, who had been supplying him with mercenary troops, and Hastings badly needed these funds to finance the wars in the south. He decided that the quickest way of getting them was by persuading the Nawab to recover some of his father's huge wealth, which had been appropriated by the late Nawab's widow and mother.

The Begums and their treasure were housed in the palace-fortress of Faizabad, and their household was managed by two powerful eunuchs. Egged on by Hastings, the Nawab marched on Faizabad, with the British resident and Company troops to support him, and laid siege to his wealthy mother and grandmother. The Begums were made of sterner stuff than young Asaf, and they obstinately refused to part with their inheritance. The Nawab responded by arresting their two favoured eunuchs, putting them in irons and starving them of food. These tactics appear to have worked, because the eunuchs coughed up "from the most secret recesses of their houses" the huge sum of 100 lakhs of rupees (about £80 million now).

At Hastings's impeachment, his treatment of the Oudh dowagers provoked some of the most emotive and colourful outbursts from speakers like Edmund Burke, always a champion of princesses in distress. Most dramatic of all were the carefully rehearsed attacks of Richard Brinsley Sheridan, the Whig MP who was also the most popular playwright of his day. His speeches were full of what he called "love-passion" for the wronged Begums. London's fashionable society queued from dawn to buy tickets for his court performances, and tickets changed hands for as much as £50 each (£4,000 today). Sheridan's rhetoric painted the spoliation of the Begums as a Renaissance tragedy, with the Nawab incited to gross filial impiety by the villainous British Governor-General. Even seasoned MPs could not recollect weeping "so heartily and copiously on any public occasion."

Macaulay later accused Hastings of instigating physical torture of the imprisoned eunuchs and also starving the Begums into submission. Penderel Moon was more judicious, pointing out that the Begums themselves were later reconciled with Hastings, sent messages of support

---

[1] A lac or lakh is the Indian expression for 100,000 rupees, which would have been £10,000 then or roughly £800,000 in today's money.

to him at his trial and bore him no ill will, "rightly believing him to be the well-wisher of the family and the helper and protector of their weak and foolish Asaf-ud-Daula." The Begums retained at least half their great treasure, even though their legal right to it under the late Nawab's Will was never proved.

Hastings certainly felt a special responsibility to put the affairs of Oudh in order. In 1784, on the eve of his return to Britain, he travelled to the kingdom's capital Lucknow and spent five months there retrenching the Nawab's expenditure, recovering his debts to the Company, settling the land revenue due from his tax-collectors and reforming his army. "The Nabob [Nawab] solemnly promised", a self-satisfied Hastings concluded, "that he would not break a single thread of my arrangements, and these, if undisturbed, will discharge all his debts to the Company in the course of a year, and leave him a free and independent man. His uncle, his mother and his grandmother, the most respected of his family, are all in my interest, and look upon me as the guardian of their house."

Duty apart, Hastings's special fondness for the cultural riches of the court of Lucknow and his ambivalence about the Nawab are illustrated by a remarkable painting he commissioned from the famous society portraitist Johann Zoffany, who spent several years in Oudh in the 1780s. Entitled "Colonel Mordaunt's Cock Match", this extraordinary canvas, now at Tate Britain, is full of visual puns and ambiguities. It shows Asaf-ud-Daula, possibly with an erection, in a supplicant pose in relation to the arrogant but androgynous figure of his handsome English captain of guard. They are surrounded by Indian and European notables, clearly meeting on an equal footing. Even the Indian servants and water-sellers are portrayed as individuals, with no evidence of any ethnic stereotyping. The painting was done over a period of three years, in the course of which several historical figures were added in, but Hastings himself is conspicuous by his absence.

Since the painting hung in his study back in England till the end of his life, one must assume that it encapsulated a way of life which he had enjoyed and wanted to remember, without wishing to be tarred by association with its more dissolute aspects. "It is lamentable to observe," wrote Penderel Moon, "how deeply he had now fallen under the influence of incessant adulation. When Nawabs, Begums, Rajahs and Ministers told him that he was their sole resource, that they depended entirely on his wisdom and understanding – he who knew everything! – he veritably believed them." When the Mughal Crown Prince arrived at Lucknow to seek his military aid, Hastings was so flattered that he even toyed with the idea of restoring the Mughal Empire and through it dominating the whole subcontinent, a project vetoed by his Council. Hastings, never shy of singing his own praises, wrote somewhat immodestly to the Company's Directors:

> "I do not know a man who may be more safely entrusted with extraordinary powers than myself, or who would be more likely to make moderate use of them, as I am neither vehement in the pursuit of gain, nor apt to convert an authority which I possess to an instrument of partial favour or enmity to others."

Macaulay, though critical of Hastings's capacity for self-congratulation, conceded that "he made himself beloved by both the subject many and by the dominant few" and "enjoyed among the natives a popularity…such as no other governor has been able to attain." During his own years in Calcutta half a century later, Macaulay could still hear "nurses sing children to sleep with a jingling ballad about the fleet horses and richly caparisoned elephants of Sahib Warren Hostein".

As against the contemporaneous disasters being suffered by the British Empire across the Atlantic, Hastings left British administration in India on a sounder footing than ever before. The corrupt excesses of the Company's servants had been significantly curbed, French and other local military threats had been resoundingly beaten off, and the "Company Sahib" was now the dominant power in the subcontinent, its favour courted by the Mughal Emperor himself. But Hastings, to Macaulay's lasting disapproval, "did little…towards introducing into India the learning of the West". Instead, he famously declared: "I love India a little more than my own country".

When Hastings retired from his post in 1785 and took ship back to England, it was at his own instance and not at the behest of his opponents and critics. He was looking forward to investing his Indian savings in a restored country-house at his old family seat of Daylesford. He also expected his Indian successes to be rewarded with the same favour that Clive continued to receive at Court and in the counsels of both the Company and the government. His London agent, Major Scott, had led him to expect no less than a peerage and probably also a Cabinet post as head of the government's newly constituted Board of Control for Indian affairs. But as Macaulay later pointed out, Scott was "the greatest bore of his time", and his predictions proved wildly inaccurate, due partly to his own complacency.

At first, all seemed to go well. Hastings was warmly received by George III, although the Whig wits ridiculed him for showering the royal family with "fine diamonds" and "a certain richly carved ivory bed which the Queen had done him the honour to accept from him." London gossip, always envious of the fabled wealth of India-returned Nabobs, was particularly cruel about the extravagance and ostentation of Hastings's beautiful, German wife, Marian, who allegedly appeared at one function wearing jewels worth £25,000 (a staggering £2 million in today's money), woven into her hat and clothes. She became the subject of a tabloid lampoon:

" Gods! how her diamonds flock
On each unpowdered lock!
On every membrane see a topaz clings!
Behold her joints are fewer than her rings!
Illustrious dame! on either ear,
The Munny Begum's[2] spoils appear!"

Hastings's old enemy, Philip Francis, now an active Whig backbencher in Parliament, had been feeding Edmund Burke with ammunition against Hastings. Burke had threatened in the House to "make a motion respecting the conduct of a gentleman just returned from India", but then let the matter slide. In a display of hubris that would cost him dear, Hastings dared Burke to make good his threat. The trial that ensued cost Hastings the modern equivalent of eight million pounds, almost his entire fortune, and put paid to any prospect of a future political career. Although he was eventually acquitted of all charges, the impeachment left permanent scars on his reputation.

For nine years, Hastings's trial in Westminster Hall was the most popular show in town, and the packed audiences included Queen Charlotte, her daughters, the Prince of Wales and sundry dukes and society hostesses. Hastings, always a poor public speaker, had to reckon

---

[2] Stepmother of the Nawab of Bengal, from whom Hastings was alleged by Nandakumar to have accepted bribes.

with the oratory, not merely of Burke, but of other prominent Whigs like Charles James Fox, Charles (later Earl) Grey and the playwright Sheridan. Their very theatrical performances, Macaulay tells us, excited the ladies present to "a state of uncontrollable emotion" and "handkerchiefs were pulled out; smelling bottles were handed out; hysterical sobs and screams were heard: and Mrs. Sheridan was carried out in a fit."

Hastings survived all this and lived on in semi-retirement till the grand old age of 85. In 1813, both Houses of Parliament rose spontaneously to give him a standing ovation when he came to give evidence on new legislation about India. Although he received no honours, historians have been generous in their verdict on his remarkable achievements. Even Macaulay, while accepting the Whig view of his alleged abuses of power, credited him with "great public services" and "a title to be considered as one of the most remarkable men in our history".

In 1812, in a letter which would be his last political testament, Hastings warned his successor Marquess Hastings (no relation) that Indians had been misrepresented "as sunk in the grossest brutality and defiled with every abomination", thereby justifying British attempts "to reform them, nay to 'coerce' them into goodness". Instead, he exhorted his namesake, "it will be better to leave them as they are..." In stark contrast to Macaulay's later diatribes against the superstition, deviousness and corruption of Bengali Hindus, Hastings proclaimed them to be "as exempt from the worst propensities of human nature as any people upon the face of the earth, ourselves not excepted.... They are gentle, benevolent, more susceptible of gratitude for kindness shewn them than prompt to vengeance for wrongs sustained, abhorrent of bloodshed, faithful in service and submission to legal authority." Hastings concluded with a plea for racial equality that was remarkable for its time:

> "Among the natives of India, there are men of as strong intellect, as sound integrity and honourable feelings, as any of this Kingdom. I regret that they are not sufficiently noticed, sufficiently employed nor respected...Be it your Lordship's care...to lessen this distance: be their especial Patron, friend and protector, and by your example make it the fashion among our countrymen to treat them with courtesy and as participators in the same equal rights of society..."

Such views make Hastings an unlikely candidate for the role of colonial oppressor, in which he was cast by Whig champions of human rights. In the long term, his "Orientalist" approach to Indian administration lost out to a far more Anglicist sense of imperial mission, summed up by Burke's dictum that "it was the duty of a British Governor to enforce British laws, to correct the opinions and practices of the people, not to conform his opinion to their practice". But Penderel Moon, with his own extensive Indian experience, argued that Hastings did far more than Burke to establish standards of human rights which future British rulers would respect. "It was Hastings' example rather than Burke's eloquence," Moon concluded, "that transformed, ennobled and, to some extent, redeemed the naked greed and violence of the Company's early rule…"

Jeremy Bentham

A.C. Grayling[1]

For many years Jeremy Bentham lived in the house once occupied by John Milton in Queen's Square Place, Westminster, not far from the famous school at which he was educated (and about which he was

[1] My thanks to my colleagues Dr David Mitchell and Dr Naomi Goulder for helpful comments on this essay.

scornful: he described it as "a wretched place for instruction"). He owned not only Milton's house but the house next door, the garden of which he incorporated into his own so that he had a larger space for his daily walks. In this next-door house lived his colleague and helper James Mill and the infant John Stuart Mill, then busy learning Latin and Greek before the age of five. Later the house was occupied by William Hazlitt, who from its windows often watched Bentham perambulating his extended garden, and who famously anatomized him in the *The Spirit of the Age*.

In that celebrated collection of essays Hazlitt wrote about those of his contemporaries who he thought would still be known a century and more later. His judgment, as so often, was impeccable; Bentham appears alongside Coleridge, Wordsworth, Byron, Scott, Godwin, Malthus, Southey, Lamb and more. How many of us could make as assured a judgment as this about our own contemporaries' future fame? And just as his judgment was impeccable in this respect, so was Hazlitt's assessment of each of his subjects. When included by Hazlitt among those who would survive, Bentham had no reputation in England but was famous outside it: "His name," wrote Hazlitt, "is little known in England, better in Europe, best of all in the plains of Chili and the mines of Mexico. He has offered constitutions for the New World, and legislated for future times. The people of Westminster, where he lives, hardly dream of such a person; but the Siberian savage has received cold comfort from his lunar aspect."

The chief reason why Bentham was then a prophet in many lands other than his own was that the part of his voluminous writings which were published in his lifetime appealed only to technical tastes in law, legislation, social and political reform, ethics and economics, and therefore had a small readership at home; yet one of the most immediately influential of his works was first published in translation – in French, then in Russian, Spanish, German and other languages, only appearing in English a decade after his death.

Another reason for his neglect in England was that he was a radical in politics, and a republican, which put him in opposition to the Establishment of the day, which meant that – like Hazlitt and others who were independent-minded – he received neither public recognition nor honour. Who now remembers that he coined the words "utilitarian," "codify" and "international," was the first to propose an international court of arbitration in the interests of peace, correlatively laying down principles of international law; and that several dozen prisons around the world, and a number of hospitals and other institutions besides (including the original buildings of University College Hospital in London) are constructed on the "panopticon" principle he and his brother Samuel devised? Nevertheless his influence on the course of practical affairs has been great, not just in his own country but in many parts of the world, even if the influence has often been diffuse, sometimes indirect, and to begin with rarely acknowledged, though now his significance is far more appreciated than hitherto.

Bentham was born on 15 February 1748, and lived to the ripe age of 84, dying in London on 6 June 1832. His father was a lawyer, his younger brother Samuel was a naval engineer and diplomat. Bentham attended Westminster School, leaving it at the age of twelve for Queen's College Oxford, where he took his B.A. three years later. He was no more impressed by Oxford than Westminster, disliking its pomp and idleness, and in particular the obligation it imposed on him to attend chapel, swear oaths and subscribe the articles of the Church of England.

He then read for the Bar. As part of doing this he observed proceedings in the Court of King's Bench at Westminster, and returned for a while to Oxford to hear Blackstone on the common law in lectures later published as the famous *Commentaries on the Laws of England*. Both these experiences left a mark. In the Court of King's Bench he sat through the trial of John Wilkes the radical journalist, and came to admire the presiding judge, Lord Mansfield. By contrast he found the views of Blackstone flawed and tendentious, and attacked them in his later writings.

Bentham's career at the Bar, to which he was called in 1769, was brief: indeed he only had one brief, and then decided to devote himself to the reform of law and society. This was because he had been inspired by his discovery of the principle of utility in the thought of Hume, Helvetius and Beccaria, among others. In Cesare Bonesana-Beccaria's treatise on crime and punishment he found the phrase *la massima felicita divisa nel maggior numero* – the greatest happiness of the greatest number. In Hume he found the idea that utility is the criterion of virtue. In Helvetius he found the idea that utility can guide conduct by effecting a connection between it and pleasure and pain, the respective pursuit and avoidance of which Bentham took to be the only motivators of action, as Epicurus long before had argued. He believed that a range of social problems could be remedied by the application of the fundamental principle thus implied, namely, that "the greatest happiness of the greatest number" is the infallible and invariable guide to what is right and wrong. Accordingly he dedicated himself to the task of putting this principle into practical effect.

Bentham argued that what he came to call "utilitarianism" imposes an obligation on legislators as well as individuals to "minister to general happiness," an obligation which, he said, is "paramount to and inclusive of every other." He used the term "utility" to denote "[whatever] tends to produce benefit, advantage, good or happiness," these all being synonymous in Bentham's usage. He defined the principle of utility itself as "that principle which approves or disapproves of every action whatsoever, according to the tendency which it appears to have to augment or diminish the happiness of the party whose interest is in question." Although Bentham refined and developed these ideas during the course of his long life and many writings, this was the core of what he sought to put to work across the whole range of his interests.

Note that utilitarianism, whether of Bentham's or later more elaborate kinds, is a "consequentialist" theory of morality, that is, one which understands moral value in terms only of the consequences of actions, leaving aside any questions about the intentions of agents or their characters. Other theories of morality focus on the latter, but the distinctive feature of utilitarian theories is that they measure right and wrong, good and bad, wholly as a matter of expected outcomes. Bentham and John Stuart Mill, who are jointly known as the "Classical Utilitarians" though the latter made a number of advances over Bentham's version of the view, agreed in regarding happiness as the greatest good, and each person's happiness as being equal in value to anyone else's. This means that working to produce the greatest happiness for the greatest number – that is, the greatest good – is done impartially; anyone's reason for promoting the good is the same as anyone else's reason for doing so.

It is immediately obvious that there is a tension at the heart of this view. Bentham regarded pleasure and pain as "sovereign masters" which, as he put it, "govern us in all we do, in all we say, in all we think." This view is known as Hedonism, and it is in essence an egoistic or self-regarding view. How is this fact about each of us, if fact it is, consistent with the demand to promote the greatest happiness of the greatest number, when my own "sovereign masters" might drive me to act in ways that advantage me at the expense of the general happiness? Life demonstrates that this tends to happen rather more often than does generalised altruism.

Bentham was made aware of this difficulty, and tried different ways of overcoming it. One was to say that we promote our own happiness by promoting as much happiness as possible for the majority of others. Another, which he adopted later in life, was to moderate the Hedonistic view, and to accept that we sometimes act out of benevolence towards others. This latter is more plausible than the former, given that Hedonism explicitly makes self-interest the ground of action, and has to reduce altruism to self-interest in such a way as to render the former only apparent. Some theorists, such as J. L. Mackie, have indeed sought to make "enlightened self-interest" the rule of action, but two obstacles lie in the way of accepting this: first, the empirical fact that we sometimes do indeed act in others' interests at a cost to our own, and second, the bad taste left in the mouth by the idea that in the end all we do is ultimately self-serving.

Although Bentham was influenced by Hume he rejected the latter's moral psychology. Hume thought that actions tell us about a person's character, and he held that character is the morally interesting matter. For someone interested in applications of moral principle to actual social affairs, as Bentham was, character is too subjective and inaccessible to be useful. Only individuals themselves can know what they intend or desire, yet the reasons they have for their choices and actions can often be opaque even to themselves. How can this be a practical basis for judging right and wrong? It was a practical basis Bentham sought.

Bentham's patron was the first Marquess of Lansdowne, a leading Whig politician who, having been appointed Prime Minister by a reluctant King George III, brought about peace at the end of the American War of Independence, having always supported the Colonies' side in the dispute. He introduced Bentham to a Genevan exile called Étienne Dumont, the tutor to his sons. Dumont was the person responsible for Bentham's fame in Europe, for he translated a number of Bentham's manuscripts into French and published them in three volumes as *Traités de législation civil et pénale* (1802), the first two volumes of which were re-translated into English much later as *The Theory of Legislation* (1840).

Prior to this Bentham visited his brother Samuel in Russia – hence Hazlitt's reference to his influence on Siberian peasants. Samuel was an interesting individual who had a successful and extremely varied career. At the time of Jeremy's visit he was working for Prince Grigory Potemkin, an advisor and minister (and for a time much more) to the

Tsarina Catherine the Great. Potemkin, as the parenthesis suggests an amorous man, knew of Samuel because of his very public unhappy love-affair with a Russian countess, and apparently on this basis offered him a job – although no doubt Samuel's training as a naval engineer was relevant too. The result was a series of adventures in which Samuel was decorated for bravery in military action against the Turks, built an amphibious vehicle for Catherine the Great, and imported a number of craftsmen from Wales and Tyneside to set up an industrial estate on one of Potemkin's country properties.

Samuel travelled across Siberia to China, then returned to England in 1791 where he engaged in a career as a naval architect and engineer, building a number of ships for the Royal Navy, rising to become Inspector General of Naval Works, and receiving a knighthood. He later went back to Russia for a short spell as a diplomat, and retired to France at the end of the Napoleonic Wars.

Jeremy Bentham used his time in Russia to good effect. He wrote a rebuttal of Adam Smith on interest rates; Smith had argued that they should be legally capped, but Bentham replied that this was inconsistent with Smith's commitments to free trade, investment and business innovation. The book containing these views, *A Defence of Usury* (1787), was admired by J. S. Mill, and came to have a huge influence in the United States, where it was repeatedly reprinted and cited in public policy and economic debates throughout the nineteenth century.

Another product of the Russian visit was a joint scheme Bentham and Samuel devised for panopticon prisons. When the brothers returned to England they worked to persuade the government to build such a prison, and Parliament indeed passed a Bill commissioning one, but the scheme eventually died, leaving Bentham so out of pocket that the government had to pay him compensation of £23,000, a fortune in those days.

The prison scheme was part of Bentham's desire for penal reform generally; he was horrified by the squalid and inhumane conditions in which prisoners were kept – in old dungeons and rotting hulks of ships moored off-shore – and he believed that surveillance made people behave better. Accordingly he and Samuel devised the idea of a circular, cruciform or stellate building which enables supervisors stationed at a central point to observe all the inmates easily – hence the name "panopticon," which might be translated "see-all." The idea was intended not only for prisons but schools, hospitals, workhouses and factories, indeed any institution in which residents or inmates need to be supervised.

When Bentham returned to England from Russia he was encouraged by Lansdowne to address the then-burning question of how "perpetual peace" was to be achieved in the international order, together with other questions of foreign policy with particular reference to how law might be applied to the relations between states. In the process of drafting the essays that came to form his book *Principles of International Law* Bentham coined, as noted, the word "international" itself, and put forward the idea of a court for settling disputes between states. His sympathies for both Russia and France led him to oppose the belligerent attitude to both countries of the then Prime Minister, William Pitt; in the course of 1789 he published a series of letters in *The Public Advertiser* criticizing Pitt's foreign policy.

The situation in France especially engaged Bentham's interest. Even before the Revolution broke out he began to write a series of pamphlets, with Dumont's help, proposing political solutions and judicial reform for France. They were published in French and disseminated among leading figures in Paris. In the period after the fall of the Bastille the proposals were discussed by France's National Assembly. His support for the Revolution resulted in his being given honorary French citizenship in 1792.

He had no parallel influence on contemporary matters at home in England. Both interest and effort directed at social and political reform were chilled by the repressive measures introduced by Pitt's government in its fear of revolution, so Bentham turned his attention elsewhere; to poor law reform, the question of policing, economics, and above all legal reform, the latter giving him an opportunity to vent his highly critical attitude to what he saw as the muddled nature of the common law and the arbitrary nature of "judge-made law."

Bentham's interest in poor law reform was stimulated by the fact that war-time conditions were raising the price of food and exacerbating the difficulties of both the rural and urban poor. In line with his practical bent, he wished to see a more uniform and systematic treatment of the problem, based on a chain of "industry houses" in which the indigent, disabled and sick could be provided with work and welfare. He envisioned that these forerunners of workhouses would be operated by a joint stock company (he proposed the name "National Charity Company") which would finance its activities out of the produce of the "industry houses". The man later responsible for the provisions of the Poor Law Act of 1832, Sir Edwin Chadwick, was a friend and disciple of Bentham, and much influenced by him; neither foresaw the grinding misery inflicted by these institutions on those who entered their bleak doors, for they were no sooner set up than they were given a disincentive purpose, the harshness of their regime being intended to dissuade people from seeking in them a refuge from want.

Bentham also devoted himself to political economy and the question of taxation during the 1790s, the decade that saw the introduction by Pitt of income tax (two pence in the pound for annual incomes over £60, two shillings in the pound for incomes over £200; the measure was intended to be temporary). His writings on these subjects were not published during his lifetime. Although they reflect his responses both to the writings of Adam Smith and the practical dilemmas of that period, they contain a number of original ideas still of interest today. Among his chief dissatisfactions with society and its institutions those relating to law and the administration of justice troubled him most.

The law reforms Bentham proposed were the replacement of technical with natural procedures of evidence, and the introduction of legislation in place of judge-made law. Another of his neologisms which has remained in the language is the verb "to codify," which he introduced in urging the codification of law. He expressly opposed the Blackstone view that obsolete or unsuitable laws should not be repealed but adapted, wherever necessary by the means of "legal fictions." An example of such is treating a corporation as a natural person for legal purposes, or forbidding MPs to resign but in effect allowing them to do so by appointing them to an office forbidden to MPs (the Chiltern Hundreds).

Bentham accepted the view that law is by its nature negative, in the sense that its whole essence lies in imposing restrictions and limits, thereby reducing individual liberty. His idea of liberty was, like that of Hobbes, what is now called "negative liberty," that is, absence of restraint. This view has a straightforward consequence when conjoined with Bentham's version of utilitarianism. It is pleasant to be free and painful to be restricted; since pleasure and pain are the criteria of value, it follows that liberty is a good. But Bentham would have no truck with the idea that liberty is a "natural right," an idea on which he poured unreserved scorn, calling all talk of natural rights "nonsense on stilts." This is because he rejected the idea of a social contract which had brought people out of a "state of nature" in which they had enjoyed primitive rights and freedoms, some of which they forfeited in exchange for the benefits of community. He thought that people had always lived in society, and that laws are the commands of whoever or whatever holds authority in it. This anticipated the "legal positivism" of the theorist John Austin later in the nineteenth century, the view that law is expressly the product of the will of a sovereign. This view entails that whether or not a law is good or bad, moral or otherwise, it is nevertheless law if so enacted. This idea further entails that all rights are created by legislation, and that liberties are conferred either explicitly by law, or implicitly by the law's silence.

A more attractive feature of Bentham's legal views concerns the question of evidence. He viewed the law of evidence and its admissibility as extremely muddled; it was full of distinctions, exceptions, and a host of obscure technicalities that had accumulated through the process of judge-made decisions over time. Bentham saw the legal profession's adherence to this unsatisfactory state of affairs as malignly self-interested because it prolonged hearings and added much to lawyers' purses. Previous legal theorists had attempted to impose order on the chaos, and to justify some of the more bizarre doctrines that underlay evidential practice. Bentham took a more robust approach; he sought to sweep aside all "rules of evidence" and to replace them with a natural approach on utilitarian grounds, an approach premised on ordinary daily experience and common sense.

When eventually his writings on the subject were published in the 1820s they were seen to be sharply at odds with other reform proposals from legal theorists. Because Bentham's views represented a wholesale criticism of the law profession and the tradition of judge-made law, it provoked a mixed reaction, even from followers like Dumont and Henry Brougham. But they made a difference to practice, if only in piecemeal fashion at first, though some commentators argue that, since his time, most reform to the law of evidence has moved in the direction he indicated.

As a result of his letters to President Madison in the United States on the subject of codification of laws, and to each of the State legislatures in America, his views bore indirect fruit in another direction; one example is the partial codification of civil procedure in the state of New York (the Field Code) as a result of the indefatigable labours of David D. Field II, who had been influenced by Bentham while on European travels undertaken to research legal codes.

But in fact Bentham's ideas had an ever wider though less specific ripple effect than this; his ideas on constitutional questions in general attracted attention in Spain, Portugal, Italy, France, Poland, Russia and both North and South America. He received letters and requests for information and advice from government ministers, civil servants, reformers, politicians, liberals and even heads of state and monarchs: from the Cortes in Spain, from reformers in France and Italy, from governors of several American states, from the Polish statesman Count Czartoriski, and from Tsar Alexander of Russia.

A chief reason for this wide-ranging influence began, as noted, with Dumont's translation of his unpublished manuscripts as the *Traités de législation*. Tsar Alexander had a Russian translation made, and it was followed by translations either in full or as excerpts in German, Polish, Hungarian, Spanish and Portuguese. In these last two languages it was widely read in South America, and it laid the basis for Bentham's later works to be read there and taught in nascent Latin American universities. His writings provoked controversy in Chile and Colombia; in the latter Simon Bolivar, as President, succumbed to pressure by the Catholic Church (not least for reasons explained by Bentham's religious views: see below) and banned them. Bolivar's successor as President, Francisco Santander, revoked the ban and restored them to the university curriculum.

In Greece after liberation from Ottoman rule Bentham's writings influenced the drafters of the new constitution, chiefly as a result of the writings of Anastasios Polyzoides, a Bentham disciple. A similar service to Benthamite ideas was performed in the United States by David Hoffman, the legal scholar, who introduced utilitarian ideas into law studies at the University of Maryland in the 1820s. All this bears out Hazlitt's comment on Bentham's fame abroad and relative anonymity at home. It also bears out Isaiah Berlin's comment, premised chiefly on the examples of John Locke and Karl Marx – Locke's writings on politics were quoted *verbatim* and *in extenso* in the documents of the American and French revolutions – that a philosopher sitting in his study can change the history of the world within a generation. For as this observation implies, ideas are the cogs that drive the wheels of history.

All of Bentham's schemes for the improvement of society and its institutions, from penal reform to his urgings on political economy and the law, faced formidable barriers at home in Britain because of tradition and vested interests. He came to realize that the only hope for them lay in fundamental political reform. He was encouraged in this by James Mill, who in 1808 became his lieutenant and coadjutor. Bentham had written about political reform earlier in his career, but had put his manuscripts aside; now with Mill's encouragement he dusted them off and extended them. He had come to think not only that substantive reform was impossible without political reform, but that the only alternative to political reform was revolution; and he preferred the former.

In his view the key to the problem lay in the "influence" exercised over political institutions by individuals and claques in the Establishment from the King downwards, acting through an unrepresentative Parliament which was in the pockets of wealthy patrons. To combat this, parliamentary representation needed to be reformed. He therefore set about arguing in favour of an extension of the franchise, annual elections by secret ballot, basic qualifications for those who stand for Parliament, a system of fines to enforce regular attendance by MPs, accurate reporting of Parliamentary debates, and abolition of royal patronage in offices and honours. He associated himself with James Mill's published condemnation of the exclusion of women from the franchise, though he said the franchise should be extended to them only once all adult males had it.

Reform of the system of representation was by itself not yet quite enough; he further argued that there was waste and corruption in government, that public expenditure needed to be reduced and the efficacy of the civil service improved, chiefly by better selection and training of civil servants.

When his proposals on parliamentary reform were published in 1817, and his attacks on waste and incompetence in public administration were published in 1824, he was confirmed as the country's leading voice of political radicalism. This by itself would have been enough to marginalize him in Establishment terms, but he exacerbated his exclusion from direct influence on public affairs by his attitude to religion. He was an atheist, and wrote scathingly about Christianity – and in particular about the Church and its hold over education, as witness his attack on the "National Society for Promoting the Education of the Poor in the Principles of the

Established Church" (for such madrasa-style objectives as here connoted, Bentham would think the word "Indoctrination" a more accurate alternative to "Education" in that title).

For someone who saw superstitious beliefs as a barrier to progress, religion as a bulwark against reform of minds as well as institutions, and the clergy as possessing unwarranted influence over educational and public affairs, he was a powerful voice in favour of secularism. His *Of the influence of natural religion on the temporal happiness of mankind* (1822) rejected the religious apologists' standard claim that faith is a force for good in the world. As with others (Richard Dawkins comes to mind) who are criticized for not engaging with the nuances and refinements of theological theory but restrict themselves to "superficial" attacks on religious beliefs and influences, Bentham has an answer: there is no point in engaging with theology if the fundamental premise that gives it a *raison d'etre* is rejected, this premise being that there are deities or at least one deity or even just supernatural agency of some kind in the universe. In the absence of grounds for thinking that there is a rational possibility of such a thing or things, theology is vacuous.

The harm done by religion to people and societies throughout history, and the distorting influence of reverence for holy writings and religious hierarchies, were a particular target for Bentham. He shocked many of his contemporaries with his *Not Paul, But Jesus* (1823) in which he described Jesus as a political revolutionary and St Paul as a liar.

Characteristically, though, Bentham was in favour of religious liberty, and in particular defended Nonconformists against the disabilities they suffered as a result of refusing to subscribe the Thirty Nine Articles of the Church of England. This kept them out of the universities, public schools, Parliament, and any civil or military office. As a result nonconformists had founded their own schools, mostly superior by far in curriculum and teaching to established institutions. When therefore proposals were put forward for a secular school in London and then a university – University College London, today one of the world's great institutions of higher education and research – Bentham was enthusiastically in favour. James Mill and the radical Francis Place were behind the idea of a secular school, and Bentham suggested curricula for it, emphasizing science and practical subjects and de-emphasizing the classics. (Despite this latter point he called his book on the subject *Chrestomathia*, Greek for "useful learning". He was not one to appreciate ironies.) The school project fell through, but then its proponents decided to establish a university instead; and this was the beginning of University College London.

There is a certain irony in the fact that Bentham died just before the signing into law of the Reform Act of 1832, the first step in Parliamentary reform and the extension of the franchise. In his last years he described himself as "the hermit of Queens Square Place," though in fact he was the focus of constant pilgrimage by people who shared his interests and concerns, among them many foreign dignitaries of the kind listed above in connection with his work on constitutional reform. The idea that he lived hidden in his garden in introspective isolation is contested not only by this fact, but by his continued engagement in the tasks of information, persuasion and campaigning; in these final years he gave money for the founding of the periodical *Westminster Review*, among the later leading contributors to which were George Eliot and John Stuart Mill.

As a thorough Utilitarian it was inevitable that Bentham should wish his corpse to be useful after his death. He provided in his will that his body should be publicly dissected to illustrate the value of donating one's body to medical science. His funeral eulogy was delivered over his dissected remains by the physician Thomas Southwood Smith. Bentham also directed that his body should become an "auto-icon," dressed in his habitual clothes and put on display to serve an educational purpose for the public. Accordingly he sits, thus clothed, in speculative mood in a glass cabinet in University College London, and can be visited there to this day.

Bentham's influence on thinkers and societies other than his own has already been indicated. It began to be more apparent in his home terrain when John Stuart Mill in effect reintroduced his countrymen to Bentham's thought, first by editing and publishing the five volumes of the *Rationale of Judicial Evidence* (1838-43) and then by developing the utilitarian doctrine that he had inherited from him. Mill was no mere disciple, though, as his father had largely been; he recognized that there could be an argument to the effect that pleasures are not all equal, but can come in higher and lower forms, and he recognized that minorities needed protection from the possible tyranny of majorities, which means that democracy has to be tempered by constitutional restraints and protections for individual liberty, which he valued as an intrinsic good.

But once Benthamite themes started to gain a wider audience in the decades after his death, their influence grew too. This was especially noticeable in economic theory, where the utilitarian calculus Bentham had sought to devise (the "felicific calculus" intended as a practical metric for deciding what would maximize the utilities in a given case) influenced the development of cost-benefit analysis. While starting from the same premise as Adam Smith, that the pursuit of their own interests by individuals would aggregate to the overall prosperity of the country, and agreeing therefore that the legislative burden on economic activity should be light, Bentham nevertheless saw that there would be a need for government to deal with the unequal distribution of benefits that would result from diminishing marginal utility. This inspired later economists such as W. S. Jevons and Sydney Webb to develop welfare economics, though theorists on the other side of the political spectrum were also able to mine Bentham for ideas about individualism and even libertarianism. That this is so is a characteristic mark of the work of anyone as wide-ranging and multiple as Bentham; perhaps one should say that he cannot be held wholly responsible for what others made of his ideas.

With growing influence came growing criticism. Thomas Carlyle perhaps captures the most severe opposition; he decried Bentham's views as "pig-philosophy" extolling "virtue by profit and loss." More gently the French philosopher Benjamin Constant criticized the concept of utility for its vagueness. Almost all critics from Hazlitt to Macaulay and Mackintosh commented unfavourably on the picture of human nature that underlay Bentham's views, a rather impoverished, mechanistic picture in which he neglected wholly that side of human beings where – as Hazlitt in particular complained – imagination, love and sentiment play their typically dominating part. In Hazlitt's opinion Bentham's neglect of these factors rendered his philosophy "fit neither for man nor beast." This view of Bentham was shared by Marx, who called Bentham an "arch-Philistine," and regarded utilitarianism as irredeemably superficial and bourgeois.

Above all – and predictably – Bentham was vilified by the clerical lobby, who were delighted by the expose written by one John Colls, an Anglican clergyman who, before becoming such, had briefly served as secretary to Bentham, and who wrote a rather unChristian attack called *Utilitarianism Unmasked* (1844) portraying Bentham as a dangerous, bigoted and unpleasant subversive.

Among philosophers the consensus is that Bentham erred in seeking to reduce all human motivation to the desire for pleasure and avoidance of pain, and in holding that only one thing – happiness – is to be identified as the *summmum bonum*, given that there are arguably other good things that people seek for their intrinsic – which is to say non-instrumental - value.

But whatever one might think about the detail of Bentham's many views on many subjects, it remains that they continue to be relevant – indeed, they increase in relevance as scholarship advances – to debates in moral philosophy, economics, legal theory, politics, history and psychology. The truly admirable thing about him is that he resolutely and unswervingly saw *gnosis* as the servant of *praxis* – that the reformation of society and the condition of humankind was a task worth devoting an entire lifetime to – and that he lived as he thought, hoping to achieve the betterment of the world.

I think that his severest critic, Carlyle, would now, in longer hindsight, see that Bentham had what Carlyle said the Normans brought to the "gluttonous race of the Jutes and Angles…lumbering about in their pot-bellied equanimity," namely, a preparedness to engage in "heroic toil and silence and endurance, such as leads to the high places of this Universe, and the golden mountain tops where dwells the Spirit of the Dawn." For Bentham was a mighty labourer in the causes he believed in, and though the dawns sought by reformers typically take far too long to break, quite a few of the things Bentham valued have indeed come to morning in the two centuries since he argued for them: aspects of constitutional reform, welfare economics, legal practice, applied ethics. These aspects, therefore, are his monument, and in not a few respects – and not just in British and British-influenced societies – one can exhibit it just by saying: *circumspice*.

Henry Mayhew

Gareth Stedman Jones

enry Mayhew was born in 1812, the fourth son of Joshua
Mayhew and one of seventeen children. He attended Westminster
School between 1822 and 1827. Excited by the progress of
science at a time when dramatic discoveries had been made by Humphry
Davy and others about the nature of chemical elements including sodium,

potassium and calcium, his youthful ambition was to become a chemist.[1] In a book written in 1842, *What to Teach and how to Teach it*, he argued for a school curriculum, which would include science, history and modern languages and for forms of teaching which inspired curiosity and encouraged practical experience. All this was in strong reaction against the deadening classics-based education current at the time in major public schools. At Westminster, he wrote:

> "we were not even taught our own language, nor even writing nor reckoning, but bored to death simply with the dead tongues…We were sent into the world to get our living out of the elements by which we were surrounded… in the same beastly ignorance as any Carib – not only of the physical world about us, but of our own natures and of our fellow creatures, as well as of all that was right, true, beautiful, or indeed noble in life."[2]

But the antagonism towards the classics may also have had a more personal origin. At the age of fifteen, he ran away from Westminster. He had reached the top of a list of candidates in the school's Latin Challenge, but he had been threatened with a beating for neglecting to write out some accompanying Greek lines. Such baffling swings between impressive achievement and seemingly self-induced failure formed something of a pattern in his life, and it seems to have been engendered as a response to the tyrannical household in which he grew up.

Mayhew's father, Joshua, was a wealthy and prominent solicitor, who was worth £50,000 at the time of his death. He was keen to advertise his wealth, employing, in addition to the normal complement of household servants, a coachman, footman and page. But he was also – or so at least he was portrayed by his children – a miser and a stern and unrelenting disciplinarian. Joshua's miserliness and vindictiveness were amply

---

[1] Later in 1855, Mayhew wrote The Wonders of Science: Or, Young Humphry Davy.

[2] Cited in Humpherys, A. *Travels into the Poor Man's Country: The Work of Henry Mayhew*, Athens, University of Georgia Press, 1977, pp. 3, 12. This book provides the most informative account of Mayhew's life and particularly of his early writings.

recorded by his sons.[3] He was notorious among local cabmen, who would drive away on seeing him approach, not least because it was known that he would not hesitate to prosecute when he considered himself to have been over-charged. At the age of twenty-one, each son was given an allowance of £1 per week and expected thereafter to maintain himself upon it. 16 Fitzroy Square, the house where the Mayhews lived, was locked at midnight, and according to a family story, even adult sons arriving after that time, were thrown a shilling and told to find a bed elsewhere. Sons were obliged to address him as "Sir" and to remain standing until permitted to sit. Mrs Mayhew seems also to have been an object of her husband's ill-temper; it was said that her jewellery collection was assembled from peace offerings given to compensate her after his outbursts of uncontrollable rage.

Following the end of his schooling, Henry's father sent him to India as a mid-shipman. But this did not work, and by the early 1830s, he was back in London working as an apprentice to his father. Joshua wanted all his sons to become solicitors and apprenticed each of them to him (defraying their costs from their inheritance). But it is some measure of their resistance to his ambitions, that only one son, Alfred, followed his father as a solicitor, while all the other brothers, except Julius (a failed photographer) – Thomas, Edward, Horace and Augustus – became journalists. In Henry's case, the apprenticeship ended as disastrously as had his schooldays. Whether through resentment or neglect, Henry neglected to file some important papers, and as a result, a bailiff came to arrest Joshua, while the family was at dinner. Henry hurriedly left the table and did not see his father for several years.

Having left home, in the 1830s and 1840s Henry formed part of a bohemian world of comic and radical journalists, who set up short-lived clubs, met in pubs and conversed over punch and tobacco. In this milieu, he became friends with Mark Lemon, Henry Baylis, Gilbert à Beckett

---

[3] All this was recounted in a poem written for the 1848 edition of the *Comic Almanac* written by Henry and his brother, Augustus. It was entitled "A Highly Respectable Man". After recording the injuries, suffered by Mrs Mayhew, the stanza went on:
"That his Children, on hearing his knock,
To the top of the house always ran –
But with ten thousand pounds at his Banker's
He's *of course* a respectable Man."

(OW), Stirling Coyne and the cartoonist, George Cruikshank, and also got to know, Dickens, Thackeray and Douglas Jerrold. The radicalism of these journalists mainly found expression in their mockery of the pretensions of Henry Brougham's *Society for the Diffusion of Useful Knowledge*, the bland publications of Charles Knight, and above all, the hypocrisy of much of the advocacy of free trade in knowledge.

Much of their inspiration came from France. In 1832, for instance, Henry joined forces with Gilbert à Beckett to produce *The Thief*, a direct copy of a Parisian journal, *Le Voleur*, started in 1828. This was "scissors and paste" journalism, in which everything except the leader columns and answers to correspondents was stolen from elsewhere. *The Thief* criticised copyright laws, defended its use of journalistic piracy and criticised "respectable" papers, who practised the same thing, without avowing it. It justified its own activity as the promotion of the free diffusion of knowledge among the working classes.[4]

Together with à Beckett, between 1835 and 1839, Mayhew also edited another of these French-inspired papers, *Figaro in London*, whose success was largely the result of its theatre criticism and its political cartoons (some by Cruikshank). But his most successful venture in this area – and in most accounts, his original idea - was the foundation of *Punch* in 1841. It was launched by a group of three proprietors – Mayhew, Mark Lemon and Stirling Coyne – with contributions from Douglas Jerrold, Thackeray and à Beckett. It became the most famous comic and satirical journal in Britain and lasted through to 2002. In line with Mayhew's own approach the satire was light, its radicalism was moderate and it was not connected with any particular party. In 1842, however, there was a change of ownership, Mark Lemon became sole editor, and Mayhew drifted away. His last contribution was made in 1845. Why he withdrew or became marginalised is not clear. But in the same year, he tried out an educational series, *What to Teach and How to Teach it*, followed by a similar primer in 1844. Neither of these series was completed.

In 1844, Mayhew married Jane, the daughter of Douglas Jerrold.[5] Mayhew had first met the Jerrolds in Paris in the mid-1830s, where

---

[4] See Feely, C. (2014) '"What say you to free trade in literature?" *The Thief* and the Politics of Piracy in the 1830s', *Journal of Victorian Culture* 19 (4): 497-507.

[5] Douglas Jerrold (1803-1857) was known as a wit and a radical. He was briefly a midshipman, and then a journalist, comic sketch writer and playwright. He was best known for his melodrama of 1829, *Black-Eyed Susan*, a play about

Douglas was avoiding arrest as the result of a law-suit pursued by Henry's father, while Henry himself was living cheaply and keeping at a safe distance from home. Henry offered to act as a go-between with his father and this seems to have resulted in some form of reconciliation as well as a successful settlement of Jerrold's law-suit. It also formed the basis of his close friendship with the Jerrold family. After *Punch* and his educational ventures, Mayhew attempted to take advantage of the great railway boom of 1844-1847. At the height of the 'mania', he launched his *Iron Times*, which retailed railway gossip together with news about the market. Backed by a publisher and a salary of around £300 a year, the couple bought a new and lavishly furnished house in Parsons Green. But the attempt to capitalise upon the railway mania came too late. In 1846, his publisher went bankrupt and in 1847 he followed suit, with debts of over £2,000. Jane returned temporarily to her father, while Joshua, who regarded bankruptcy as the ultimate disgrace, never forgave him, and, apart from his £1 per week, cut him and his children out of his will.

Once more Mayhew attempted to recoup, this time mainly by resorting to novels or moral fables, co-authored with his brother, Augustus, and published under the authorship of the 'Brothers Mayhew'. These included *The Good Genius that Turned Everything into Gold* (1847), *The Greatest Plague in Life* (1847), *Whom to Marry and How to Get Married* (1848), *The Image of his Father* (1848) and *The Magic of Kindness* (1849).

In 1847, the Palmerstonian owner of *The Morning Chronicle*, Sir John Eastlake had sold the paper to a group of Peelites, particularly interested in health and sanitary reform. In the following autumn, there was a major cholera epidemic in London, in which 14,000 died; and this appears to have been the main reason why the *Chronicle* embarked upon its survey of 'Labour and the Poor'. Although the precise connection between cholera and infected water was not understood at the time (it was believed to be produced by the 'miasma' arising from sewer and slum waste), it

---

corruption and press gangs in the navy. Relations between Mayhew and Jerrold appear to have broken down at the end of 1850, perhaps in connection with the termination of the *Chronicle* series. Jerrold's daughter, Jane (1825-1880) had two children with Henry. There is no evidence to suggest that the relationship was lacking in affection. Their periodic separations seem to have been occasioned more by financial than by emotional problems. But for whatever reason, Jane ended up living alone with her daughter.

was clear enough that the disease was related to the poverty and appalling sanitation of the slums. This was the context in which Mayhew on September 24th 1849 wrote his *A visit to the cholera districts of Bermondsey*, highlighting the pestilential "rookery" and centre of leather-tanning, Jacob's Island – already notorious from Dickens' account in *Oliver Twist*. This item formed the prelude to his first letter on the *The Metropolitan Districts* as "our special correspondent". In all, there were to be 82 letters between September 1849 and December 1850 from the "Metropolitan Correspondent" as his contribution to the national survey produced by the *Morning Chronicle*.[6]

The reports of the "Metropolitan Correspondent" were a great success. They took the form of testimonies from a wide variety of those who "will work", "can't work" or "won't work", delivered in response to (unpublished) questions put to them by Mayhew. Mayhew himself was highly paid and assisted by an army of assistant writers, stenographers and hansom cabmen. Apart from *The Economist*, his contributions were widely praised in the press. They were excerpted by Julian Harney and G.W.M. Reynolds in radical and Chartist newspapers, while a special "Labour and the Poor" fund was established at the *Chronicle* with money collected for Mayhew interviewees. But by the spring of 1850, interest had begun to wane. The letters, which had appeared three times a week, were now appearing only once, and by December 1850 had ceased altogether.

Why Mayhew parted from the *Chronicle* is not entirely clear. There were complaints that criticisms of free trade had been removed from the interviews, and there was a particular dispute over the juxtaposition between Mayhew's reports and a prominent advertisement for the large ready-to-wear tailor, Nicholls of Regent Street. Mayhew had exposed of the sweated piece work system employed in ready-made tailoring, which, as he told a meeting of tailors on October 28th 1850, led to the impoverishment of needlewomen and their resort to prostitution.[7]

---

[6] The series included reports from Angus Reach from the manufacturing districts, Alexander Mackay and Shirley Brooks from the rural districts and Charles Mackay on Birmingham and Liverpool.

[7] Cited in Roddy, S.; Strange, J.M.; & Bertrand Taithe, B. (2014) 'Henry Mayhew at 200 – the "Other" Victorian Bicentenary', *Journal of Victorian Culture* 19(4): 481-496.

Mayhew continued his enquiry, published in the form of weekly pamphlets under the title, *London Labour and the London Poor,* which ran between December 1850 and February 1852. These concentrated on the life of costermongers and "street folk". He was able to sell around 13,000 copies at 1d or 2d per issue.[8] In 1851, he also attempted to extend his range with the serial publication of an alternative political economy, entitled *Low Wages* - mainly an elaboration of the answers he had already written in answer to the queries of readers in his earlier series. But this lasted only for a few numbers. In June 1851, he informed readers that *London Labour and the London Poor* would probably take another five or six years, but either for legal or commercial reasons, publication came to an end in 1852.

In 1856, backed by his friend and publisher, David Bogue, a three-volume edition of *London Labour* was planned together with a new series on London life entitled *The Great World of London*. The volume started grandly with a view of London from the "Royal Nassau Balloon".

"As we floated along, above the fields in a line with the Thames towards Richmond and looked over the edge of the car...the sight was the most exquisite visual delight ever experienced. The houses directly underneath us looked like the tiny wooden things out of a child's box of toys and the streets as if they were ruts in the ground."

But as dusk approached and the wind changed direction, the scene radically changed.

The Metropolis was covered by a "dense canopy of smoke", which hung over "the Leviathan City", so that "it was impossible to tell where the monster city began or ended."[9] There followed studies of "professional" and "legal" London, while the bulk of the work went on to describe London's "criminal prisons."

This new burst of activity was brought to an end by Bogue's sudden death, and thereafter, the series was abandoned unfinished. It was completed by John Binny and published as *The Criminal Prisons of London* in 1862. Similarly, a further volume, which was to follow the

---

[8] Taithe, B. (ed.) (1997), *The Essential Mayhew: Representing and Communicating the Poor*, (London: Rivers Oram Press), p. 18.

[9] Mayhew, H. (1856) *The Great World of London*, (London: David Bogue). p. 9.

three volumes of *London Labour* collated in 1851-2, did not appear. A new and amplified edition in four volumes was published in 1861-1862. But there was no revision of the original text, and the fourth volume was the work of other writers. A further edition was published in 1865, but by then, there was little political or economic interest in the work. By the 1870s, the project had become quaint – a development abetted by Mayhew himself in his 1874 *London Characters. Illustrations of the Humour, Pathos and Peculiarities of London Life* – and there it remained until his work was rediscovered by social historians in the 1960s.[10]

Concurrently, with *London Labour* in 1851, Mayhew had written a comic sketch of the Crystal Palace Exhibition. He then intermittently spent several years in Germany, where he wrote two studies of the "picturesque scenery" of the Rhine.[11] It appears to have been a place in which he could both live more cheaply and avoid creditors. He was there again in the early 1860s, where he wrote *The Boyhood of Martin Luther* and in 1864, a study of *German Life and Manners as seen in Saxony at the Present Day.*

After 1856, he appears to have abandoned any serious attempt to restart his London project, opting instead to make random use of the material for fictional or theatrical purposes. In 1857, he joined with his brother, Augustus, to draw upon *London Labour* in a novel, *Paved with Gold*, but withdrew after five issues. Around the same time, he organised comic recitations using *London Labour* to imitate London street sellers, assisted at the piano by James Hatton, who sang comic songs. A successful performance in St Martin's Hall led to a planned three-month provincial tour, beginning in Brighton. But on the first night, he was traumatised to find himself confronted by his sternly disapproving father sitting in the first row and fled the stage.

In the 1860s and 1870s he attempted various journalistic ventures, including a book on department stores, an attempt to set up a rival to *Punch* and some reporting of the Franco-Prussian War. But he wrote

---

[10] See Thompson, E.P. & Yeo, E. (eds.) (1971), *The Unknown Mayhew: Selections from the Morning Chronicle 1849-50.* (London: Merlin Press).
[11] Mayhew, H. & Cruikshank, G. (1851), *1851; or, The Adventures of Mr and Mrs Sandboys.* London, David Bogue. In 1853 Mayhew campaigned for the opening of Crystal Palace on a Sunday. On Germany, see Mayhew, H. (1856) *The Rhine and Its Picturesque Scenery: Rotterdam to Mayence.* See also Mayhew, H. (1858) *The Upper Rhine and Its Picturesque Scenery*, (London: Routledge).

nothing that recaptured the originality and importance of his *Morning Chronicle* and *London Labour* enquiries. Living alone, he died from bronchitis on July 25th 1887.

Estimations of Mayhew's importance as a social investigator have shifted radically during the last half-century. Up until the 1970s, Mayhew was only known from various reprints and selections from the 1861 four-volume edition of *London Labour and the London Poor*. It was therefore easy to believe that he was overwhelmingly concerned with street traders, street performers and prostitutes – to such an extent that the title of his book seemed a misnomer. It was not until Edward Thompson and Eileen Yeo presented a selection from Mayhew's forgotten contributions to the *Morning Chronicle* that it could be argued that his work provided more than a quaint collection of cameos and that it in fact represented a pioneering empirical survey of poverty in London and a radical questioning of conventional assumptions about its cause.

But such claims did not go uncontested. Gertrude Himmelfarb in her large-scale historical study of poverty continued to argue that Mayhew's interviews were not representative of the London poor as a whole and that they were an unreliable assemblage of "sensationalist anecdotes."[12] The subsequent republication of the complete series of *Chronicle* articles by Caliban Press in 1980 diminished the strength of this argument. The *Morning Chronicle Survey* did cover a major cross-section of the artisan and labouring trades of London. Among the skilled and the semi-skilled, there were descriptions and accounts of discussions among tailors, shoemakers, hatters, cabinet-makers, toymakers, carpenters, turners, joiners, sawyers, coopers, shipbuilders, weavers and leather-makers. The survey of the unskilled included most branches of land and water transport – dockers, ballast heavers, coal-whippers, cabmen, carmen, watermen and seamen. The major omissions related to parts of the building trade, the metal and engineering trades, printing and paper work, precision manufactures and domestic service. The main reason for these omissions was the fact that the project remained unfinished. While not comprehensive, Mayhew produced an unprecedented investigation into the nature of the workshop and outworking trades of Victorian London and of the various forms of heavy and unskilled labour connected with London's importance as a port and a centre of distribution.

---

[12] Himmelfarb, G. (1984) *The Idea of Poverty: England in the Early Industrial Age*. (London: Faber & Faber).

It is true that some of this treatment was uneven - hatters got much more hurried treatment than tailors, for example. It was also true that skilled trades with a higher standard of living received far less attention than poor and overcrowded occupations. Nevertheless, some of the best accounts of the culture and life-styles of the "honourable" trades were to be found in Mayhew, as were a series of uniquely detailed analyses of the diet and purchasing habits of the working classes and their relationship with pawnshops and alcohol consumption. His work also contained an assessment of the significance of such well-publicised contemporary charities as *Asylums for the Houseless*, and *Ragged Schools*. Taken together, *London Labour* and the *Morning Chronicle Survey* offered a broader survey of London labour than previous historians had been prepared to acknowledge.

The central importance of the occupations, which Mayhew investigated, is now accepted to have been far greater than once thought. Despite the industrial revolution, London in 1851 and 1861 remained the largest centre of manufacturing activity in the country, and hand-labour one of the principal components of the economy as a whole. Hand-labour of a skilled, semi-skilled or unskilled kind was the basic means by which the elementary demands of an expanding population for housing, clothing, footwear, furniture and other consumer durables were satisfied. Because labour was plentiful and cheap, and because demand was fashion-prone, in addition to being seasonally and cyclically variable, increasing demand was met by the addition of new units of production rather than by economies of scale. The new technologies in these trades were capital- rather than labour-saving. This is exemplified by the role of the band-saw, the sewing machine and the hand-lathe in the clothing, furniture and metal trades. Effectively, these were *new* industries of the mid-nineteenth century, just as novel in their manner of organisation and use of labour, as had been the pioneer factory sector in cotton spinning at the end of the eighteenth.

As the population began to drift off the land, which it did at an accelerated rate from the 1830s onwards, it was to an increasing extent in London and other major cities rather than in the countryside that the largest captive pools of cheap labour were to be found. Therefore, at least until the 1890s, when factory production began to make serious encroachments upon this sector, the so-called "sweated trades" expanded at least as fast as the urban populations whose needs they served.

There was no more acute observer of the character and development of these new industries than Mayhew, especially in the *Morning Chronicle Survey.* His account of the sweating system and the development of the "dishonourable" sector in the clothing, footwear and wood-working trades was the first substantial account of the process and by far the best source we possess on these developments in the first half of the century. In his attention to the changing forms of work organisation and in his analysis of the means by which labour productivity was increased in these trades, Mayhew stood alone at the time in which he wrote. One need only compare his reports with the bland accounts of George Dodds, *Days in the Factories,* or the blind and unfocussed polemic of Charles Kingsley's *Cheap Clothes and Nasty* to take the measure of his achievement. Before the parliamentary enquiries of the 1860s, Mayhew was virtually alone in attempting to investigate the world of work, working conditions and wage payment concealed behind the façade of conventionally accepted wage statistics and the usual litany of complaints about the laziness, indiscipline and intemperance of the working classes.

If some historians found the authenticity of Mayhew's picture of the "dishonourable" trades and the labouring poor difficult to accept, others, while endorsing the accuracy of his reporting, were disappointed by his apparent inability to organise his findings into an alternative political economy.[13] Such criticism was also misdirected, since it ignored what his findings revealed. Although some have wished to compare him with Marx, to the extent that he wished to uncover the hidden reality behind the façade of popular political economy, in the picture assembled by Mayhew, the removal of the façade revealed no simple polarity between capital and labour. Rather, as Donna Loftus has argued, Mayhew's supposedly confused thinking about the conundrums and contradictions in the metropolitan market was really no more than "an echo of the messiness of the London economy" itself.[14]

This was especially true of the pervasive role of small-masters in workshop and outwork trades. Setting up as a small-master, as Loftus had shown, was a response to poverty, which afforded workers a chance of

[13] See Samuel, R. (1973) 'Mayhew and Labour Historians', *Society for the Study of Labour History*, 26: 47-52.
[14] Loftus, D. (2014) 'Work, poverty and Modernity in Mayhew's London', *Journal of Victorian Culture* 19(4): 507-519.

income and a degree of autonomy, even a hope of social mobility; but small-masters also caused poverty by adding labour and goods to an already overstocked market. [15]

Mayhew claimed both to be applying "the laws of inductive philosophy" to "abstract questions of political economy and to be engaged in establishing an understanding of work, based on real life" and taken from the "lips of the people themselves."[16] His aim was to discover reasons for the connection he discovered between overwork and underpay, and to challenge the prevalent arguments found in popular political economy, which ascribed low wages to the impact of overpopulation upon the supply and demand for labour. But in some cases, his attempt to refute this Malthusian picture through the testimony of operatives themselves, led him astray. On this basis, for instance, he claimed in *London Labour* that the demand for labour had kept pace with population and that in the particular trades like shoemaking and tailoring, living standards had fallen without a marked rise in numbers in the trade.

Here he had to retrace his steps. For much of the evidence supplied by his informants clearly did suggest that oversupply of labour and as a result, excessive competition in the labour market played a fundamental role in accounting for the poverty associated with sweated labour. Where he had a case against Malthus was not in contesting the fact of oversupply of labour, but rather in showing that the causes of low wages had little to do with the size of population as such and much more to do with the practices of artisans and small masters themselves, especially in their use of family work. Workers overstocked the labour market by increasing the number of apprentices or by employing their own family to meet orders. As one representative of the clothing trade told Mayhew:

"I date the decrease in the wages of the workmen from the introduction of piece work and giving our garments to be made off the premises of the master; for the effect of this was, that the workman making the garment, knowing the master could not tell whom he got to do his work for him, employed women and

---

[15] *Ibid* at 508.

[16] Mayhew, H. 'Answers to Correspondents, no.16, March 29th 1851' in *London Labour and the London Poor,* cited in Loftus at 508.

children to help him and paid them little or nothing for their labour."[17]

This indeterminacy in the status of the artisan positioned in the no-man's land between employer and employee disrupted the clarity of the different roles assigned to labour and capital in Victorian political economy. The transformation of workers into employers and of small-masters into middlemen might have begun as a "survival strategy", but its effect was to accentuate the underselling of each by the others, pushing the labour of themselves and their dependents in a downward spiral ending in prostitution or destitution.

Mayhew was writing at a time when in the new industrial towns a clear distinction between labour and capital was becoming increasingly visible.[18] But this was not the case in London or in other capital cities in mid-nineteenth-century Europe, where workshop trades, family labour and casual work were also the norm. From the mid 1840's the volume of rural-urban migrations had greatly increased, and it had been further augmented by the Irish potato famine and crises in domestic linen weaving. The Webbs contrasted the new industrial regions in which society was divided horizontally between employers and wage earners with untransformed urban structures in which society was divided vertically trade by trade. London did not fit either of these schemas. It remained an artisan economy, but one in which the influx of semi-skilled or unskilled labour had in some occupations contributed to a breakdown of pre-existing trade customs or diluted the strong economic and cultural distinctions between "honourable" and "dishonourable" trades. This was not a situation, simply to be ascribed to a process of transition. For half a century later, Booth's description of these trades in the 1890s highlighted similar problems associated with "sweating" and the oversupply of labour.

The disorganisation of important sectors of the London economy in which many artisans and small-masters were both "victims and perpetrators" of their condition was paralleled in the mid-century years by political confusion associated with the decline of radicalism From the 1830s, the radical alliance between shopkeepers, small-masters and skilled artisans had been weakened. But by 1848-9, the forces which had

---

[17] Mayhew, H. (1851) *London Labour and the London Poor*. London: Office, 16 Upper Wellington Street, Strand. Vol.2, p.313.
[18] Use of the terms 'labour' and 'capital' became standard in the 1850s.

challenged traditional radicalism were themselves in crisis. Owenite socialism after the failure of the Queenwood community had splintered and Owen himself had moved towards spiritualism. Chartism, despite the efforts of its leaders, did not recover from the fiasco of Kennington Common and was further demoralised by the failure of the democratic and social republic in France. This left little to identify with, and helps to explain why significant numbers of artisans and street sellers were prone to blame free trade for their misfortunes: a contention to which Mayhew himself was sympathetic. In Mayhew's own case, he respected the social functions of unions and showed some sympathy with the schemes of partnership between labour and capital discussed in Mill's *Principles of Political Economy.* But he kept clear of schemes of co-operation, whether of an Owenite or Christian Socialist kind, and his own attempt to establish a "Tailor's Guild" was noticeably moderate. Commentators have sometimes wondered why in Mayhew's later writings the openness to radical ideas shown in the *Chronicle* and *London Labour* series had disappeared. But Mayhew's active commitment to reforms was spasmodic and by the time he discontinued his series – as much as anything, in the face of falling sales – panic about cholera had receded, hopes of radical reform and anxiety or curiosity about the labour question had ebbed away.

In the end, historical assessments of the importance of Mayhew depend upon the credibility of his witnesses in the streets and in the workshops. Did he polish their language or shape their narratives according to standard literary or theatrical expectations? It was of course inevitable that in the process of transcribing shorthand and writing up his notes, Mayhew transformed the broken, contradictory or repetitious character of actual speech into sustained monologues and coherent prose. But, as John Seed and Caroline Steadman have in a different way argued, there is no evidence that Mayhew attempted to reframe their narratives according to melodramatic or other literary tropes. In this sense, he more than any other observer of the period reproduced the unedited interests and preoccupations of his respondents, this was an achievement almost unique in this period. Or to translate his achievement into the terminology of contemporary social theory about the tendency to edit or transform the language and yearnings of the poor and oppressed, John Seed has written: "Far from indicating the inarticulate subordination of the subaltern, *London Labour and the London Poor* is a chorus, or a cacophony, of other and disaffected voices. The subaltern did speak incessantly."[19] And this in the end is his main claim to greatness.

---

[19] Seed, J. (2014) 'Did the Subaltern Speak? Mayhew and the Coster-girl', *Journal of Victorian Culture* 19 (4): 536-549 at 548; and see also Steedman, C. (2014) 'Mayhew: On Reading, about Writing', *Journal of Victorian Culture* 19 (4): 550-562.

A.A. Milne

Philip Waller[1]

Geta
(Mr. A. A. Milne).

A. Milne needs no introduction. Since this isn't one, still less a Grand Introduction, it must be a Contradiction. So Owl pronounces at the start of *The House at Pooh Corner*;[2] and Owl is

---

[1] The author thanks Westminster's archivist Elizabeth Wells and history master Tom Edlin for their help. The illustration is of A.A. Milne as Geta in the school's Latin Play, 1899.
[2] A.A. Milne, *The House at Pooh Corner* (London: Methuen, 1928), ix.

unmistakably authoritative, being "very good at long words" and having both bell-pull and knocker outside his residence, the first directing "PLES RING IF AN RNSER IS REQIRD" and the other "PLEZ CNOKE IF RNSR IS NOT RQID".[3]

Paradox is the key to Milne and his work. It is epitomised by his finest creation Winnie-the-Pooh, now 90 years' young. In that time he quit the nursery and, having discovered the North Pole on an Expotition in the Hundred Acre Wood, only to be told that a South Pole existed too and doubtless "an East Pole and a West Pole, though people don't like talking about them",[4] he went on to traverse the world, fusing fact and fiction. One inspiration for Pooh was real enough, an orphaned female black bear cub bought for $20 (about £4) at White River, Ontario, by Harry Colebourn of the Fort Garry Horse Regt. and Canadian Army Veterinary Corps; it was Colebourn who named it Winnie after his home town Winnipeg and deposited it with London Zoo when going off to war in 1914. A decade later, among countless visitors captivated by Winnie was Milne's son Christopher Robin, whose tubby teddy Edward Bear his father had already versified.[5] Christopher Robin also liked feeding a swan by a lake; this he nicknamed Pooh "because, if you call him and he doesn't come (which is a thing swans are good at), then you can pretend that you were just saying 'Pooh!' to show how little you wanted him".[6] Comingling the two in Milne's imagination brought forth Edward Bear reborn as Winnie-the-Pooh, a short (and stout) hero of the eponymous story-book and its successor published in 1926 and 1928, which became instantaneous and persistent best-sellers. Winnie herself would die in 1934 and, her fame resplendent, a commemorative statue was unveiled at the Zoo in 1981. Winnie-the-Pooh meanwhile travelled a fair way along the career track to immortality.

For a Bear of Little Brain, frequently a Bear of Very Little Brain and occasionally a Bear of No Brain at All, Pooh is cheeringly resourceful. Faced with a flood, Pooh saves himself by paddling his biggest honey jar,

---

[3] Milne, *Winnie-the-Pooh* (London, Methuen, 1926), chap.4. The bell-pull turns out to be Eeyore's tail.
[4] *Winnie-the-Pooh*, chap.9.
[5] 'Teddy Bear', in Milne, *When We Were Very Young* (1924). The teddy, made by Farnell, was bought for Christopher Robin (1920-96) by his mother for his first birthday, from Harrod's.
[6] 'Just before we begin', in *When We Were Very Young*.

re-corked, having first risen to the challenge of eating its contents and those of nine more jars; then, alarmed that pocket-sized Piglet was "entirely surrounded by water", Pooh has an additional flash of genius to improvise a lifeboat from an upturned umbrella. Justly, he composes a modest epic, saluting his (temporary) transformation into "a Bear of Enormous Brain".[7] Among Pooh's other unsuspected gifts, manifested subsequently, has been his talent as an impressionist, articulating convincing impersonations of the voices of, among many, Willie Rushton and Stephen Fry. As a wordsmith, he has impressed those gatekeepers of the English language, the *Oxford English Dictionary*, four neologisms deriving from his books.[8] Above all, Pooh has been disclosed as a true internationalist, not so much multilingual as omnilingual, fluent in some ninety languages and dialects, from Albanian through Mongolian to Zulu. In 1960, undaunted even by the ordeal of conversing with the dead, Pooh demonstrated a mastery of Latin that saw him once more storm the best-seller charts.[9] Naturally, Pooh has attracted major scholars: Raphael Loewe, Goldsmid Professor at University College London and Honorary Fellow of St John's College Cambridge, produced a Classical Hebrew version. The oriental philosophy fraternity likewise mobilised in tribute, with a suitable decennial interval for meditation, their devotions led by Benjamin Hoff's *The Tao of Pooh* (1982) and *The Te of Piglet* (1992). Poets everywhere have paid homage, notably Boris Zakhoder (1918-2000), whose *Vinni-Pukh I vse-vse-vse* (1965) made Pooh Russia's favourite bear. Nearer home, the poet-novelist James Robertson rendered *Winnie-the-Pooh in Scots* (2008) and *The Hoose at Pooh's Neuk* (2010).[10] Amid this acclaim, it is only to be expected that Pooh should require a couple of sessions of psychoanalysis and deconstruction, administered by

---

[7] *Winnie-the Pooh*, chaps. 9-10.

[8] These are: Eeyorish, heffalump, kanga, and Pooh-sticks.

[9] Alexander Lenard's *Winnie Ille Pu* (1960) is the only Latin book to make the *New York Times* best-seller top ten. Brian Staples then Latinized *The House at Pooh Corner* as *A.A. Milnei Domus Anguli Puensis* (London: Methuen, 1980).

[10] Both published in Edinburgh by Itchy Coo, in which Piglet appears as Wee Grumphie and Eeyore as Heehaw.

those specialists in mumbo-jumbo, literary theorists. Frederick C. Crews twice devised foolometers by which to measure their delusions.[11]

It is chiefly as a film star that Pooh now straddles the globe. Fyodor Khitruk animated him three times in the USSR from 1969, in a style superior, according to connoisseurs, to the Disney twenty-six-minutes' cartoon of 1966. Not only connoisseurs bristled at Disney's displacement of Piglet by a gopher, done to give the cast a folksy touch thought more appealing to American audiences. Outraged Piglet fans pointed to his proud pedigree. His grandfather sported two names – "in case he lost one". This was evidenced by the board outside Piglet's beech-tree home, unfortunately broken but with "TRESPASSERS W" still visible, that being "short for Trespassers Will, which was short for Trespassers William".[12] Notwithstanding his distinction, Piglet has suffered many a ban elsewhere than in America, apparently because he is comprised of pork; but Disney restored him in three feature-length animated films, beginning in 1977. Twenty years later, Pooh officially overtook Mickey Mouse as Disney's most popular character, although with the release of *The Tigger Movie* (2000) these interpretations had long departed from the stories, merely being, as the formula has it, "based on the 'Winnie-the-Pooh' works". To the distress of admirers of E.H. Shepard, [13] whose "decorations" garlanded the books, the Disney image hereafter dominated; yet it is not inevitable that Milne himself would have been hostile.[14]

---

[11] Frederick C. Crews, *The Pooh Perplex: A Freshman Casebook* (New York: Dutton, 1963), and *Postmodern Pooh* (New York: North Point, 2001). Crews is Emeritus Professor in English at Berkeley.

[12] *Winnie-the-Pooh*, chap.3.

[13] "Decorations by E.H. Shepard" features on the title page of *The House at Pooh Corner*. Shepard (1879-1976) was born not far from Milne in north London; they first met as colleagues at *Punch*. Their inaugural collaboration was on *When We Were Very Young*. Pooh was drawn from Shepard's own son's Steiff teddy, Growler, the other characters from toys in Christopher Robin's nursery. Eeyore's stoop is explained by a damaged neck. Shepard is equally loved for illustrating the 1931 edition of Kenneth Grahame's *The Wind in the Willows* (1908), which Milne dramatized as *Toad of Toad Hall* (1929).

[14] Ann Thwaite, *A.A. Milne: His Life* (London: Faber, 1990), 212, quotes Milne writing to Grahame's widow in 1938, when Disney was reportedly interested in *Toad of Toad Hall*: "It is just the thing for him, of course, and he would do it beautifully." Thwaite, whose biography is indispensable for understanding Milne,

There had been merchandising associated with the Pooh characters since 1930, when Milne sold the non-book rights to a New York literary agent Stephen Slesinger. Such exploitation was no new phenomenon. As youngsters, Milne and his brothers had been kitted out in Little Lord Fauntleroy gear, after the fashion of Mrs Hodgson Burnett's best-seller.[15] Had the Milne boys been girls, the Kate Greenaway industry would have targeted them. The most aggressive model for Pooh as entrepreneur was Beatrix Potter. Having patented and licensed a multitude of spin-off manufactures, she reported with satisfaction in 1917, "all rabbits *are* called Peter now", before qualifying it: "either Peter or Brer Rabbit".[16] Her allusion to a different American market was apt. Disney added muscle to Pooh's sales pitch following a contract in 1961 with Slesinger's widow, whereupon Potter enterprises became a cottage industry by comparison. From the 1990s a series of lawsuits ensued over the division of spoils between Disney and the Slesingers, unsurprisingly when Merrill Lynch in 2000 valued Pooh products at $6 billion annually, double his worth in 1995 and accounting for about one-fifth of Disney's revenue. The Pooh output is practically infinite in variety: there are not just the videos and stuffed, wooden and plastic toys, but towels and duvet covers, clothes and confectionery, greetings cards, maps, jigsaws and board games, garden statuary, bookends, fridge magnets, friezes and wallpaper, nursery china, pencil cases and school satchels, lunch boxes, picnic boxes and all. Nor have Milne's literary agent Curtis Brown, and publishers Methuen in Britain and Dutton in the USA, been shy about vivisecting and repackaging Pooh. All manner of imprint from miniature to giant, and de luxe and box sets, were just a beginning, for there are baby and buggy books, birthday and party books, diaries and annuals, sticker, painting, drawing, colouring and chalkboard books, sparkly, tickle, pop-up, peek-through, lift-the-flap, and touch-and-feel books, alphabet and counting books, cookbooks (*Pooh's tasty smackerels*) and exercise books (*Pooh's little fitness book*), to go alongside teatime and coffee companion books, not forgetting *Winnie-the-Pooh's trivia quiz book* (1996) and *Winnie-the-Pooh's little book about weather* (1997). The romantic and thinking man's

---

otherwise shows him contemptuous of cinema-goers and of much cinema fare, although a tenacious negotiator concerning film rights.

[15] Photo in Thwaite, *Milne*, opp. 204.

[16] Philip Waller, *Writers, Readers, and Reputations: Literary Life in Britain 1870-1918* (Oxford: University Press, 2006; 2008), 343.

and woman's Pooh is catered for by *Positively Pooh: a book for your inner bear* (2005) and *Positively Pooh: timeless wisdom from Pooh* (2007).Pooh has also been orchestrated, with song books for soloists and choirs and music for pianos, recorders, and other instruments. Finally, there is a chess set, featuring Tigger as rook, Owl as bishop, Eeyore as knight, and the hapless Piglet as pawn. Pooh and Kanga are King and Queen, a marital union beyond imagining or satire.

A.A. Milne requires no introduction, but Alan Alexander Milne does. Known by his first name, Milne was born on January 18th 1882; still, as Eeyore devastatingly remarks, "after all, what *are* birthdays? Here to-day and gone tomorrow."[17] Alan was the youngest of three children – all boys – of John Vine Milne and his wife Maria who ran a private school in Kilburn. Since demolished, Henley House acquired retrospective fame from a pupil and a teacher. The pupil was Alfred Harmsworth, who left the school two years before Milne was born. He started the school magazine, finished as Viscount Northcliffe, and between times founded the *Daily Mail*. Milne hailed that achievement: "Harmsworth killed the penny dreadful by the simple process of producing a ha'penny dreadfuller."[18] The teacher was H.G. Wells, about whom Milne was considerably warmer: Wells "taught me all the botany I never learnt".[19] It was Wells who took Milne and other boys to London Zoo, and added to the school's sunny atmosphere that generally radiated from Milne's parents, particularly his father, "the best man I have ever known...He differed from our conception of God only because he was shy, which one imagined God not to be, and was funny, which one knew God was not."[20] The school, however, was financially parlous and as an educational institution feeble, no more than "a sketch of good intentions".[21]

---

[17] Milne, *Pooh Corner*, chap. 2. On the list of National Awareness Days, January 18th is designated Winnie-the-Pooh Day. He thus trumps the philosopher Montesquieu and everyone else born on that day.

[18] Reginald Pound and Geoffrey Harmsworth, *Northcliffe* (London: Cassell, 1959), 116.

[19] Milne, *It's Too Late Now. The Autobiography of a Writer* (London: Methuen, 1939), 50. The American edition appeared as *Autobiography* (New York: Dutton, 1939).

[20] Milne, *Too Late*, 25.

[21] H.G. Wells, *Experiment in Autobiography* (London: Cape, 1934; 1969), vol.1, 322.

Milne started life on the precarious lower rungs of the middle class. His father was born in Jamaica, one of ten offspring of a Scots Congregationalist missionary who never earned more than £80 p.a.[22] This origin and Jamaican cousins made the family "a little suspect" in social class terms, Milne mused, noting that back then "there was something called Society, into which (unless you were born there) it was almost impossible to enter; and if you were outside it, as I was, you read about it in the society papers with awe or indifference or an assumed contempt". Later, codes relaxed, to Milne's benefit, though he never cared for it, writing in 1939 that "a study of the society papers shows that there is no barrier through which the sports car of the gigolo has not crashed, no frontier over which the passport of the interior decorator... will not take him."[23] Milne's mother also came from a big family and Nonconformist background, from Derbyshire, with the downright surname Heginbotham and little else to fall back on. Fully engaged in their school, the Milnes in many respects lived well. Their boys had a governess and enjoyed improvident treats, such as bicycles with new-fangled pneumatic tyres, and holidays to Ashdown Forest in Sussex, that "enchanted place", the Hundred Acre Wood; but it was made crystal clear that if they were to progress to public school and university, this would be by the scholarship route and not by parental means. Hence the desirability of BRAINS. This appears as a comedic refrain throughout the Pooh sagas. "You and I have brains. The others have fluff," Rabbit remarks to Owl, the particular joke here being that shallow learning and a superior air combine to create a brace of bores.[24] Pooh has Rabbit's measure:

"'Rabbit's clever", said Pooh thoughtfully. "Yes", said Piglet, "Rabbit's clever." "And he has Brain." "Yes", said Piglet, "Rabbit has Brain." There was a long silence. "I suppose", said Pooh, "that that's why he never understands anything."'[25]

---

[22]*The Congregational Year Book, 1873* (London: Hodder & Stoughton, 1873), 302, where James Milne was listed among "European Missionaries in Heathen Lands in connection with the London Missionary Society", stationed at First Hill, Jamaica, since 1840.
[23] Milne, *Too Late*, 40, 262.
[24] Id., *Pooh Corner*, chap. 5.
[25] *Ibid.*, chap. 8.

Milne knew that different qualities matter in people; nevertheless, he was deadly serious about the importance of brains and not without self-conceit that he possessed them. His own cleverness was precociously expressed in mathematics; and when the crossword fad spread in the inter-war, Milne proved a crack hand. Arithmetical jokes abound among Pooh's circle; again, such aptitude is ostensibly downplayed. Christopher Robin fails to teach Pooh the "Twy-stymes" table, and takes comfort from having Piglet with him when he himself is "not quite sure whether twice seven is twelve or twenty-two".[26] It was Milne's mathematical ability that bagged him a Queen's Scholarship to Westminster in 1893, following his older brother Ken, whom he generally outshone,[27] in 1892.

Milne's attitude to Westminster also contains contradictions, some stemming from selective memory. About the food he was emphatic: it was abominable, beginning with breakfast. This was a dispiriting repast of inedible bread and unsalted butter, served with undrinkable tea topped by a scum of boiled milk, in contrast to the uplift Pooh would gain from contemplating his breakfast – "a simple meal of marmalade spread lightly over a honeycomb or two".[28] Westminster's peculiar slang and conventions offended the rationalist in Milne. Among the most bizarre was that juniors were forbidden to think; that is, not allowed to preface an observation by "I think". That's why he sent Christopher Robin to Stowe, a new foundation of 1923 which under J.F. Roxburgh's headship did away with that kind of daftness, along with fagging; yet he financially supported Ken's two sons through Westminster. The Head Master during Milne's time, Rev. William Gunion Rutherford,[29] agreed about the ridiculousness of school customs, with a caveat: "Nine-tenths of the Tradition may be rubbish, but the remaining tenth is priceless, and no one who tries to

---

[26] *Ibid.*, chap. 7; and *Winnie-the-Pooh*, Introduction.

[27] Milne was always conscious of Ken's good-natured forbearance and of how much he learned from Ken, who was just sixteen months older. Distressed by his early death, Milne dedicated his autobiography: "To the memory of Kenneth John Milne who bore the worst of me and made the best of me."

[28] Milne, *Winnie-the-Pooh*, chaps. 8 and 10.

[29] On Rutherford (1853-1907), Head Master 1883-1901, notice by John Sargeaunt, *rev.* Richard Smail, *Oxford Dictionary of National Biography* (*ODNB*).

dispense with it can hope to do anything that is good."[30] Thus, while Rutherford ruffled feathers, he was only a half-reformer. His towering passion was for Greek, beside which both divinity and Latin shrank. When moved, he could deliver a fine line in exasperation, boomed in broad Scots: "I thought people were *born* knowing the date of the battle of Leuktra!"[31] Rutherford did deviate from the model of heroic Head Master in one significant respect. He was not an intemperate flogger, unlike Westminster's own Richard Busby in another age and Wellington's first Head Master E.W. Benson, later Archbishop of Canterbury. At Westminster it was the prefects – the school Captain and monitors – who dished out a "tanning". Ultimately a monitor himself, Milne looked back on these thrashings with a shudder, blaming "not the actual pain but the perpetual fear of it" for dimming pupils' "enthusiasm for life."[32] Milne's own father never caned him. He kept a birch in his office as a headmaster's symbol, but was remembered more for not using it.

Rutherford did more damage to Milne by a dismal report at the end of his first year, fired off before Milne's exam result, in which he came top in maths, was known. This injustice, he would claim, dashed his dream of one day becoming Senior Wrangler; yet Westminster was not geared up for maths or indeed much else apart from the classics. "With the English language we never had any official dealings", Milne witheringly recalled.[33] No essay was demanded from him throughout his time at the school; nevertheless, he utilised the hour 5.15 to 6.15, allocated for "Occupations", to browse in the library. Another enjoyment was sport, although again Westminster did not shine in this department, with singular exceptions such as Leonard Moon,[34] who played cricket for Cambridge and England. Conditions were primitive, with an absence of baths and hot water. Still, as Milne remarked charitably, if mistakenly, it was enough

---

[30] Christopher Hassall, *Edward Marsh: Patron of the Arts. A Biography* (London: Longmans, 1959), 17. Marsh (1872-1953) preceded Milne at both Westminster and Trinity College Cambridge.

[31] Hassall, *Marsh*, 17.

[32] Milne, *Too Late*, 99-100.

[33] *Ibid.*, 103.

[34] Leonard Moon (1878-1916), a Lieutenant with the Devonshires, died at Salonika. His brother Billy (1868-1943) became England's youngest national goalkeeper in 1888. Oddly, Milne's son Christopher Robin enjoyed being called Billy Moon, 'Moon' from his mispronunciation of 'Milne'.

that Wren designed College: "One cannot have everything; probably there are no baths in St Paul's Cathedral."[35] Milne too played cricket, and as a modest-performing all-rounder was awarded colours ("Pinks") in his final year. He was also a footballer, his debut coming in a match lost 1-3 to Old Brightonians. Scoring Westminster's solitary goal brought damnation by faint praise from the school magazine – "Milne made a fairly successful first appearance, but he plays in lazy fashion, and requires much more dash and energy."[36] Cricket remained an enthusiasm, with age supplanted by golf, in which he came to have a single-figure handicap. Football he kept up for several years, even turning out for Westminster Old Boys after joining *Punch*; but professional football was among his aversions, along with blood sports and all forms of gambling. It was at Westminster also that he developed a repugnance to smut and lavatory humour.

Whatever Milne's reservations about Westminster, he retained enough fond feelings to include it, apart from his family, as a beneficiary of his estate, together with the Garrick Club and Royal Literary Fund.[37] A new day house at 5A Dean's Yard was named Milne's in 1997, in recognition of his generosity.[38] Milne's mathematics had remained sufficiently plausible even after seven years at Westminster to pitchfork him into Trinity College, Cambridge, in 1900. He failed to win an open scholarship, but Westminster had closed scholarships there and Milne was awarded one, worth £40 p.a., supplemented by an exhibition bringing in another £23. It was at Cambridge that his maths, if it didn't altogether beat a retreat, then scarcely advanced. He fetched up with a Third in 1903.

---

[35] Milne, *Too Late*, 100.

[36] *The Elizabethan*, March 1899, 131-2.

[37] Milne joined the Garrick in 1919. His first club was the National Liberal, proposed by H.G. Wells and the Ibsenite drama critic William Archer in 1903-4, for utilitarian purposes, as a free-lancer to meet editors. Later, he belonged to the Athenaeum, Beefsteak, and Savile, but the Garrick was favourite and he remained a Tuesday regular for lunch even after buying Cotchford Farm, near Hartfield, Sussex, in 1924. As for the Royal Literary Fund, begun in 1790 to aid impecunious authors, income from Milne's bequest financed its Fellowship Scheme in 1999, placing writers in universities and colleges to encourage others' writing skills.

[38] As well as two nephews at Westminster, Milne had a third family connection: Ken's eldest child Marjorie, born in 1906 and an inspiration for Milne's story-telling before Christopher Robin, became Bursar's Secretary. She married T.M. Murray-Rust, maths master (1926-48) and Grant's Housemaster (1935-48).

Playing games most afternoons hardly helped, but the chief culprit was the undergraduate magazine *Granta*. He and Ken had collaborated in composing light verses over Christmas in 1899, and Milne's first publication in *Granta* was a joint effort. Ken would withdraw from the partnership, but the writing itch never left Milne. He acquired the professional writer's prop, a pipe; he also peppered *Granta* with contributions before becoming editor in Lent 1902. Being at Trinity was no disadvantage, because *Granta* was almost a house magazine. Milne's predecessor, who nominated him, was at Trinity, likemost editors since its foundation by Rudie Lehmann in 1889.[39] Lehmann was one of those versatile types – oarsman, Cambridge Union President, pugilist, politician, and parodist for *Punch*[40] – and it was he who encouraged Milne to start sending his confections to *Punch*.

However useful Milne found such connections then and later, he made his own luck by being an outstandingly gifted writer. He was naturally funny, though the 'natural' bit rather annoyed him when people supposed the stuff just flowed from him without effort. He certainly tried miraculous conception – "I have even gone to sleep in the afternoon, in case inspiration cared to take me completely by surprise"; but, no, "the only way I can get an 'idea' is to sit at my desk and dredge for it", by putting in a shift like anyone else.[41] Milne was also irritated by critics' propensity to caption a new writer as a second X or Y – in his case, a second Lewis Carroll or J.M. Barrie – instead of acknowledging the original A.A. Milne. With Barrie he would share the curse of being styled "whimsical", an epithet first attached to him in 1910, as if all his work was lightweight and without serious purpose or prospect of permanence. The year 1910, by coincidence, was when he sent *The Day's Play* (a collection of his *Punch* pieces) to Barrie, who invited him to lunch and to join his cricket team of celebrity authors, the Allahakbarries.[42] Milne

---

[39] Up to 1914 Trinity contributed 31 editors of *Granta*; the next most was Clare, with four. Thwaite, *Milne*, 90.

[40] On Lehmann (1856-1929), Eric Halladay's notice, *ODNB*.

[41] Milne, *Too Late*, 253-4. Pooh's muse was of the other kind: "Poetry and Hums aren't things which you get, they're things which get *you*. And all you can do is go where they find you." *Pooh Corner*, 144.

[42] Milne, *Too Late*, 197-8, 203-4. Sometime members of the Allahakbarries included Conan Doyle, Jerome K. Jerome, P.G. Wodehouse, and Milne's *Punch*

admired Barrie; he also had ambitions as a playwright; but he did not imitate him. Milne was his own man.

This is to get ahead of ourselves; still, Milne's Cambridge period need not detain us longer. Here the current writer, being from Oxford, must respect Milne's dictum: "What distinguishes Cambridge from Oxford, broadly speaking, is that nobody who has been to Cambridge feels impelled to write about it."[43] Milne's parents, like others of the aspiring sort, harboured hopes of their boys entering the professions, secure, salaried, and pensionable, ideally Whitehall where with a clean nose and the right manner a senior civil servant might eventually merit a gong. Both Milne's brothers were articled to a solicitor, a family friend in Weymouth, and after qualifying Ken joined the Estate Duty Office in 1904, transferred to the Ministry of Pensions in 1917, and rose to Assistant Secretary with a CBE in 1920.[44] Milne half-heartedly obliged by attending the civil service crammer Wren's, after leaving Cambridge; but, seized by the writing bug, he joined the republic of letters instead. The Milne family finances had much improved meanwhile. After Henley House, his father established another school at Streete Court, Westgate-on-Sea, in 1894.[45] So successful was it, he settled £1,000 on each of his sons. Milne used this to cushion himself at Cambridge. It buttressed him again during his struggling period as a freelancer until, at the end of 1904, he had £20 left and moved into cheaper lodgings. All the while, his submissions appeared in a variety of papers and periodicals. *Vanity Fair* published his first, a spoof of the return of Sherlock Holmes, at the conclusion of which Watson asks about Moriarty: "'There was no such man', said Holmes. 'It was merely the name of a soup.'"[46]

---

colleagues: the editor Owen Seaman, chief cartoonist Bernard Partridge, and staff writer E.V. Lucas, who became chairman of Milne's principal publisher Methuen.
[43] Milne, *Too Late*, 131.
[44]*Who Was Who*, for Kenneth John Milne (1880-1929): he retired in 1924, afflicted by tuberculosis.
[45] Among his pupils was St John Philby, the traitor Kim Philby's father. Both went on to Westminster and Trinity College Cambridge. Milne's nephew Ian Innes ("Tim") Milne (1912-2010), at Westminster with Kim Philby, was recruited by him into MI6: see his onetime suppressed memoir, *Kim Philby: The Unknown Story of the KGB's Master Spy* (London: Biteback, 2014).
[46] Milne, *Too Late*, 160.

The *Granta* editorship gave Milne confidence and contacts, and at the age of 24 he had made it, becoming assistant editor of *Punch* at £500 p.a. This was shortly raised to £550; by 1913, including freelance sums, he was clearing £1,000. When income tax was 1s. 2d. (5.8%) in the pound, levied above £160, this was a tidy sum. It placed Milne in the comfortably solid middle class, a position which he armour-plated by marrying the goddaughter of his boss Owen Seaman. This was Dorothy (known as Daphne or Daffy) de Sélincourt, who came complete with personal maid and private income; her father, a mantle manufacturer, became chairman of the swanky department store Swan & Edgar. There was also a cerebral side to the Sélincourts, an uncle who became Professor of Poetry at Oxford and an aunt Principal of Westfield College London. Best man at the Milnes' wedding was a contemporary at Westminster and Trinity, Roland Kitson, afterwards Lord Airedale.[47] Moreover, the beauty of being a writer was that Milne could distribute his own honours. Thus, at the last, Sir Pooh de Bear arises, having earlier been dubbed "F.O.P. (Friend of Piglet's), R.C. (Rabbit's Companion), P.D. (Pole Discoverer), E.C. and T.F. (Eeyore's Comforter and Tail-finder)."[48]

Milne spent his first nineteen years a Victorian. He even met Gladstone, although that term is used loosely. Milne attended Gladstone's funeral at Westminster Abbey in 1898, exiting behind the supreme thespian Sir Henry Irving. In 1922, J.M. Barrie recommended to the young, "Don't forget to speak scornfully of the Victorian age"; he then added, "there will be time for meekness when you try to better it."[49] The Victorians contained many an awkward squad, and that was the party to which Milne naturally gravitated. He pretended that he left Westminster "the conventional public-school boy", with conventional views on everything from religion and politics to love of games and "good form";[50] but that was not strictly true. In his final year, as treasurer of the Debating

---

[47] Roland Dudley Kitson (1882-1958) succeeded his half-brother as 3rd Baron Airedale in 1944. He won the DSO and MC with the West Yorks., and was a director of the Bank of England, 1923-47.

[48] Milne, *Pooh Corner*, chap. 10, and *Winnie-the-Pooh*, chap. 9. Note, by contrast, "O.B.E.", Milne's tart poem about those who prospered from the war, in *The Sunny Side* (London: Methuen, 1921).

[49] J.M. Barrie, *Courage* (London: Hodder & Stoughton, 1922), 41. This was his Rector's address at St Andrews.

[50] Milne, *Too Late*, 127.

Society, he argued for "the State to take control of all railways".[51] While his father separated from Gladstone over Irish Home Rule – "ratted", Milne called it – and became a Liberal Unionist, Milne when he reached maturity was a stalwart Liberal, or "unpatriotic Radical" according to his crusty Conservative editor Owen Seaman, who was knighted in 1914.[52] He canvassed for the Liberals in the "Peers versus People" General Election of December 1910 and, though increasingly disillusioned, he remained a dedicated democrat throughout his life. This explains his decision in 1945, the first time he voted Conservative. For Milne, the Liberal party being practically defunct, this constituted the strongest voice against totalitarianism, Communism to his mind having replaced Nazism as the principal enemy of liberty. In the inter-war, his disdain was unbridled for ministers such as Joynson-Hicks, the narrow-minded zealot who was Home Secretary in the Baldwin cabinet, and his colleague at the Admiralty Lord Bridgeman, "an utterly uninspired, unimaginative, rather bewildered mediocre little man" who was paid £5,000 a year for being "red in the face saying 'Yes. Yes' and signing something".[53] Mussolini drew multifarious admirers, from Lord Londonderry, the ultra-Tory Air Minister ("that half-wit" was his cousin Winston Churchill's verdict)[54] to Hugh MacDiarmid, the vituperative Anglophobe poet and proto-Scots Nationalist; but Milne was not one. "Oh, do you like murderers?" he politely asked a fellow golfer who was fulminating against the government and demanding a British Mussolini.[55]

Above all, Milne's radicalism was expressed in his anti-war philosophy. It was A.J.P. Taylor who, having traced a dissentient British foreign policy tradition, denominated its adherents "the trouble makers". Taylor also contrived to distinguish between "pacifism" and "pacificism", a distinction later elaborated by Martin Ceadel: pacifism is "the belief that war is *always wrong* and should not be resorted to, whatever the consequences of abstaining from fighting", and pacificism "the assumption that war, though *sometimes necessary*, is always an irrational and inhumane way to solve disputes, and that its prevention should always

---

[51]*The Elizabethan*, Oct. 1899, 180.

[52] Milne, *Too Late*, 163, 193.

[53] Milne to his brother Ken, 1926, in Thwaite, *Milne*, 315.

[54] Ian Kershaw, *Making Friends with Hitler: Lord Londonderry, the Nazis and the Road to World War II* (New York: Penguin, 2004), 96.

[55] Thwaite, *Milne*, 273.

be an overriding political priority".[56] Being rather messier than academics would prefer, people commonly resist neat categorisation. Anti-militarism was widespread before 1914, and Milne himself oscillated between pacifism and pacificism.[57] Of three types of pacifist inspiration advanced by Ceadel – religious, political, and humanitarian – the first scarcely registered with Milne. His father was a Presbyterian elder, and Milne was brought up a Nonconformist. This he delighted in asserting at Westminster, by refusing to turn east and bow for the recital of the Creed.[58] Thereafter he lapsed into agnosticism and enjoyed playing the iconoclast, after the manner of Samuel Butler's *The Way of All Flesh* (1903), which he proclaimed "the best novel in the English language".[59] He took pot shots at prelates, such as the Bishop of Gloucester who moaned to *The Times* aboard a Cunarder in 1924 that he could no longer afford three gardeners; and the irony did not escape him that in wartime "all the nations are praying to the same God."[60] He set out his position in a pamphlet *The Ascent of Man* (1928) and in verse *The Norman Church* (1948). Christopher Robin was not christened.

Milne's pacifism stemmed from rationalism, not religion. His enlightenment conversion came from reading Norman Angell's *The Great Illusion* (1910), which substituted realism for sentiment in the pacifist armoury by arguing that modern States' economic and financial interdependence made war ruinous for all, therefore fatuous.[61] When war came in 1914, Milne was a married man of thirty-two. No compulsory military service obtained until 1916, but Milne did not abstain. It became a commonplace to think of that conflict as "The War That Will End War"[62], yet for Milne that was precisely his hope. His own war was slight.

---

[56] A.J.P. Taylor, *The Trouble Makers: Dissent over Foreign Policy, 1792-1939* (London: Hamish Hamilton, 1957), 51; Martin Ceadel, *Pacifism in Britain 1914-1945: The Defining of a Faith* (Oxford: Clarendon Press, 1980), 3.

[57] Milne was aware of the terminology. In the preface to *Peace with Honour* (1934), he noted: "Purists, I'm told, write of 'Pacificists' and 'Pacificism'." Milne himself generally used "pacifists" and "pacifism".

[58] Milne, *Too Late*, 26, 97.

[59] Thwaite, *Milne*, 78.

[60] *Ibid.*, 168, 258.

[61] Ceadel, *Living the Great Illusion: Sir Norman Angell, 1872-1967* (Oxford: University Press, 2009).

[62] H.G. Wells, *The War That Will End War* (London: Frank & Cecil Palmer, 1914).

A signalling officer with the Warwickshires, he contracted fever on the Somme and recuperated on the Isle of Wight, where he penned plays before providing propaganda ("horrible word") for War Office Intelligence. He knew how fortunate he was: 20% of Westminster's 224 war dead were his school contemporaries. He wrote: "it makes me almost physically sick to think of that nightmare of mental and moral degradation, the war... It seems impossible to me now that any sensitive man could live through another war."[63] With cruel mistiming, this was in 1939.

Punch paid him half-salary for three years of the Great War, but he resigned at war's end to lay siege to the theatre. He won immense fame, although his plays were more lucrative than lasting. His biggest hit was *Mr Pim Passes By* (1921). In 1922 he was making from £200 to £500 *per week*; in 1924, £2,000 from amateur rights alone. His only play now routinely staged is *Toad of Toad Hall* (1929), his adaptation of Kenneth Grahame's *The Wind in the Willows* (1908).[64] Milne tried his hand at detective fiction, *The Red House Mystery* (1922), which still has readers; but all was eclipsed by his children's poems, *When We Were Very Young* (1924) and *Now We Are Six* (1927), and by the double dose of Pooh. Yet, in the 1930s his prominence as a pacifist soared. He publicly endorsed the Oxford Union declaration, "That this House will in no circumstances fight for its King and Country"; in the same year 1933, he began writing *Peace with Honour* (1934). Its subtitle was *An Enquiry into the War Convention*, by which he meant the readiness of modern States to use war as a tool of foreign policy, a habit he decried as a "medieval".[65] The book was a powerful, widely-selling polemic. Published on 27 September 1934, it entered a third printing in November, and the 4th edition contained an Appendix, in which Milne addressed his critics. He was a sought-after speaker, but shyness precluded him becoming a platform star. The crux of his thesis was this: "It is often said that Germany prepares for war while paying lip-service to peace. The truth may be that she prepares for peace while paying lip-service to war."[66] He was wrong, and his recantation came in a pamphlet, *War with Honour* (1940). "I am still a Pacifist", he

---

[63] Milne, *Too Late*, 211.

[64] Thwaite, *Milne*, 194, 222.

[65] Milne, *Peace with Honour. An Enquiry into the War Convention* (London: Methuen, 1934; 4th ed., 1935), 137.

[66] *Ibid.*, 144.

wrote, "but I hope a practical Pacifist". Hitler he execrated as "the enemy of humanity", Nazi rule as "the foulest abomination with which mankind has ever been faced". Only force could crush them: "Victory for Britain is a victory for democracy over autocracy. There is no hope for the Cause except through democracy".[67] It was a brave attempt to salvage something from the wreck.

Pooh's world is non-violent: a burst balloon, that's all. We should not gloss over Milne's disappointments. The painful premature death of his brother Ken was not compensated by closeness to his older brother Barry; in fact, estrangement deepened after Milne suspected Barry of manipulating their father's will. Between Milne and his wife a distance developed. They stayed together, but it was a separate bedrooms sort of marriage. Daphne prescribed for herself extensive retail therapy, shopping in Manhattan. Worse, Christopher Robin found unbearable the weight of fame and popular image arising from Milne's children's poetry ("Vespers", especially) and Pooh books. Milne regretted his own typecasting by critics. He was more than a children's author, but the legend stuck. Still, he was proud of Pooh, and it is with his benign philosophy that this account can properly close. It's the scene on the bridge where, after playing Pooh-sticks, the friends are in reflective mood:

'For a long time they looked at the river beneath them, saying nothing, and the river said nothing too, for it felt very quiet and peaceful on this summer afternoon.
"Tigger is all right, *really*," said Piglet lazily.
"Of course he is," said Christopher Robin.
"Everybody is *really*," said Pooh. "That's what *I* think," said Pooh. "But I don't suppose I'm right," he said.
"Of course you are," said Christopher Robin.'[68]

---

[67] Milne, *War with Honour* (London: Macmillan, 1940), 17, 25, 28, 31. To elicit American entry into the war, it appeared in book form, together with essays by A.P. Herbert, E.M. Forster, Austin Duncan-Jones, C.E.M. Joad, Ronald Knox, J.R. Clynes, and Harold Laski: *England Speaks. A Symposium* (New York: Macmillan, 1941).

[68] Milne, *Pooh Corner*, chap. 6. Milne may have been astonished, and not a little pleased, to find that the Archbishop of Canterbury telling his successor Justin Welby, "There is almost no situation on earth which cannot be explained with the hermeneutical tool of Winne the Pooh." *The Times*, 15 Oct. 2015

John Spedan Lewis

Peter Cox

In May 1909 the young John Spedan Lewis had an enviable commute. Each morning he would saddle up at the family home in Hampstead, ride down through the Heath and Regent's Park to stables in Weymouth Mews, and walk the last few hundred yards to the family shop in Oxford Street. When his father John Lewis first rented it in 1864 and started selling silks it had a narrow single frontage, and he had scraped the plaster off the walls to increase its sales area. Painstakingly he had acquired all the nearby shops over the next thirty years and rebuilt them as a substantial department store. In 1909 Oxford Street wasn't the major shopping destination it is today, but a few weeks earlier the flamboyant American, Gordon Selfridge, had opened his astonishing new store at the far end of the street, shaking up the staid old world of traditional London shopping, of which John Lewis was an exemplar.

On this particular May morning in 1909, however, Spedan's horse shied in Regent's Park and threw him. He was severely winded, but ignored the increasing pain and worked on for a couple of days. A rib had penetrated a lung, his condition rapidly deteriorated, and he collapsed with pleurisy and empyema, which is as unpleasant as it sounds: its main symptom is extreme chest pain, especially when breathing in. His condition needed a novel and dangerous operation, followed by another in the late summer of 1910. The protracted illness meant that he spent much of the next three years shuttling between spells in the business and recuperation on the coast and the continent. That gave him the time to think, and the topic he increasingly dwelt on was how to improve his father's business. Spedan's conclusions eventually led to what he called his experiment in industrial democracy. He created something entirely unique and, after many vicissitudes, including a devastating bombing in 1940, it was ultimately an enormous success.

His father, John Lewis, had come a long way from the ailing country town of Shepton Mallet, where he'd been born in 1836, at a time when Somerset's wool-based prosperity had leached away, taken over by the cheaper steam-driven mills in the north. One of the few expansion areas was the workhouse, where John Lewis's widower father, a baker who suffered from epilepsy, died in 1843. Along with his five sisters John was now an orphan, brought up by an aunt, a former milliner, and all were apprenticed to drapers in various Somerset market towns. John escaped to the city as soon as he could, going at first to Liverpool, where he was sacked after a year for bloodying the nose of a fellow assistant, a pugilistic instinct which he would later take enthusiastically to the courts. With just a borrowed sovereign he came to London, where his commercial shrewdness and industry brought him to the attention of Peter Robinson, whose extensive drapery emporium was in Oxford Street. He was soon

Robinson's silk buyer, but in 1864, keen to be his own master, he bought a little shop on the other side of the new station at Oxford Circus.

Twenty years later, apparently a confirmed bachelor, he found himself on the open top deck of an Oxford Street omnibus next to Eliza Baker, a girls' school deputy head from Bedford who had met him in passing four years before in the company of her brother, a Bristol draper. He hadn't taken much notice of her then, and she needed to remind him who she was, but within weeks they were married – Lewis was nothing if not decisive, and they were both getting on. He was forty-eight and had left school at fourteen. Eliza had just turned thirty, one of the first intake at Girton College, Cambridge, and by then marriage was not on her horizon. On the face of it, and indeed temperamentally, they had little in common, but she too had been orphaned at a young age by the death of her father, recently bankrupt. Within three years of their marriage Eliza duly delivered an heir and a spare: Spedan and Oswald, born in 1885 and 1887.

It was soon clear that Spedan was precociously clever, and perhaps his mother's early teaching had left him streets ahead of the other boys, because he was sent home from his first school as a result of being "scandalously idle and insolent". Doubtless he was bored and unchallenged, but the Head Master at his second school kept him up to the mark, so that in 1899 he won a Queen's Scholarship to Westminster at the age of fourteen but 'did not board' becoming a member of Grant's House; Oswald followed in 1901. Spedan later recounted that he had been inclined to laziness, doing only what was essential, but said that the Master of the Sixth, the brilliant John Sargeaunt, had told the Head Master that Spedan would make a revolution in whatever he went into. Sargeaunt was a polymath who "taught by digression", and was perhaps a role model for the boy, who took a vigorous part in school debates. On one occasion Spedan successfully opposed a motion to restrict immigration. On another he echoed his father's criticism of a system which allowed a landlord to profit by increasing the rent on a property which the tenant had improved at his own expense. That was in 1903, the year his father spent three weeks in Brixton prison for contempt of court, at one stage of an acrimonious twenty-year battle for exactly that reason with his own landlord.

What next for Spedan after Westminster? Oxford beckoned, and his father was happy for him to go to university and then enter a profession, but Eliza was uneasy about the strain the business was imposing on her husband, and wanted Spedan to help out in the firm. When he left school his father was approaching seventy, often in poor health, and had been talking of getting a business partner or becoming a public company. Eliza wanted her sons in the business to discourage him from any rash decision. Spedan had no objection to foregoing a university career and joined the business in 1904, with Oswald following suit a year later. Spedan subsequently said that he would never had done so had he realised his father would live into his nineties, still gripping the reins of the Oxford Street business tightly well into the mid-1920s. Courted at one time by the Liberal whips, Spedan considered entering politics, because increasingly he found working for his father extremely trying. "The perversity of some of his notions and the arbitrariness of his temper made the strain of working with him considerable."

But he became intrigued by retailing and stuck at it, and both brothers continued working in the Oxford Street business. On their 21st birthdays in 1906 and 1908 John gave them each a quarter share, but was not keen to share responsibility for major decisions, and father and sons began increasingly to fall out. Spedan admired his father's fundamental shopkeeping tenets – keen and fair prices, excellent customer service, a wide assortment of stock, and complete honesty in trading – but lamented that the shop was not living up to these ideals. For example, John had devised a meticulous system for dating merchandise as it arrived, to ensure that old stock was cleared out quickly, but the scheme was poorly administered:

> I actually found a vest for a very small baby that had been bought in the year before I was born. At home we regarded my father as a superman, virtually infallible in matters of business. I had not expected … to find that it was in fact no more than a second-rate success achieved in a first-rate opportunity.

From the outset Spedan wanted to know about everything, and he investigated each aspect of the business forensically. Typically he insisted on going out on the horse-and-cart rounds to customers, subsequently improving the delivery system and the quality and treatment of the horses. He had no office, just a desk in the counting house, but he devised a means of note-taking that allowed him to carry masses of information in tiny script on cards he kept in his pocket. He soon discovered that two

department heads had been robbing the business for years, and his brother
Oswald found appalling inefficiency in the counting house. The two sons
were particularly struck by the slovenly way the profits were invested.
Almost everything would be sunk in purchases of houses and small shops.
Once their father had bought them – often at auction, usually when he was
made aware he had too much in the bank – he then promptly forgot about
them. Events came to a head in early 1909, when, after a lengthy and
acrimonious family row, Oswald decided to leave and demanded his
quarter share. It was refused point-blank, but Oswald took advice from his
father's eminent lawyer Sir Edward Carson and John backed down. Father
and younger son both sat as Liberal councillors on the new Greater
London Council, but didn't speak to each other for the next six years.

This was the fractious family background when Spedan was laid up in
1909. One particularly contentious point at issue was his father's policy of
paying employees as little as he could get away with, which Spedan
regarded as short-sighted and wrongheaded. Only recently had he been
allowed sight of the company accounts, which gave him plenty to ponder.
He'd discovered that the 300 employees were receiving close to £16,000 a
year in total. But Spedan, his brother and his father were together paying
themselves almost exactly that £16,000, to which could be added £10,000
a year in interest on their capital. Each was making therefore the
equivalent today of about £800,000 a year, with a very low rate of income
tax, while the vast majority of their employees were being paid no more
than a pound a week, the equivalent today of £4,500 a year. No other
major employer thought twice about that disparity, then as now. As
Spedan was to write later:

> As a whole the staff were getting just a bare living, with very little
> margin beyond absolute necessities and correspondingly little
> chance to get much fun out of life, and at the same time feel they
> were saving adequately for their retirements … Moreover the pay
> rates were not supplemented in any way. Absence for illness
> almost always meant stoppage of pay. Only in very special cases
> was there any help for that or in any other trouble… Not a penny
> was spent on playing-fields or any other amenity for the staff. In
> all such ways the management could hardly have been more
> ruthlessly close-fisted. Obviously such a state of affairs could not

have existed unless the general conditions at the time had been more or less similar. To me ... all this seemed shocking.

This led him to conclude that someone who controlled a business should not take out of it more than he would pay anyone else to do the same job. Moreover no one who ran a successful venture should pay his workers less than "a decent living wage". His father profoundly disagreed, and contended that many of his workers were lazy, and only did the minimum they could get away with. Spedan's retort was that since they had no stake whatever in the success of the business, and were not even paid for overtime, they gained nothing by extra effort.

> I came to see that an enterprise, a business, is a living thing with rights of its own. Its earnings ought to be used with real care for its own efficiency, exactly as a good farmer feels a duty to maintain and develop the fertility of the land that he farms and to leave it in better, rather than worse, heart than when it came into his hands.

During 1910, the year after his accident, Spedan considered whether a more humane and inclusive way of doing business could mitigate the destructive effects of capitalism on society, effects that were then particularly acute in pre-revolutionary Russia. They were becoming rife in Britain too, where strikes were being vigorously suppressed, as they were most notoriously in the summer of 1911. The cooperative movements had emerged in the mid-nineteenth century and thrived from tentative beginnings with the twenty-eight Rochdale 'Pioneers' of 1844. They were societies of consumers: they worked well and became very substantial. But cooperative societies of *producers* were more difficult to establish and sustain, as the great social reformer Robert Owen had discovered in Scotland and America nearly a hundred years earlier. There were many entrepreneurs with a social conscience – Cadbury, Salt, Lever – but their measures to improve the lives of their employees didn't provide an explicit share in the profits of the business, didn't allow them to participate in decision-making, didn't undermine the deep-embedded pillars of capitalism. Spedan strove to devise a method of including employees in a business's success while safeguarding its health. He concluded that "capital should have a moderate fixed interest with a reasonable *but never unlimited* reward for taking a risk. All further earnings should go to all workers alike, from top to bottom." But how exactly to do it?

It was while recuperating from another operation in the first few days of October 1910 that he finally worked out the crucial details. He said it came upon him in the bath, for which there was an ancient precedent. He knew he wanted to treat any business of his as a partnership of all its workers, but he couldn't decide how to make it self-financing. The idea was to distribute shares instead of cash. The shares needed to be freely saleable, but they must not have votes, otherwise outsiders could build up a share of the business and take it over. The solution hadn't occurred to him earlier because his father's business was still in private hands, had no shareholders, and he had no first-hand experience of the stock exchange at all. "The notion was so obvious that I am puzzled that it did not occur to me sooner."

Spedan was now a man with a plan, but with no business of his own to try it out on, and it took until 1914 for the opportunity to arise. In 1906 his father had decided to buy Peter Jones, a once successful department store in Sloane Square, by then severely run down and perversely downmarket after the death of its founder. But now John was too old to adjust to running a second department store, lost interest and neglected it. It had been losing money heavily for years by the time he grudgingly asked Spedan to join him on the Peter Jones board in 1913. The following January it posted losses of £8,000 on sales of £100,000 – multiply by about 100 to get today's equivalent – and after a blazing row John in exasperation said Spedan could take over its day-to-day running. Spedan asked if that meant he could do what he liked at Peter Jones. Yes, but: "You must not neglect the Oxford Street shop. You must not go down there before five o'clock." Spedan took a cab to Peter Jones each evening, took a magnifying glass to everything, and was even more aghast at Peter Jones than when he'd lifted the covers at Oxford Street. As there, ancient stock needed to be jettisoned immediately. So did several buyers. Spedan waited four weeks and then sacked five of them in one day. He said that in the next week the total turnover started to rise and in the first six months overall sales rose by 12%: "I put into Peter Jones almost all my leisure. Night after night I got home about nine o'clock so tired that my voice was nearly gone."

Faced with mounting bills for essential repairs, he asked his father for a loan and was refused. After a series of violent arguments he cut himself adrift by swapping his shares in the Oxford Street shop for his father's in Peter Jones.

> That was an exchange of a quarter-partnership in one of the soundest businesses in England, and the prospect of being my father's sole heir, for a controlling interest in about as forlorn a derelict as could easily have been found in the whole of the drapery trade.

This was in 1915, when retailing was struggling during World War I. His father was nearly eighty, Spedan not yet thirty but convinced his methods would work if only he were allowed full rein. Once in charge at Peter Jones he tackled his employees' pay and conditions. He introduced a minimum wage, way ahead of its time – he would later, even more remarkably, introduce a *maximum*, expressed as a multiple of the average shop assistant's salary. Next on his list was the living-in accommodation for unmarried staff. The standard of such hostels was notoriously poor throughout the retail industry, despite an undercover newspaper exposé a few years before. One of his selling assistants would recall:

> One of the very first things he insisted on was that each room should have running water, both hot and cold, hitherto unheard of… Then, in order to further a feeling of freedom, the occupants of the rooms were each allowed to visit the fabric department and choose the material for their own curtains and bedspreads.

At the same time Spedan removed all restrictions on personal freedom in the hostel. Anyone over twenty-one could come and go as they liked at any time. Night porters were engaged so that the hostels were open all night, not locked up early as before. The resulting accommodation was scrupulously hygienic, which a doctor later identified as the reason the hostel was completely free from the terrifying 1919 flu epidemic. Another contribution to the health of the store was the food, whose standard Spedan set out to improve, turning the drab and slovenly staff canteen, with its filling but dull fare, into a proper restaurant. It was heavily subsidised, with a choice of main meals, one of which was very cheaply priced, a policy that continues today. Spedan was later to say:

For most people eating is one of the chief pleasures of life, immensely important to good temper and liveliness of mind. Our dining room ought to be so managed that, when people leave the Partnership, they regret it regularly every meal-time.

For the rest of the war Spedan, against all financial advice, continued to improve working conditions and the fabric of the shop, funding it partly out of increased profits but largely from his own pocket. Once the war was over the mass influx of returning servicemen led to a rapid surge in trade, and he was at last able to enact the plan he had formulated ten years before. The critical moment was the 1920 meeting of the long-suffering Peter Jones shareholders, who had received no dividend for years. He stunned them by proposing something totally new and outside their experience, a staff profit-sharing scheme. He planned to reorganise the capital structure of the company. He would write down the Ordinary share capital to a quarter of its nominal value, and cancel the substantial arrears of Preference dividend, with the promise of a higher dividend in future as compensation. He told them he was drawing no salary for himself whatsoever, nor would he pay himself any dividend on his holding of over 80% of the Ordinary shares. His scheme was ingenious, and he so dazzled the shareholders that his disarming honesty persuaded them. He recalled telling them:

Sad experience of a wicked world may make it extremely difficult for you … to believe that a programme so unusual and financially so disinterested can really be honest and have no catch in it… I could sell my interest immediately without bothering to put through any scheme at all, for a vastly larger sum than I could possibly get for it when the scheme is through.

He then summed up blithely: "The scheme was then adopted on a show of hands without any need for a vote." Some of the shareholders felt they were being taken for turkeys and asked to vote for Christmas. But his sheer openness and self-confidence persuaded the majority that, at the very least, if they were turkeys he was turkey-in-chief. There was indeed no catch, neither for the old shareholders nor the nervous new, for each employee of Peter Jones received a proportion of a total of 7,000 new Preference shares, or rather share 'promises' – he did not want them traded on the Stock Exchange for fear of alerting his father – representing 15% of their pay. It was the first annual Partnership Bonus payout. And soon afterwards he told them they were no longer employees, but 'Partners', joining him in a new kind of enterprise. What did that mean? It all seemed too good to be true. Could they trust him? He recalled one exchange which was typical of the time:

> Oh, Matron, Florrie's got her share money! What about it? But are these things really money? Of course they're really money, as I keep on telling you silly girls, and now perhaps you'll believe it. But I've got thirty of them! Fancy me worth thirty pounds! And she burst into tears.

So what were the reforms that Spedan gradually brought into Peter Jones that would make it so different from all other department stores, and ultimately from almost any other business? How would he convince his employees that he meant what he said? From the outset he defined the key components of a genuine Partnership as the sharing of Knowledge, Gain and Power. He started a weekly journal he called the *Gazette*, introduced regular two-way communication meetings with elected staff representatives, and augmented their pay with an annual profit-sharing scheme that would give all employees the same extra proportion of their income. He understood in particular that a sense of the power of joint ownership would only emerge through shared knowledge:

> Another innovation that made them gasp … was the admission of the whole of the staff to knowledge of figures normally reckoned to be highly confidential. It had an extremely tonic effect upon the minds of the recipients.

One initiative was particularly farsighted. He started a *Gazette* letter column, and insisted that writers could be anonymous, and that they should be answered without fail and in full. At first people were wary, and to encourage them he wrote critical letters (anonymously, but few were fooled) to himself, and then answered them at great length. Gradually employees, now readily accepting the term Partners, realised that he bore no grudges, and began to write more freely. He was honest and open, and imposed the same rules on himself as he did on them. The anonymous letter system remains in place today, and every director knows that an inadequate answer will lead to a flurry of further letters and consequent public opprobrium, so it has a profound deterrent effect on ill-thought-through or poorly explained decisions.

Apart from information promulgated weekly in the *Gazette* he organised regular meetings with the shop assistants – not the managers – from different parts of the shop. They would elect representatives who could make him aware of any grievance, while he could keep them abreast of events. He recalled how bitterly it was opposed by the Peter Jones department heads, the middle tier of management of the shop, who were used to ruling without question. "I listened to their objections and persisted. An important buyer tendered her resignation next morning. I ignored it and no-one left." Later he created an elected council for the whole staff, which he didn't attend himself, and as the business expanded country-wide in the 1930s each local department store had one. He subsequently went on to reorganise the company's central board to include five elected members in a total of twelve.

One immediate effect of these changes was to markedly improve trust between managers and managed at Peter Jones, in stark contrast to Oxford Street. There his father's irascible intransigence led to a major strike at Oxford Street in 1920, strongly supported by all the Press (there has never been a serious strike in the Partnership itself). The relationship between father and son had been poor for years, but the birth of a grandson eventually helped pave the way for a reconciliation, a timely one because John, now approaching ninety, was persuaded to inject spare cash into Peter Jones when it suffered dangerous liquidity problems as trading conditions worsened in the early 1920s.

Spedan's marriage in 1923 had come about following a decision triggered by a growing conviction that you needed first-class brains to make a real difference to any difficult venture, and he knew his ideas needed to be challenged. Spedan's second big innovation was to have almost as profound an effect as his first – and it would change his life. He went to the university authorities at Oxford and asked for details of their top woman graduates, and then invited them to work for him. Retailing was at that time a profession hitherto beyond the pale for a graduate. One woman became general manager of Peter Jones at 24, many became top class buyers – and one became his wife. Beatrice Hunter was an Oxford graduate in her early thirties who had been a factory inspector during the war, a strong feminist with a sharp mind and an engaging directness, who gave Spedan as good as she got throughout their life together. She bought into his ideas completely, and was just the sounding board he needed. She was fully engaged both in the business and its important social side, directing and acting in the plays and revues that Spedan encouraged, and which would become a strong tradition, as would its music.

Later in the 1920s he recruited from Oxford and Cambridge a future management team, largely of men with first class degrees, who would help with the rapid expansion he initiated after his father's death in 1928. Until the day he died at ninety-two John was still in nominal control at Oxford Street, and though Spedan ran it in practice he was careful to keep two sets of paysheets, one for his father to see, and the real ones... In total charge at last, and full of pent-up energy, Spedan brought the original shop into his Partnership, which he named after his father and not himself, in respect for his trading principles. He devised a complex trust that would own the business on behalf of all its Partners, and which remains in place today. In essence he gave his business to its employees. In the 1930s he expanded the business at a furious rate, making up for lost time. As his successor as Chairman put it later, "1927 to 1939 was a time of youthful zest and energy spilling over in all directions; nothing was too zany to look into and everything was possible." Spedan wanted people with brains and original ideas, and recruited people from all walks of life – retired generals and admirals, women who impressed him irrespective of experience and background, as long as they could stand toe to toe with him in debate. As a county chess player himself, he was particularly impressed by brilliant chess minds, and in the 1930s recruited the British champion Hugh Alexander, who went on to Bletchley Park – as did several other senior Partners – and later to GCHQ as head of cryptoanalysis, and the long-standing world women's champion Vera Menchik.

By 1939 he had several department stores and a host of small factories supplying them, as well as a then tiny grocery business called Waitrose, just acquired, and at Cookham in the Thames Valley a heavily subsidised residential country club with wide-ranging sports facilities available for every Partner. He had great ideas for the place, including a residential further education college for Partners, and open-air opera – his financial support would later be instrumental in rescuing Glyndebourne – but World War II abruptly ended those plans. However, initially it didn't stop

---

opportunistic business expansion, and in early 1940 the Partnership bought a provincial store chain at a knockdown price from Gordon Selfridge, a shrewd purchase that would help buttress the business when disaster struck that September.

Despite the installation of an elaborate fireproof roof long before the war, ten days after the London Blitz began in September 1940 a stick of eight high-explosive incendiary oil-bombs, almost certainly intended for the BBC, burst through the roof of the Oxford Street shop and burnt it virtually to the ground. Some of the shops he had bought in the 1930s, those in port cities, were also severely damaged. But Oxford Street, whose size had doubled in the 1930s, was the great profit powerhouse. His was the only London department store to be so devastatingly hit, a misfortune that would gnaw at him for years.

Despite the shock of the loss of the Oxford Street shop, the war brought out the best in Spedan. At its outset, when trade everywhere slumped by half, he was forced to release 300 of the Partnership's 6000 Partners, but with the offer of re-engagement when trade improved; he asked the better-paid to 'defer' a proportion of their income, which was paid back at 5% p.a. interest in 1942; and for those conscripted he topped up service pay to their Partnership rate. He had already put his own early Welfare State in place, with subsidised medical care, a form of family credit, support for Partners suffering hardship, and generous paid holidays. Now in 1941 he brought forward plans for the first non-contributory pension scheme outside the civil service and armed forces. Despite the business's parlous position following the bombing, he felt it would be good for morale, and it had the benefit that payments would only start gradually.

After the end of World War II, with Britain not far from bankruptcy, trade barely picked up, and the delay in rebuilding the Oxford Street store was crippling. Such was the shortage of steel for businesses deemed low priority that the shop wasn't fully rebuilt until 1960. Indeed the Partnership Bonus, which had usually been over 10% since 1928, subsided to an average of just 2% between 1940 and Spedan's retirement in 1955. The post-war period sapped Spedan's confidence, particularly at a time in the Korean War when profitability was so poor that those earning over a threshold level had to take a temporary pay cut. That was the Partnership at its lowest ebb, a period during which, as one competitor put it: "they talk endlessly about sharing their profit, but there's none to share." This was bad enough, but worse for Spedan was the sudden death in 1953 of Beatrice, the companion who supported him and helped him work out – or discard – some of his more ambitious ideas. Two years later he retired as was planned on his 70th birthday, regarding his life's work as unfinished business.

Spedan's ultimate success can be gauged by the fact that all his major innovations still exist in the business today, in a very different trading world increasingly dominated by the Internet. The John Lewis Partnership still has profit-sharing in proportion to pay for everyone in the business, a maximum salary as well as a minimum (one which keeps the top income at round about £1m p.a., far far less than in equivalent businesses), elected staff councils and a part-elected Board, a weekly journal with an anonymous letter column and full public accountability, and still provides a non-contributory final-salary pension. It continues to operate with the same strong trading principles that he inherited from his father. And, not least, it has admiring and loyal customers. In the sixty years since his retirement the annual bonus has averaged over 15%, now entirely in cash, eight weeks extra pay each year. It gives the staff, all Partners, such a strong sense of shared ownership of the business that it's apparent every day in their dealings with their customers. There is no public equity, hence no shares quoted on the Stock Exchange, thus allowing the business to consistently take a long-term view.

To finish, here are two quotes that illustrate the man. The first comes from an eighteen-year-old taken on in the mid-1940s. He had been one of the so-called Bevin Boys who worked down the coal mines as an alternative to war service. It was typical of Spedan that, after being impressed by a wartime article the young man had written for the *Spectator* about the primitive pit conditions in Kent, he summoned him to his Hampshire home:

> I was picked up at the station in an old horse and carriage. We had lunch, where he and Beatrice had a quarrel over some obscure ornithological point. She gave as good as she got. He was an absolutely riveting man... You had to listen to every word and be totally direct and honest. Otherwise he'd play with you like a cat with a mouse, and every now and then he'd jump on you and ask a question out of the blue. He had great delivery and pace – he could have been an old actor of the Shakespearean school.

The second comes from Sir Bernard Miller, the man who succeeded him as Chairman in 1955 and led the Partnership's recovery from its post-war travails. He had come with a History First straight from Cambridge, where he had beaten his famous contemporary AJP Taylor to the annual essay prize. Miller had no intention of becoming a retailer, but Spedan bowled him over:

> I was expecting to teach or enter the Civil Service. An interview with Spedan Lewis changed all that. I was so swept away by him that I forgot all the things I had in mind; he seemed to be on the point of explosion all the time.

Had Spedan's novel industrial experiment been analysed at the point he retired, it would probably have been considered an intriguing but doomed failure. The sad bitterness in which he spent a restless solitary retirement up to his death in 1963 would have been mitigated if he could have foreseen what would happen. Spedan himself said that the time to judge the success of his idea would be in the tenure of its third Chairman. It's a pity that he died while the jury was still out, ten years before that point, but it has gone on to prove an outstanding business model. He would have been delighted at that, astonished by its sustained profitability and size, now approaching 100,000 Partners, but puzzled and disappointed that it has not been emulated on any substantial scale in Britain, despite much blithe recent talk of the "John Lewis model". Few business owners are as farsighted and tenacious, and as outstandingly generous with their own money in pursuit of an ideal. Spedan was a rare and shining exception.

Richard Doll

Conrad Keating

Millions of people are alive today who would otherwise be dead had Richard Doll not made his enduring contribution to medical science. In 1950, when Doll and his mentor, the medical statistician, Bradford Hill, demonstrated that smoking was "a cause and an important cause" of the rapidly increasing epidemic of lung cancer in

Britain, his path in life was set. Adapting the old science of epidemiology, which had evolved in the nineteenth century to identify the causes of infectious disease, Doll expanded the discipline to discover the causes of the devastating diseases of modernity: stroke, heart attacks and, in particular, cancer. Uncovering the dangers of tobacco and showing the benefits of quitting to educationalists, politicians and the public formed a major part of Doll's career in medical science. His approach was heavily reliant on the science of statistics, rather than of the stethoscope, and Doll's belief in statistical evidence was firmly rooted in its efficacy for the common good. In 1951, Doll and Hill wrote to every doctor in Britain, which marked the beginning of their great experiment, the prospective study of smoking and mortality in British doctors, that Doll continued for 50 years, showing that half of all smokers are prematurely killed by their habit and that stopping smoking is remarkably effective. Epidemiology is both an art and a science and Doll used it to cause a revolution in thinking and helped to change the health of the nation. Between 1950 and 2005, overall UK death rates decreased by half in middle age; more than half of this decrease was due to the decrease in mortality from smoking.[1]

Doll became the leading cancer epidemiologist of our time, contributing new concepts of humanity's relationship with the environment and opening up new fields of study. Although best known for his work on tobacco, his research covered a wide spectrum including – radiation, asbestos, drugs, diet and infection in relation to cancer. The trajectory of Doll's career was shaped by his political radicalism. Appalled at the "anarchy and waste" of the economic depression in the 1930s, Doll jettisoned his establishment background and joined the Communist Party. This prevented him from pursuing a conventional career in pre-NHS medicine, but in so doing, allowed him to follow his two innate interests, "mathematics" and "public health medicine". During the course of his lifetime Doll's prodigious output helped to usher in a new era in medicine; the intellectual ascendancy of medical statistics. In 1966 Doll co-wrote *Cancer Incidence in Five Continents*, the book that crystallised his general theory of carcinogenesis: "no cancer that occurs with even moderate frequency, occurs everywhere and always to the same extent". What Doll was saying, and the reason why his name will have an enduring link with cancer epidemiology, is that the main causes of cancer

---

[1] Peto, R. and Beral, V., (2010) "Sir Richard Doll CH OBE. 28 October 1912-24 July 2005", *Biographical Memoirs of Fellows of the Royal Society* 56:63.

are environmental and therefore they are in principle avoidable. He showed, more clearly than anyone, that each case of cancer arises from a combination of nature, nurture and luck.

In later life, Doll became the Regius Professor of Medicine at the University of Oxford and dedicated himself to developing clinical medicine, establishing the Oxford Medical School into the leading position it occupies today, and to the founding of Green College in 1979 (now Green-Templeton College, with 600 graduate students). Doll's early ambition was to be a "valuable member of society"; he sought to understand the world and to help people enjoy their lives, free from the unnecessary burden of avoidable disease. Doll never retired and his Indian summer of scientific research continued up until his death, in his ninety-third year, in 2005.

Perhaps more than any other physician, Doll's work enabled people to understand how knowledge of their smoking habits allowed prediction of the relative risks of dying from lung cancer, and from various other diseases. As a result of the twentieth-century epidemiological studies of smoking, of which Doll's were among the among the most persuasive, many millions of deaths have already been prevented by the time he died; according to the World Health Organization, hundreds of millions of deaths from tobacco will be prevented during the twenty-first century. Richard Doll's lifework forms an indelible chapter in the history of modern medicine.

Richard Doll was born at 15 Park Road, Hampton Hill, Middlesex, on 28 October 1912 into a middle-class family, a mix of the conventional and the artistic. His father, Henry William Doll, was a physician and surgeon. His mother, Amy Kathleen May Doll (née Shaboe) was a celebrated classical pianist.

The poverty in which many Londoners lived in the 1930s would come to have a radicalising effect on Doll, but his childhood was lived in a protected oasis. The family home at 42 Montpellier Square, Knightsbridge, was a magnificent eighteenth-century house, set in leafy seclusion in one of London's most select areas. The family had a chauffeur, and Doll's playgrounds were Hyde Park and the Natural History Museum.

At the age of twelve, Doll stood at the threshold of a new challenge, a place at Westminster School. His world was expanding and he wanted to find his place within it. During his six years at Westminster Doll excelled at mathematics and immersed himself in religious and political ideas as a way to make sense of his existence and to seek a role in life. These rites of passage led him initially to become a Christian fundamentalist, but when he lost his faith, he then embraced pacifism, before eventually rejecting its conciliatory ideals for party political action that he increasingly recognised would be necessary to bring about social change. As a King's Scholar Doll could go into the House of Commons gallery at any time. On one occasion he saw James Maxton, of the Independent Labour Party, being thrown out. As Doll recalled, "He was a fine representative of the real left. I had great respect for him, he was an honest man who stuck to his beliefs, and wouldn't bend".[2] Like Maxton, Doll was becoming more resolute in his beliefs. After witnessing the 1926 General Strike and the subsequent economic decline and growing numbers of demoralised unemployed, Doll lost his faith in the capitalist system. Accordingly, he joined the Young Communist League as a schoolboy; he remained an active communist until May 1957. Doll contemplated a career in mathematics, but instead took his father's advice and decided to study medicine at St Thomas's Hospital (1931–37). There he would lay the intellectual foundations for his future career in epidemiology while refining his political philosophy.

The young idealist soon recognised the effects of poverty on health when, as part of his medical training, he had to deliver twenty babies, half in people's homes. Lambeth had some of the worst slums in London, and Doll became convinced that addressing social deprivation, the effects of malnutrition, and people's living conditions was crucial to improving the nation's health. Under the leadership of the surgeon and MP Somerville Hastings, Doll joined the Socialist Medical Association and campaigned for building more and bigger houses and for a universal and free health service to combat the suffering of the poor. He also came under the influence of the Swiss Marxist physician Henry Sigerist, who called for a "people's war for health". Doll envisioned a society in which the benefits of medical science would be distributed to all. He sought to be a valuable member of society and in many ways epitomised Sigerist's concept of the politicised doctor: "We still need, more than ever, a scientific physician well-trained in laboratory and clinic. But we need more: we need a social physician who, conscious of the social functions of medicine, considers

---

[2] Keating, C., *Smoking Kills: The Revolutionary Life of Richard Doll*. (Signal Books, 2009), p. 7.

himself in the service of society. There is no point training doctors primarily for city practice among the upper-middle class".[3] Doll, in his role as a physician, joined in the struggle for the improvement of conditions and to combat the injustice of health inequality. Compelled to take some action against the moral paradox of hunger in the midst of plenty, Doll worked for the Committee against Malnutrition, established the St Thomas's Socialist Society – much to the disgruntlement of the dean – and participated in the Jarrow Hunger March in 1936, treating the blistered feet of the protesters against mass unemployment. His political beliefs led him to raise funds enthusiastically for medical aid to the republican cause in the Spanish Civil War and visit the Soviet Union, while his medical studies led him to visit Nazi Germany in 1936, where he witnessed at first-hand how deeply anti-Semitic propaganda had corrupted medical teaching.[4]

Coterminous with his political activism, Doll was looking for ways to apply his interest in mathematics to medicine. After reading R.A. Fisher's classic book *Statistical Methods for Research Workers,* he grew to understand how the science of statistics could influence his work. This led Doll to write an article on the use of the Chi-squared test in the *St Thomas's Hospital Gazette,* and the use of statistics in evaluating the efficacy of medical interventions. The article, his first scientific paper, can be seen as prescient, signposting Doll's future career as an epidemiologist, while advancing a thesis that became one of the guiding principles of modern clinical medicine.

"Were physicians to abide more strictly to the rules of statistics they would find it very much easier to assess the values of their

---

[3] Milton. T, 'The Contributions of Henry E. Sigerist to Health Service Organisation', *Journal of Public Health Policy,* 1995, vol. 16, pp. 152-93.
[4] Doll attended a lecture on radiotherapy in Frankfurt, in which the SS radiologist Professor Dr Hans Holfelder showed students in attendance a slide in which cancer cells were portrayed as Jews. "We were told that the radiotherapist was a keen Nazi and he would expect us all to stand up and say "Heil Hitler" in response when he came in, which of course we didn't. But he came in and "Heil Hitler"-ed and then, in the course of the lecture, he showed slides in which the X-ray beams were illustrated as Nazi storm troopers and the cancer cells had all got Jewish emblems on them. So, we didn't require many experiences of that sort to realise there was something evil that had to be eliminated from the world"

methods of treatment... To facilitate this, a qualified statistician should be available to co-operate with clinical workers at any centre of research. Not only would they be able to help in evaluating the results obtained, but he could also help beforehand in designing the experiment to suit the conditions. Advantage would accrue to the medical profession, for they would have to waste less time in disproving ill-founded claims, and to the general public, for they would be less liable to suffer from the continued use of a useless remedy".[5]

Later in his career, Doll played a central role in expanding the frontiers of epidemiology and teaching a largely innumerate medical profession to think quantitatively. One of the phrases that became associated with Doll was, "the play of chance" and with the use of the Chi-squared test, it was possible to evaluate whether the effect of a given treatment was real, or merely a chance event.

Doll's visit to Germany made it clear to him that war was inevitable. As a consequence, a week before the declaration of war on 3 September 1939, he was already in Preston in Lancashire acting as medical officer to a regular battalion, the First Loyals. A week later he was in France, where he treated and helped evacuate wounded soldiers through the disorderly retreat to Dunkirk. Despite sustained shelling and strafing from the air, he led men to safety. In 1941, he was sent to Egypt and served as medical officer in a Cairo infectious disease ward and then on a hospital ship in the Mediterranean that was closely involved with the Salerno landings.[6] He developed renal tuberculosis and was repatriated in 1944: the left kidney was removed by his colleague from St Thomas's, T.W. 'Gaffer' Mimpriss, and he recovered.

On 8 May 1945 (VE Day), among the enormous crowd celebrating in the bright sunshine of Piccadilly Circus was Richard Doll. There he met Joan Faulkner (1913–2001); they fell in love while singing the socialist anthem, "*The Red Flag*". It marked the date of their engagement, and it changed the direction of his life. In Joan he had found a friend, lover and scientific companion. They had met a decade before at a meeting of

---

[5] Doll, R., 1936. 'Medical statistics'. *St. Thomas's Hosp. Gaz.*, pp. 294–97
[6] His friend Archie Cochrane remembered Doll arranging concert parties on the boat to Cairo and organising the singing of "You'll get no promotion on this side of the ocean".

communist doctors, but Joan had dismissed him as a "callow youth". However, the war had transmogrified him into someone she now saw as "solid and reliable". The resulting fight for Joan was one of the most "upsetting periods" of Doll's life, as she was married to Hugh Faulkner and had a young son. Eventually, she divorced, and Richard and Joan married on 4 October 1949, at Kensington register office, with Doll becoming stepfather to her son Tim. Like Richard, Joan was medically qualified and was committed to social change, and they both campaigned for the establishment of a national health service in Britain, in 1948 jointly writing a pamphlet entitled *Humanise the Hospitals*. During his final illness at the John Radcliffe Hospital in Oxford, I gave Richard a copy of the pamphlet which he had not seen in over fifty years. After a period of concentrated reading, he pronounced, "some of our recommendations have still to be implemented".

Joan and Richard Doll remained "democratic communists" (although with increasing unease after the 1948 Lysenko debacle) until 1957, but after the Soviet invasion of Hungary in 1956, and Khrushchev's "Secret Speech" describing the realities of the Stalin era, they resigned and came to accept the undesirability of planned economies. Nevertheless, in the late 1940s, Doll's communism was preventing him from finding a career in conventional medicine.

His salvation came in the form of two events that were career-defining. Doll's interest in mathematics and social medicine led him to enrol on Bradford Hill's part-time course *Essentials in Statistics* at the London School of Hygiene and Tropical Medicine. Secondly, Joan, in her professional capacity as a member of the Medical Research Council's headquarters' administrative staff, alerted Richard to a research project being carried out by the gastroenterologist, Francis Avery Jones at the Central Middlesex Hospital. In 1946, Doll, under the aegis of Avery Jones, embarked upon his first epidemiological study – of occupational factors in the causation of gastric and duodenal ulcers.[7] Hill was the first person to introduce the medical profession to the idea of randomisation, and Doll's work on peptic ulcers was perhaps the first randomised clinical trial to use a factorial design (evaluating the treatment effect of more than one intervention in an experiment). Such was the completeness of the study – he succeed in following up and interviewing 98.4% of all the

---

[7] Doll, R. and Jones, F.A., 'Environmental Factors in the Aetiology of Peptic Ulcer', *The Practitioner,* 1949, vol. 162, pp. 44-50.

participants, even climbing up a haystack to speak to one recalcitrant farm worker – and attention to detail, that the work came to the attention of Bradford Hill, Britain's foremost medical statistician. In 1947, when the Medical Research Council (MRC) asked Hill to conduct a large-scale study into the aetiology of the epidemic of lung cancer deaths in Britain, Hill recruited Doll to assist him in the undertaking. Somewhat prophetically, Hill wrote these comments to Harold Himsworth, Secretary of the MRC: "…I regard him as a very good worker to whom it is well worth while giving a wider experience in medical statistical work with an eye to the future. As you know, the number of medical persons who take at all kindly to careful statistical work is still small".[8]

After the Second World War, British men had the highest incidence of lung cancer in the world. For the first time lung cancer deaths exceeded those from tuberculosis, and no one knew why. Hill and Doll began planning their search for an explanation on 1 January 1948, at a time when smoking was generally regarded as innocuous. More than eighty per cent of men smoked, while the economic and social emancipation led to the habit being taken up by some forty per cent of women. Smoking was even more entrenched among doctors and scientists than it was in the rest of society, as they were not impecunious in retirement. At the time, Doll smoked a pipe and non-tipped cigarettes, and Hill a pipe. Later Doll wrote: "I was not antagonistic to tobacco when I began to study its effects".[9] Originally Doll thought the increase in motor cars and the tarring of roads were likely to be responsible for the epidemic. Hill, typically, was reported to have entered the study "with an open mind".[10]

Doll and Hill were dispassionate scientists and the results of their first study published in 1950 were clear. The one consistent difference between lung cancer patients (cases) and other patients (controls) was that almost all of the lung cancer patients had smoked. Doll and Hill concluded that smoking was "a factor and a major factor, in the production of carcinoma

---

[8] Keating, C., 'Smoking Kills: The Revolutionary Life of Richard Doll.' Signal Books (2009) p. 82.

[9] Doll, R., 'Tobacco: a medical history', *Journal of Urban Health: Bulletin of the New York Academy of Medicine,* 1999, vol. 76, pp. 289-313

[10] Austoker, J., *History of the Imperial Cancer Research Fund, 1902-86.* (Oxford University Press, 1988), p. 194.

of the lung".[11] However, as history has shown, their revelatory findings were not inimitable. Four American studies also published in 1950, independently found the same association, as had two smaller German studies (published in the era of National Socialism), that had been generally unnoticed in Britain and America. Doll and Hill's second report, published in 1952,[12] cited all these American, German, and British studies as being mutually supportive and Doll consistently referenced all of them in his subsequent historical reviews.

In 1950 Doll and Hill established smoking as a major cause of preventable disease. The knowledge that a fatal cancer could be largely eradicated by epidemiological science was revolutionary and would have a far greater impact on public health than could ever be achieved by curative medicine alone. Unfortunately, with the exception of Himsworth at the MRC and a few notable others, their discovery was widely doubted and generally ignored. For the conclusion as to whether an observed association is causal or not is one of the most difficult things epidemiology has to achieve. Non-infectious epidemiology had no intellectual standing within the medical establishment, and the political class was as addicted to tobacco as the democracy it represented. Clearly, some new type of evidence was going to be needed if doctors, politician and the general public were going to be convinced that smoking was dangerous.

Both Doll and Hill believed their findings, and at the age of thirty-seven Doll stopped smoking cigarettes while Hill, because of his deep devotion to his habit, ceremoniously buried his pipe in his back garden! Doll was one of the great medical experimentalists of his time, and was devoted to retaining a sense of scepticism to accepted beliefs, even if they were based on his own research. As he wrote: "Our responsibility – having concluded in our 1950 study that smoking was a cause of lung cancer – was to see if we could disprove it and the obvious way to try to disprove it was to say, 'Well, does it predict, does knowledge of smoking habits predict whether someone will get lung cancer or not?'"[13] Their

---

[11] Doll, R. and Hill, A.B., 'Smoking and Carcinoma of the Lung, preliminary report', *British Medical Journal,* 1950, vol. 2, pp. 739-48.
[12] Doll, R. and Hiill, A.B., 'A study of the Aetiology of Carcinoma of the Lung', *British Medical Journal,* 1952, vol. 2, pp. 1271-86.
[13] Doll, R., 'Tobacco: a medical history', *Journal of Urban Health: Bulletin of the New York Academy of Medicine,* 1999, vol. 76, pp. 289-313

original experiment following the classical methods of epidemiology was a *retrospective* study, now Doll and Hill's minds turned towards a *prospective* enquiry. The idea was to identify a specific population, ask them to describe their smoking habits, follow them for some years, obtain the causes of death of those who died and see if knowledge of their smoking habits allowed prediction of the relative risks of dying from lung cancer, and from various other diseases. Their choice of a population fell on the medical profession. In 1951, Doll and Hill sent a letter to 60,000 British doctors useful replies were received from 34,000 men and 6,000 women – it took one year to open all of the replies – and within three years the researchers were able to confirm the validity of their previous observations. On 26 June 1954 the *British Medical Journal* published the first prospective results from the British Doctors Study, confirming that lung cancer rates were much higher in smokers and increased with the amount smoked. In an epidemiological investigation a *dose-response* relationship gives increased confidence to a finding. In 1956 Doll and Hill reported that smokers also had higher death rates from heart disease, chronic lung disease, and many other conditions.[14] In 1957, thanks to Doll and Hill, the British government was the first to officially accept that smoking caused lung cancer; now, all governments do. Their prospective study had an added societal impact; once doctors realised that smoking wasn't just killing their patients, that it was also killing them, they began to give up. Moreover, this awareness of the dangers of smoking moved them into the forefront of the public health campaign to warn their patients of the dangers of smoking, and benefits of quitting. Non-infectious disease epidemiology was now firmly established in the medical armamentarium.

The 1950s was the definitive decade of Doll's professional life. In 1950, he became a full-time member of Hill's Statistical Research Unit, and elected to make his career in medical statistics and epidemiology. Moreover, in that decade Doll initiated a variety of epidemiological studies which established the leitmotifs of the discipline of epidemiology. The most important breakthrough in the history of cancer epidemiology was the carcinogenic effect of tobacco, a discovery to which Hill and Doll made a major contribution. Building on this achievement, in the 1950s Doll embarked on a series of studies with Michael Court-Brown of the

---

[14] Doll, R., and Hill A.B., 'Lung cancer and tobacco'. The B.M.J.'s questions answered. *British Medical Journal*, 1956, vol. 1, pp. 1160-1163.

long-term effect of medical exposures of X-rays.[15] Although heavy exposure to X-rays was already known to cause cancer, particularly to the skin, they demonstrated that moderate doses could also cause cancer, particularly leukaemia, establishing for the first time within one study a dose-response relationship between radiation and cancer. For the rest of his life, Doll collaborated extensively in several quantitative epidemiological studies of low-dose radiation of various types.

Moreover, Doll's research often revealed some unpalatable findings for industry. This was the case in 1955 when Doll completed a study (in collaboration with the company) of the mortality of men who worked at Turner Brothers Asbestos in Rochdale, in Yorkshire.[16] The striking results, with a tenfold increase in lung cancer in heavily exposed workers, led the company's lawyers to attempt to suppress the research, claiming the military importance of asbestos, the irrelevance of long-past occupational exposures, and private ownership of the employment records. Despite legal threats, Doll promptly published his findings, after which the company agreed to continue indefinitely to provide Doll with current and past employment records for independent analysis, which were eventually used to demonstrate a significant continuing hazard. Doll was expanding the frontiers of the burgeoning new science of epidemiology by the originality of his work. According to Sir Donald Acheson, the benchmark 1955 paper was, "a classic in its own right, which would have gained Richard Doll a place in the history of epidemiology, had it been his only publication... Almost as an aside Sir Richard's paper also gives one of the first and unquestionably one of the simplest descriptions of the man-years method of calculating expected numbers. Subsequently this technique rapidly became established as the standard way to measure risk in cohort studies".[17]

While Doll and Hill formed an ideal collaborative synthesis in the clarity of their thought, intellectual integrity and scientific rigour,

---

[15] Court-Brown, W.M. and Doll, R., 'Leukaemia and Aplastic Anaemia in Patients Irradiated for Ankylosing Spondylitis', *Medical Research Council Special Report,* series no. 295 (HMSO, 1956).
[16] Doll, R., 'Mortality from Lung Cancer in Asbestos Workers', *British Journal of Industrial Medicine,* 1955, vol. 12, pp.81-86.
[17] Acheson, D., 'Introduction to Doll's paper, 'Mortality from Lung Cancer in Asbestos Workers', in Ashton, J., (ed.) *The Epidemiological Imagination: A Reader* (Oxford University Press, 1994), p.12.

politically they could not have been more different. The politically peaceful co-existence that had existed between the two men was tested in the early 1950s when it became apparent that Richard and Joan were not going to be able to have children of their own, and their thoughts turned to adoption. At the time, however, the adoption service was dominated by religious orthodoxy and required Christian commitment. This reality immediately placed the Dolls in a moral dilemma as both were atheists.

Prior to any formal contact with an adoption society Doll sought the support of Hill. When Doll asked Hill if he would write a reference in support of his application to adopt, the answer was as hurtful as it was truthful. "Hill thought for a moment before saying, 'I don't think communists should have children, it wouldn't be right.' I thought to myself 'Bugger you. I've got other friends'. I only asked him once. He knew it was important to Joan and I, but that was his answer. I think I forgave him for it – eventually". The rejection formed a felicitous turning point in Joan and Richard's life. Fired by an abhorrence of hypocrisy and their dedication to social justice, they decided to establish their own adoption society. With the advice of the British Humanist Society they set up The Agnostic Adoption Society. It was initially based in their home, and the Dolls used their own funds to hire its first social worker. An early policy statement setting out the aims of the society indicates their advanced thinking and still stands today: "To help would-be adopters from minority as well as majority groups, people from all religions or none, and not to turn away any child who it is within our power to help. Babies which other agencies have classified as difficult we accept gladly". In 1969, the society changed its name to the Independent Adoption Society, and it also marked the end of the Dolls' direct involvement in the society, its destiny moving to the custodianship of another generation committed to humanitarian ideals. The Dolls themselves adopted two children, Nicholas in 1954 and Catherine in 1956.

In 1967, Doll received a letter from the statistician David Cox of Imperial College London. Cox is reputed to have written that he had a very bright student, named Richard Peto, who had just completed an MSc in Statistics and would be either "brilliant or a total disaster". He turned out to be the former, and immediately immersed himself in looking for solutions to the mathematical problems of trying to link causes of disease and the effects of treatments. Just as Hill had got Doll "obsessed" with epidemiology, the process was replicated between Doll and Peto. "My first useful result got me addicted, you suddenly realise that results on paper can save lives in the real world". Peto was to dedicate his scientific life to the prevention of premature death, and Doll had found more than a collaborator; he had a protégé. Theirs became a father and son relationship, and Peto succeeded Hill as Doll's collaborator on the British doctors' study. Their collaboration made an enduring contribution to the health of the global community and continued uninterrupted until Doll's death.

By 1969, Doll had shown himself to be a worthy successor to Hill as director of the MRC's Statistical Research Unit, and he had established a world-wide reputation for scientific excellence. At the same time he had nurtured a new generation of epidemiologists whose contributions to health research would be lasting. Over the previous decade, there had been numerous unsuccessful attempts to prise Doll away from London. However, in the spring of 1969, the offer of becoming the Regius Professor of Medicine at the University of Oxford, was one he could not refuse. He was fifty-six years old and eager for a new challenge.

Doll's career in Oxford will be remembered for three lasting achievements: developing the Oxford Medical School into one of the most prestigious in the world, founding Green College (now Green Templeton), and his own scientific work. During his decade as Regius Professor (1969–79) he negotiated finance for five new chairs at the Medical School, broadened the scope of the medical curriculum and helped supercharge the standing of epidemiology and evidence-based medicine. Doll was the first Warden of Green College (1979–83), which specialised in medicine, and while this role would eventually give him great pleasure, when the new institution first opened its doors it caused unrest among some of the medical students who were antagonistic to the idea of a uni-disciplinary college that was alien to the ethos of Oxford. It took all of Doll's diplomatic skills to persuade the medical students that the new graduate college would act as a true custodian of their academic and social needs, and to raise money to ensure the college's survival. Within two years the neuralgic atmosphere between the college and the students had been transformed into one of equanimity. In 1A Observatory Street, the Warden's home, Richard and Joan would study photographs of the college's students over breakfast so that they could greet them on first-name terms.

Richard Peto's dynamism and proliferation of large-scale population studies of the causes, prevention, and treatment of major diseases, helped to extend Doll's career. In 1997 under cross-examination in a Florida tobacco trial, Doll was asked by a lawyer if he knew Richard Peto. Doll replied, "Yes. He was once my protégé, but I'm his now."

Doll never quite retired – his extraordinary Indian summer of scientific study reached its apogee with the publication on 26 June 2004 of the fifty-year results on the smoking habits of British doctors. The findings showed that lifelong cigarette smokers lost ten years of healthy life expectancy, but that stopping at ages 60, 50, 40 or 30 gained, respectively, three, six, nine or almost the full ten years. On his ninety-second birthday that year, together with his great friend and scientific collaborator Richard Peto, Doll gave a talk on the results to a packed meeting of doctors at the John Radcliffe Hospital, Oxford. Both men were relaxed and comfortable with an audience who had come to recognise the power and necessity of statistics to clinical research and hence to clinical practice.[18]

Doll was a dispassionate scientist, and the importance of his work was recognised throughout the world. Doll's integrity, courtesy, sharp mind and precise use of language made him an effective chairman of many committees and an impartial adviser to various government departments, court cases and industries.[19] Having lived through the 1930s he understood how greatly medical science in general, and epidemiology in particular, could improve people's lives.

Richard Doll was a man of deep reserve, and while for many decades he was recognised as a public figure, he was also a private man. His apparent emotional detachment led to him being respected and feared. While he unquestionably had a kind heart, it was accustomed to being subordinated to his intellect. One of his colleagues, who worked with him in the 1950s, felt that he emanated a sense of "unconscious intimidation," and when the occasion demanded he could be formidable, particularly when faced with persistent woolly thinking.[20] Primarily Doll was

---

[18] Doll, R., Peto, R., Boreham, J. and Sutherland, I., 'Mortality in Relation to Smoking: 50 years' observation on male British doctors,' *British Medical Journal,* 2004, vol. 328, pp. 519-28.

[19] Peto, R., Beral, V. (2010) "Sir Richard Doll CH OBE. 28 October 1912-24 July 2005", *Biographical Memoirs of Fellows of the Royal Society* 56:63.

[20] Avis Hutt, personal communication.

preternaturally busy. He gave the impression that every five minutes of his day was accounted for. As a result, a professional meeting with Doll was both memorable, and for the unprepared, an unnerving encounter. Compared to almost any other person, the unforgettable aspect of a conversation with Doll was that he really listened. For people not accustomed to this, it could lead to nervousness and stultified thinking, neither of which would endear the visitor to him. But if the reasoning was clear, then ideas would be exchanged, a strategy designed and inspiration distilled. Ultimately, when Doll thought the discussion had covered the relevant ground he would look at his watch and you knew that your time was up. This emotional detachment and austere exterior were tempered, particularly in later life, by a mischievousness that enjoyed nonconformity and good humoured asides.

During his time as a communist, Doll often wore jumpers and open-necked shirts but in later years he was renowned for his elegance. He embraced the debonair, dressing immaculately, and wore vivid ties that he enjoyed people noticing. He and Joan loved and depended on each other, and had similar professional values. When she died in 2001 nothing could cushion his despair. Oppressed by grief for two years, he gradually recovered, finding some inner peace, and in the last eighteen months of his life he was renascent. He liked to say that old people should take risks, and in his ninety-third year he rode on a camel, flew in a glider and climbed a jungle tree in Australia. In the last year of his life he lectured in seven different countries on five different continents.

The year 1997 was so productive for Doll that it prompted a congratulatory editorial in the *British Medical Journal*. Aptly, one of the articles he had written for the *BMJ* was entitled "There is no such thing as ageing".[21] In the week of his eighty-fifth birthday, the editor described Doll as "perhaps Britain's most eminent doctor" and commended him on his output: in that year he wrote 18 scientific papers.[22] Honouring his work on smoking and health, the editorial put his research into context: "The reduction in tobacco deaths in middle age has been greater in Britain than any other country. About half of those who smoke are killed by the habit, while among those who have never smoked or who have stopped 80

---

[21] Doll, R. and Peto, R., "There is No Such Thing As Ageing', *British Medical Journal*, 1997. Vol. 315, pp. 1030-32.

[22] Smith, R., 'Richard Doll at 85', *British Medical Journal*, 1997, vol. 315, p. 315.

per cent survive to 70 and 33 per cent to 85. Two thirds of the ex-smokers who have survived to 85 would have died if they'd carried on smoking. They owe their lives to Sir Richard".

Since 1978, Doll had asked his long-suffering doctors not only about their smoking history, but also their drinking habits. For the 1997 Christmas edition of the *BMJ*, Doll wrote the article "One for the heart" and for the hedonists among the readership it was just what the doctor ordered.[23] Doll enjoyed drinking but was aware of the dangers that alcohol had for doctors and society. His review of the evidence led him to deliver a clear message. "In middle and old age some small amount of alcohol within the range of one to four drinks each day reduced the risk of premature death". He advised that this daily consumption in people aged forty-five and above had a protective effect against vascular disease and death, and it did not matter whether they drank wine, beer or spirits since the benefit was delivered from ethanol. At medical conferences around the world, Doll could be found at the head of the queue for a glass of lunch-time wine, and his answer to any puritan enquiry was "I'm looking after my health". He hoped that his biological fate would resonate with his wishes for his own demise, to keep all of his faculties and enjoy life, which he interpreted as, 'to die young as old as possible'.

Doll's life also reminds us that though medicine is a science, healing is an art. On 8 July 2003, he gave a graduation address to medical students at Aberdeen University. While listing the great advances in medical research over the previous hundred years, he used literature as an aid to medically navigating the future.

"But if the world changes, and changes in some respects dramatically, as I suspect it will, one thing will not change, or rather will continue to change only very slowly and on an evolutionary scale, and that is the psychology of the people who inhabit it. Those of you who will deal directly with patients will still be dealing with irrational fears and jealousies, with greed and aggression, with stoicism and self-sacrifice, and, as I still believe, with a majority who are simply seeking experienced advice and are grateful for it. Our professional education does not, however, prepare us to recognise and respond appropriately to these facets

---

[23] Doll, R., 'One for the Heart', *British Medical Journal,* 1997, vol. 315, pp. 1664-8.

of human nature – at least it does not in England. What does is good literature. Tolstoy's *Anna Karenina* and *War and Peace*, George Eliot's *Middlemarch*, Vikram Seth's wonderful account of Hindu and Muslim life in *A Suitable Boy*, and Bernhard Schlink's account of German adjustment to the post-Hitler world in *The Reader*. How much more fit we are to deal with the ineluctable facts of life, when we have read such novels".

Richard Doll was one of the most important medial scientists of the twentieth century. He died with dignity in Oxford, on 24 July 2005, and was survived by his adopted children.

In December 2006, more than a year after Doll's death, an article entitled "Secret Ties to Industry and Conflicting Interest in Cancer Research" that was later published in the *American Journal of Industrial Medicine* was leaked to the *Guardian* newspaper.[24] The journal article's principal author was Lennart Hardell, and in it Hardell *et al* "revealed" that Doll had "failed to disclose" fees that he received from chemical companies. They suggested that these payments undermined Doll's work on the environmental causes of cancer. Hardell's accusations were based on letters found in Doll's archive, deposited by Doll for public scrutiny at the Wellcome Trust Library. Doll did not hide his relationship with industry and the fact that he had documented his ties to industrial epidemiology negated the idea that there was anything "secret" about the association. Doll was a man no one could legitimately accuse of being venal, he received no retainers, and gave away all of his fees to Green College. Other scientists who were also accused of a conflict of interest by Hardell *et al* said they were "honoured to be included in the company of the late Sir Richard Doll, even in such a baseless attack".[25] Perhaps a more rational explanation for the vengeful attempt to undermine Doll's status as a dispassionate scientist was that Hardell had been on the receiving end of Doll's censure twenty years before. Hardell had given evidence to a Royal Commission set up to carry out a judicial inquiry into the use and effects of chemical agents on Australian personnel in the Vietnam War. On 4

[24] Hardell L., Walker, M.J., Walhjalt, B., Friedman, L.S. and Richter, E.D., 'Secret Ties to Industry and Conflicting Interests in Cancer Research', *American Journal of Industrial Medicine,* 2007, vol. 50, pp. 227-33.
[25] McLaughlin, J.K., Boice, JD, Taronne, R.E. and Blot, W.J., letter, *American Journal of Industrial Medicine,* 2007, vol. 40, pp. 699-700.

December 1985, after "weighing the evidence", Doll wrote to the commissioner, The Honourable Mr Justice Phillip Evatt. He stated that, having examined the documents submitted to him, he was of the opinion that: "your review of Hardell's work with the additional evidence obtained directly from him at interview shows that many of the published statements were exaggerated or non-supportable and that there were many opportunities for bias to have been introduced in the collection of his data. His conclusions cannot be sustained, and, in my opinion, his work should no longer be cited as scientific evidence".[26]

On 8 September 2005, some of the world's leading epidemiologists gathered for the official opening of the Richard Doll Building in Oxford. Many had been trained by Doll and they were there to pay homage to his contribution to the health of the global community. For medical historians 8 September is an historic date in the evolution of epidemiological science, since it was the day in 1854 that John Snow persuaded the board of guardians of St James's parish to remove the handle from the Broad Street pump. Snow was the greatest epidemiologist of the nineteenth century and Doll the greatest of the twentieth century. Both men's scientific findings met with widespread disbelief among scientists, politicians and the masses but their shared concern for public health forms a great chapter in the history of medicine.

One thing that the assembled dignitaries did not know was that on 8 September 2005 Richard Doll's death certificate arrived at his own building from Stockport. He was part of the fifty-year follow-up of British doctors. His death certificate – death due to heart failure – was his final contribution to its lasting testament.

---

[26] Coombs, John, 'The Agent Orange Phenomenon: The Report of the Australian Royal Commission', in Young, A.L. and Reggiani, G.M. (eds), *Agent Orange and its Associated Dioxins: assessment of a controversy* (Elsevier Science Publishers, 1988), pp. 282-317.

Tony Benn

Ruth Winstone

W hen Tony Benn joined Westminster as a day-boy, in 1938, the Munich Agreement was about to be signed. By the time he left in 1942, aged 17, the school had been evacuated three times - to Sussex, Devon and Herefordshire.

By his own admission, notwithstanding his disrupted education, Tony was undistinguished academically or culturally. Of his school days he wrote, "The only prize I ever won at school was the Toplady Prize for Divinity and I still have the book, a Bible, with the inscription inside it. I wasn't very clever at school and my parents did not take much interest in my progress." And although the Benn family lived on the same road as the Tate Gallery, on the north bank of the Thames, he confessed later in life that he had never been through its doors.

While at the School, traits which came to distinguish his later career were discernible. His favourite subject was history. "Lively and intelligent as always," wrote his teacher. "His knowledge is patchy, e.g. he will sometimes take a political allusion which no-one else in the form sees, and at other times he is ignorant of common place matters. He has a rhetorical style of writing which is unsuitable for history essays." And later, "From being rather casual, he has now swung to the opposite extreme and takes himself very seriously. I like his enthusiasms and admire his drive but I hope he won't lose his sense of fun." (He didn't.)

His Housemaster added, "He is a strange mixture of a grown up and quite a young boy."

Both sides of Tony's family - the Benns and the Holmes - were Liberal or Radical before the Liberal schism in the 1920s. His father and later his mother adhered to congregationalism, a branch of Protestantism which had no hierarchy of priests or bishops and whose churches were free of any national or central control. (The Scots Holmes family practised a strict non-conformist brand of Christianity.) Grandfathers Daniel Holmes and John Williams Benn were MPs. Tony was never taken to the Tate Gallery but the Benns also lived five minutes from the House of Commons to which his father took him frequently.

Such were the influences on the young Tony Benn.

In his own estimation the two most important factors in his political life, although they varied in emphasis over the years, were the dissenting nature of his parents' faith; and the need for courage in the face of adversity.

Faith was a constant preoccupation, as his journals and his wartime discussions with his brother Michael (who intended to become a priest) show. He was always fascinated by the relationship of Christianity and church to political life. But over the years his Christian convictions weakened while his radicalism strengthened. In the fifties he was part of a discussion group calling itself the Christian Agnostics; in the 1980s he made a documentary with Norman Tebbit in which the latter argued for the privatisation of the Church of England while Tony put the case for disestablishment. In the last ten years of his life he became very interested in the experience of Bishop Richard Holloway whose disenchantment with the church and his religion is well documented.

For the first half of his parliamentary life, from 1950 to 1975, Tony Benn was in the centre of the Party and carefully avoided too close an association with groups to the right and left, including the Gaitskellites and Bevanites; he was regarded as an imaginative, hard working and persuasive Member of Parliament and Minister. It was not until the mid 1970s that his reputation as leader of the left took root.

I began working for Tony at the start of 1986. At that time, the leftward direction of the Labour Party with its Alternative Economic Strategy designed by Tony Banks, Margaret Beckett, and Stuart Holland, had come to a halt and the 'Bennites' were in retreat. The reversal which began under Neil Kinnock was completed by Tony Blair (there was a temporary blip under John Smith's leadership between 1992 and 1994, but Smith who died of a heart attack that year has been written out of Labour Party history). In the basement office of his home in west London, Tony prowled around, a wounded tiger. He was pretty much disregarded, as far as it was possible to do so, by the Party in parliament and by the media. He concentrated his efforts on the constituency (by then he had won Chesterfield) where he was a hard working, and diligent MP preoccupied by the year long miners' strike which began a few days after his election, and its disastrous after-effects on the Derbyshire town. It was not until he began to publish his political diaries in 1987, and more particularly through his involvement in the Middle East anti-war movement of the 1990s and first decade of the 21st century, that his rehabilitation as a left wing veteran was assured.

However, of more significance than the left-right split in Tony's career was, I think, the distinction between hierarchical and democratic control. He elaborated the original meaning of Dissent - from the Church of England and state interference in religion - into a dislike of authoritarianism in most of its manifestations. The priesthood of all believers which gave everyone a direct relationship with God without the mediation of a bishop shaped Tony Benn's attitude to most institutions. In 1980 in an essay titled Revolutionary Christianity, he wrote:

The belief in the 'priesthood of all believers' was and remains profoundly revolutionary in its impact upon the hierarchies of the Church itself. Nor was this revolutionary agitation confined to the church. The divine right of kings asserted by King Charles I as a defence of his powers was overthrown, along with the King himself, and in the ensuing revolution a furious debate began about the legitimacy of the organs of both Church and State power.

The dissenting case against the entrenchment of authority in the Church of England and the Roman Catholic Church was also true in his mind of institutions such as the Labour Party and the European Union. In the Labour Party in the 1950s and during the 1980s this manifested itself, in his view, in an intolerance of difficult people who were not prepared to toe a party line. At its worst the attempt to exert control from the top would result in the dissenters being expelled, vilified, excommunicated or, in some countries, executed. At a personal level this approach made him an increasingly awkward member of the Labour Party, the House of Commons and the Privy Council. This was a theme which informed his view of authority to the end of his life. In his last speech in the House of Commons, on 22 March 2001, he referred to this strange country that we live in. "We do not elect our head of state; we do not elect the second chamber; we elect only this House, and even in this House enormous power is vested in the prerogatives. The Prime Minister can go to war without consulting us, sign treaties without consulting us, agree to laws in Brussels without consulting us and appoint bishops, peers and judges without consulting us...." For good measure he added to his list of threats to parliament "the triple powers" of the monarchy, and the Labour and Conservative party headquarters.

The second factor - courage in the face of adversity - was for Tony epitomised by the story in the Old Testament of Daniel's trial in the Lions' den. Tony as a child was brought up on Biblical stories and loved the tale of Daniel, who having been conspired against by those jealous of his closeness to the king, Darius, is placed overnight with some hungry lions. Daniel's faith in God is rewarded and he is protected by an angel, much to Darius's relief the next morning. It is a story essentially about trust in God and the power of prayer. Tony however preferred the story as one of moral strength and principle. He often quoted a Salvation Army hymn *Dare to be a Daniel* derived from the story:

> Standing by a purpose true,
> Heeding God's command
> Honour them the faithful few,
> All hail to Daniel's band
> Dare to be a Daniel,
> Dare to stand alone,
> Dare to have a purpose firm,
> Dare to make it known.

Tony Benn himself faced fear and hostility, at various points of his life: during the Second World war, and the Suez crisis, but particularly from 1980-1984, the hey-day of the left, when sections of the media turned on him (and a minority of other Labour MPs) over his stand over the Falklands War, the Wapping printers' dispute and the miners' strike as relations between the police and the strikers turned violent and dangerous. He was fond of invoking past rebels in reference to modern controversies, - men such as John Ball the "hedge priest", Tom Paine, Francis Place, George Loveless and the Tolpuddle martyrs, Charles Bradlaugh, and the Pankhursts and women of the Suffrage battles, and the ecowarrior Swampy. *Writings on the Wall, 1215-1984*, a radical and socialist anthology edited by Tony in 1984 illustrates his awareness of the long and honourable tradition of English radicalism to which he, in historical perspective, belongs.

But despite his increasing scepticism about the House of Commons and the power of parliamentary democracy he was completely loyal to the House and fascinated by constitutional issues and was therefore perhaps closer to the parliamentary radicals of the 19th century than to earlier dissenters.

By the first decade of that century, the Radical cause had taken on the Tories and Whigs in the constituency of Westminster itself, and won - the victorious MPs in the 1807 General Election being Thomas Cochrane and Sir Frances Burdett. The former was a Scottish aristocrat and Naval officer, the latter (educated at Westminster coincidentally), a baronet who had married into the Coutts banking family. Their victory was underpinned by the work of a disciplined organising committee led by among others Place, a leather-breeches maker who became a successful tailor, and William Cobbett, a farmer's son turned journalist and editor of the weekly polemical *Political Register*. The committee campaigned street by street, kept detailed canvassing records and accounts, and printed handbills and placards, working from a gin shop in Westminster. As E.P. Thompson, much admired by Tony Benn, observed, radicalism at the beginning of the 19th century "indicated intransigent opposition to the Government; contempt for the weakness of the Whigs; opposition to restrictions upon political liberties; open exposure of corruption...and general support for parliamentary reform... Burdett, Cartwright, Cobbett, Hunt, Place are prominent in the history of radicalism for the next fifteen years." This period also established the organisational methods and practices of modern elections.

If the radical experience of this period had many lessons for Tony Benn in his own battles (by-elections in Bristol in 1961 and 1963 against the established order, to rid himself of his peerage; and his return to the political arena in the 1984 by-election in Chesterfield), his parliamentary character resembled closely, I would argue, that of the MP John Bright.

Bright was a Member of Parliament from 1843 to 1889 (for Durham, then Manchester and Birmingham) and a minister between 1868 and 1874 in Gladstone's administration. Bright was not afraid to confront the vested interests of the cotton industry in the campaign against American slavery (he was a leading cotton manufacturer himself) or oppose the Crimean war. Of slavery Bright did not mince his words. "The object is that a handful of white men on that continent shall lord it over many millions of black men, made black by the very Hand that made us white. The object is that they should have the power to breed negroes, to work negroes, to lash negroes, to chain negroes, to buy and sell negroes, to deny them the commonest ties of family... To make chattels and things of men and women and children." Bright also vociferously opposed the Crimean War. In his biography of Bright, the former Conservative MP Bill Cash, a contemporary of Tony Benn's in parliament, wrote:

> At that time there was, to put it mildly, a strong jingoistic approach to war in the Crimea, against which Bright stood almost alone in the House of Commons. Yet, when he made his famous speech which included the words: "The angel of death has been abroad throughout the land; you may almost hear the beating of

his wings," his oratory was so powerful that the House fell into complete silence. This, however, was not a view shared by his constituents in Manchester and he lost his seat at the ensuing election, although he was later vindicated. There are powerful analogies between the Crimean War and many of the protests against Iraq and Afghanistan.... His campaigns were legendary and he would address as many as 200,000 people with an energy and an oratory which had no equal.[1]

A century later, in echoes of Bright's style, Tony Benn took up the cause of abolition of the death penalty, in a searing indictment of the hanging of Russell Pascoe in Horsfield Prison, Bristol, a week before Christmas, "as the centre of Bristol was ablaze with twinkling lights and full of shoppers carrying their parcels through the jostling crowds... One of the strongest arguments against hanging is because of what it does to us. The ritual revenge we take out on murderers is a lightning conductor for our own hates, a balm to ease our own guilt, and a pleasing stimulant for our own morbidity."

Bill Cash subtitled his biography *Statesman, Orator and Agitator* and the parallels with Tony Benn are striking, not least the "oratory which had no equal" which was as true of Tony Benn in the 20th century at the height of his powers as of Bright in the 19th. Statesman, orator and agitator; all accolades which might have been applied to him but he would have been proudest to be called an agitator. He belonged to the tradition which Oscar Wilde described in *The Soul of Man Under Socialism*, a description which he, Tony, loved to quote. What is said of great employers against agitators is unquestionably true. Agitators are a set of interfering, meddling people who come down to some perfectly contented class of the community and sow seeds of discontent among them. That is the reason why agitators are so absolutely necessary. Without them in our incomplete state, there would be no advance toward civilisation.

---

[1] Bill Cash, *John Bright: Statesman, Orator, Agitator.* (London: IB Tauris 2015).